RELIGION AND SOCIETY IN ENGLAND, 1850–1914

Social History in Perspective

General Editor: Jeremy Black

Social History in Perspective is a new series of in-depth studies of the many topics in social, cultural and religious history of interest to students. The books will give the student clear surveys of the subject and also present the most recent research in an accessible way.

PUBLISHED

John Belchem *Popular Radicalism in Nineteenth-Century Britain*
Hugh McLeod *Religion and Society in England, 1850–1914*
N. L. Tranter *British Population in the Twentieth Century*

RELIGION AND SOCIETY IN ENGLAND, 1850–1914

HUGH MCLEOD

St. Martin's Press
New York

St. Martin's Press, Scholarly and Reference Division,
175 Fifth Avenue, New York, N.Y. 10010

First published in the United States of America in 1996

Printed in Malaysia

ISBN 0–312–15798–3 (cloth)
ISBN 0–312–15805–X (paper)

Library of Congress Cataloging-in-Publication Data
McLeod, Hugh.
Religion and society in England: 1850–1914 / Hugh McLeod.
p.   cm.—(Social history in perspective)
Includes bibliographical references and index.
ISBN 0–312–15798–3 (cloth). — ISBN 0–312–15805–X (pbk.)
1. Christianity—England—19th century.   2. Christianity-
-England—20th century.   3. England—Social conditions.   I. Title.
II. Series.
BR759.M37   1996
274.2'08—dc20   95–31702
                                                                    CIP

CONTENTS

Contents

ACKNOWLEDGEMENTS

The work of oral historians has provided one of the most important sources for this book. I would therefore like to begin by thanking Alan Bartlett, John Fletcher, Elizabeth Roberts, Gillian Rose, Raphael Samuel, Paul Thompson, Thea Thompson and Avon County Reference Library for allowing me to listen to tapes or read transcripts of interviews, and to quote from them. I would also like to thank the Faculty of Arts at Birmingham University for research grants, and Harry Buglass of the Department of Ancient History and Archaeology for drawing the maps. Much of the writing was done while I was a Visiting Fellow at the Research Centre Religion and Society at the University of Amsterdam, so I would like to thank the members of the Centre for inviting me and for being generous hosts and, in particular, Peter van Rooden for extensive discussions. Most of all I would like to thank my wife Jackie for many forms of help and encouragement.

Birmingham   H. MCL.

LIST OF MAPS

INTRODUCTION

This book will argue that in England during the period from 1850 to 1914, a relatively high degree of religious consensus existed, which had diminished by the early twentieth century, but had not yet broken down. Features of this consensus included acceptance by most of the population of Protestant Christianity, including acceptance of the Bible as the highest religious authority, and of moral principles derived from Protestant Christianity, practice of the Christian rites of passage, and observance of Sunday. This consensus was greatly facilitated by the pluralism dating back to the seventeenth century, which had led to the emergence of numerous Protestant denominations, catering for a huge range of theological and liturgical tastes, and varying greatly in social constituency. The deep class divisions within English society limited the ability of any denomination to attract the support of more than a limited proportion of the population. Moreover the involvement of the Church of England and of the major Nonconformist denominations in the systems of authority and social control tended to alienate those at the lower end of the social hierarchy. However, criticism of, and resistance to, these structures very frequently took a Christian form.

In its ecclesiastical structure, England stood midway between the characteristic continental European pattern and the North American pattern. Like most European countries, England had a dominant, privileged established church, allied with the forces of political conservatism. But like the United States, England had a long history of religious toleration, as a result of which large numbers of rival religious denominations were able to flourish. Class differences and class antagonisms had an enormous influence on patterns of religious affiliation and practice in this period, whereas urban/rural differences were less important than in most other parts of Europe. Gender differences in religious belief and practice, though significant, were less marked than in many parts of Europe, and certainly less so than in most predominantly Catholic countries. Important as regional differences were, they were much less extreme than in, for instance, France. Few, if any, areas of England could match the overwhelmingly high levels of religious practice found in parts of Brittany, and England certainly had no 'dechristianised' areas to match the Limousin. England was overwhelmingly a Christian and a Protestant nation. In spite of the deep social fissures produced by class, secularism remained a relatively marginal phenomenon. The crucial factor here was that liberalism, the major emancipatory movement of the middle decades of the century, was heavily shaped by religious Dissent, and the kind of secular liberalism that was so important in many continental countries remained of minor importance in England. This was also true, though to a lesser degree, of socialism, which grew out of liberalism in the later part of the century. Nineteenth-century secularisation received a large part of its dynamic from political forces. In England this political dynamic was weaker, and secularisation, when it came, did so more gradually and more evenly. On the one hand, one must be struck by the degree to which Christianity was at least passively accepted by the great majority of the population, and to which it helped to shape people's world-picture, provided a basis for widely accepted moral principles, and provided rites which were used by the great majority of the population. On the other hand, involvement in the churches was limited both by class factors, and by the inability of English Protestantism to seize the imagination of the poor.

2

Discussion by historians of the relationship between religion and society in Victorian and Edwardian England has focused on three main issues. First there has been the question of whether what E. R. Wickham, in his pioneering study of Sheffield, called the Victorian 'religious boom'[1] was an overwhelmingly middle-class phenomenon, or whether it also substantially influenced other sections of the population. Secondly, many studies have explicitly or implicitly considered whether religion in this period primarily acted as an instrument of social control, or whether it also acted as an important force for reform and for social criticism. And thirdly there has been the question of when and why the Victorian 'religious boom' came to an end. The third of these debates has been the most fundamental in its implications, since answers to this question have had a profound effect on interpretations of religious developments in this period. For some historians, such as Alan Gilbert, Robert Currie or John Kent, the whole religious history of the Victorian era is dominated by the theme of secularisation.[2] Gilbert, who makes the clearest case for this interpretation, argues that the 'religious boom' belonged essentially to the first half of the nineteenth century, when membership of Nonconformist chapels saw spectacular growth, and that by 1850 the peak of religious influence in English society had already been passed. Gilbert contends that in the short run the social upheavals associated with industrialisation increased the social importance of religion, but that in the long run industrialisation led to secularisation. This was partly because of urbanisation and the growth of a concentrated working class, both of which, according to Gilbert, assisted the secularising trend. It was partly because the increasing prosperity and sense of security resulting from economic, technological and medical progress meant that most people felt increasingly at home in the world and unwilling to seek other-worldly solutions to their problems. Among the chief critics of this view have been Jeffrey Cox and Callum Brown, both of whom believe that the Victorian religious crisis came much later, during the period 1890 to 1914.[3] They reject the assumption, implicit in Gilbert's work, that there is an integral connection between secularisation and 'modernisation', and Brown is particularly hostile to the view that the growth of cities in the nineteenth century was associated with religious decline. Both stress the enormous social role of the churches during most of the Victorian period. Gilbert, whose book was probably the most influential study of the social history of modern English religion to be published in the 1970s, argues from the standpoint of sociological determinism: secularisation was the product of inexorable social forces which the churches could do very little to direct or control. Cox, whose book was probably the most influential such study to be published in the 1980s, argues precisely the opposite: the decline suffered by the English churches in the twentieth century was primarily a result of choices that they made in the nineteenth. In particular, they devoted too many of their energies to the 'civilising mission' and the provision of social services, and not enough to the recruitment of a committed membership; as a result, the churches collapsed when the rise of the welfare state made most of what they had been doing irrelevant.

Gilbert, Cox and Brown are at least agreed in giving priority to social factors in their explanation of the Victorian religious crisis: a quite separate debate continues among those who assume that the roots of the crisis are to be found in the history of ideas. Cox is positively hostile to any explanation in such terms; Brown tends simply to ignore intellectual factors; while Gilbert recognises that some contemporaries believed that they were passing through a crisis of faith, but he argues that they misunderstood what was happening – intellectual developments which undermined the plausibility of Christianity were less important than social changes which reduced its relevance. However, many other historians, especially those specialising in the history of science or those whose interests are mainly literary, give overwhelming attention to intellectual changes. Here there are three main tendencies. The simplest approach – which continues to be the version most widely accepted by the general public – is to suggest that new scientific knowledge or advances in the study of the Bible either refuted Christianity, or refuted current Christian orthodoxies, or at least made Christianity harder to believe. The great advantage of this type of explanation is that one can actually find examples of individuals who understood their loss of faith in these terms.[4] One of the major disadvantages is the fact that many Christians of the time seem to have assimilated the arguments of the biblical scholars or the scientists relatively painlessly, and to have restated their faith in terms which they thought consistent with the new knowledge. Indeed, these Christians included many scientists.[5] Another problem, highlighted by Kitson Clark in his pioneering exploration of the social dimensions of Victorian religious history, is the difficulty of proving that more than a very small proportion of the population knew or cared much about new scientific developments.[6] So historians committed to an explanation of the crisis in primarily intellectual terms have tended to present their case in more subtle terms than any simple conflict between 'science' and 'religion'. A second approach therefore is to focus on the rising prestige of scientists or of the secular professions generally, and their growing tendency to replace the clergy in the role of carriers of mysterious wisdom hidden from the vulgar masses and of pundits privileged to pronounce on all the issues of the day.[7] A third approach is to argue that the main challenge to Christian orthodoxies came not from scientific knowledge, but from changing moral sensibilities, which rendered certain traditional doctrines unacceptable.[8] Again, a number of contemporaries left accounts of their loss of faith that stress factors of this kind – but again there were many contemporaries who saw the force of these objections, and responded not by rejecting Christianity, but by adopting more liberal versions of the faith.

One thing that most of these accounts have in common is a tendency to select one master-factor which offers the key to the religious crisis. Certainly some of the historians cited explicitly repudiate any monocausal explanation of the events; but most identify one kind of factor which they see as more significant than any other.

The factors involved in the religious crisis are so complex, and the issues which it raises are so wide-ranging, that the explanation of the crisis may never be resolved to everyone's satisfaction. The debate over the class basis of the Victorian 'religious boom' raises questions that are simpler and more readily answered. The two pioneering works in this field, published in 1957 and 1963 respectively, were a local study of Sheffield by E. R. Wickham, and a more general study by K. S. Inglis of attempts by the churches to convert and/or meet the social needs of the working classes.[9] Inglis, in particular, and Wickham in more nuanced fashion, argued that the 'religious boom' was an overwhelmingly middle-class phenomenon, and that, with the exception of the Primitive Methodists (whom Inglis regarded as too small a group to be important) and the Roman Catholics, the churches had little success in attracting working-class people. Neither of them thought that secularism was of much importance, but both concluded that religious indifference was widespread among the working class. Wickham and Inglis laid the basis of a new orthodoxy, which was accepted uncritically by many historians, refined by others, but seldom directly challenged until the 1980s.

Again Cox's study of south London, published in 1982, marks a turning-point. Cox accepted that working-class church attendance was low, but he argued that this could not be taken as an adequate measure of the importance of Christianity or of the churches in working-class life. Cox made two main points. The first, which was undoubtedly correct, was that the churches had a wide-ranging presence in Victorian working-class communities and had an important influence on the lives of many people who seldom attended services. His second, more controversial, suggestion was that the prevailing religious outlook in working-class London was not indifference, let alone 'heathenism', but what he calls 'diffusive Christianity', which had a good deal in common with what some other historians have termed 'popular religion'.[10] Cox provided the main stimulus to a school of often self-consciously 'revisionist' historians whose work appeared in the later 1980s and early 1990s, and who tended to take Cox's arguments a good deal further than he himself did. The common theme of these writings has been that the influence of the various forms of Christianity in the life of Victorian England was much more widespread than historians have generally recognised, and that the working class were not so much less religious than the middle class, as religious in different ways. Some 'revisionists', such as Sarah Williams, have concentrated mainly on interpreting the alternative forms of religious belief and practice prevalent among non-church-goers. Others, such as Callum Brown and Mark Smith, have focused on religious organisations, and have argued that they attracted a broad cross-section of the population, including many working-class people.[11]

A third major area of debate has been the social role of the churches. Clearly, historians' approaches to this question have been substantially shaped by their religious and political preconceptions, and for this reason it is unlikely that any generally acceptable consensus will be reached. One broad line of interpretation has stressed the conservative role of religion in Victorian society and the function of the churches as instruments of social control. The opposing approach attributes a much more creative role to religion, emphasising the part it played in radical and reforming movements, and the impetus it gave to humanitarian activity of many kinds. Few historians would deny that there is at least some truth in both versions, so that the argument is more over questions of emphasis. Among those historians who stress the conservative role of religion, perhaps the most cogent case is that made by

Patrick Joyce in his study of the 'factory culture' of Lancashire industrial towns.[12] He argues that in the mid-Victorian period the life of these towns was dominated by medium-size family firms, run on paternalist lines, often in close conjunction with one of the local churches or chapels. Employers tried to cultivate good relations with their workforce, and many workers were highly loyal, and took a lead from their employer in political and religious matters. Religion, as well as promoting deference to employers, also served to divide the working class on sectarian lines. When in the period between about 1880 and 1914 this 'factory culture' began to decline, one of the factors in the decline was the rise of secularism, facilitating the movement of many workers towards socialism.

On the other hand many historians have attributed a more creative role to religion. One of the most interesting alternatives to Joyce is Robert Moore's study of a coal-mining district in County Durham, which offers a similar picture in many respects, but differs on important details.[13] Here too there were a number of paternalist employers, and shared Methodist religion and Liberal politics sometimes laid the basis for friendly relations between employers and trade union leaders. But some points do not fit Joyce's picture so well. Relations between employers and workers varied considerably between one pit and the next one. Even where relations between employers and union leaders were good, union leaders were not deferential, and relations between employer and workers depended on a complex set of expectations and a certain amount of give and take. While there was a special affinity between liberalism and Methodism, there was also an important Methodist input into the emergent socialist movement. Most of the pioneers of the Independent Labour Party in this area were Methodists, so that the battle between liberalism and socialism was fought within the chapels.

This book will suggest answers to the questions at issue in these three debates. Chapter 1 provides a guide to the various forms of religion and irreligion prevalent in

Victorian and Edwardian England, and to the social and geographical bases of each religious group. While this chapter will be mainly descriptive, it will also throw some light on the question of whether organised religion in this period was essentially a middle-class phenomenon. Chapter 2, which is the longest, will focus more directly on this debate, and also on that concerning the social role of the churches. Chapter 3 will address these questions in a more indirect way, but the main objective will be to evoke some of the distinctive religious atmosphere of the period. Chapter 4 will focus on the religious crisis of the later Victorian and Edwardian periods. Rather than selecting any master-factor, I shall suggest that the crisis has to be understood in terms of the interaction of a whole series of factors, many of which were partly or wholly independent from one another.

The book is mainly based on the abundant secondary literature. The principal primary sources to be used are the various oral history projects conducted since the later 1960s. In particular, I have used: the Essex University survey, organised by Paul Thompson and Thea Vigne, which included interviews with some 450 men and women who had been born between 1872 and 1909, and who in regional and social terms represented a cross-section of the British population as it was in 1911; Elizabeth Roberts's interviews conducted in three Lancashire towns; and the Bristol Oral History Project. These projects have different strengths and weaknesses. Together they offer, in my view, unique insights into some of the questions addressed in this book. The Essex survey used standardised questionnaires and is best at providing systematic information on particular questions. On the other hand, interviewers sometimes stuck pretty closely to the questionnaire and missed opportunities for following up interesting remarks. Elizabeth Roberts provides some of the richest material on religion, because of her outstanding ability to empathise with the interviewees and to persuade them to enlarge on interesting points. The Bristol project focused more directly on questions of individual belief and unbelief, and so provided information of a kind that is often lacking from the Essex survey, where the focus is more on such topics as church-going, Sunday Schools and the relations between church and chapel.[14]

1

PATTERNS OF RELIGIOUS BELONGING

Most people in Victorian and Edwardian England would have seen themselves as belonging either to 'church' or to 'chapel'. Church people were Anglicans – those belonging to the Church of England, the established church, with Queen Victoria, or later King Edward VII, at its head. 'The Church', as it was often called, had a nationwide system of parishes and counted the whole population as its parishioners. The national religious census held on 30 March 1851 showed that 51 per cent of those attending church on the day of the census went to an Anglican service. There were no censuses of religious affiliation in nineteenth-century England, as distinct from those measuring congregations, but probably about 60 per cent of the population would have regarded themselves as Anglicans. Chapel people, also known as Dissenters, as Nonconformists, or (by the late nineteenth century) as free church people, were Protestants belonging to one of the numerous free churches. Most of these were relatively small, but when all of them were added together they attracted almost as many worshippers as the established church. In 1851, 44 per cent of those counted at worship attended one of the Nonconformist chapels. Chapel people tended to be more assiduous than church people in attending services,

11

so the percentage of Nonconformists in the total population must have been less than this – perhaps 30 per cent. Church and chapel should not be regarded as completely exclusive categories: there were some people who equally willingly attended both church and chapel services. But most people would have seen themselves as belonging to one or the other. The third major group were the Roman Catholics. They only accounted for 4 per cent of worshippers in 1851, and the proportion of Catholics in the total population was probably about the same. The Catholics were growing in importance during the second half of the nineteenth century, but their share of the population remained fairly constant at around 5 per cent.

In addition to these three very large religious communities, there were at least four other identifiable groups. The only one that might in itself be termed a religious community was the Jews. In 1850 they were about 0.2 per cent of the population; by 1914 they had increased to about 0.7 per cent. Secondly there were a variety of small religious bodies that had nothing in common with one another, except that they were completely outside the Christian mainstream. These included the very small numbers of Buddhists, Hindus, or Muslims, together with various new religious movements including Mormonism, Spiritualism and Theosophy. Finally there were two different categories of non-religious people. First there were the secularists, agnostics and rationalists, who had deliberately rejected any kind of supernatural faith. There were not many of them, but they were highly organised and active. Secondly, there were those who were so completely uninterested in religion of any kind that they acknowledged no religious or anti-religious label at all. There certainly were such people – though probably fewer than was often alleged – but it is impossible to estimate their numbers.

At the 1851 religious census, 59 attendances at places of worship were reported for every 100 people. (In the terminology that has come to be used in the very extensive literature on the census, this means a national 'Index of Attendance', or IA, of 59.) The 59 included Sunday School children and attendances by 'twicers' and 'thricers', who went to several services. The best attempt to estimate the number of individual adult church-goers has been made by Michael Watts, who suggests that in Nottinghamshire, 44 per cent of the adult population attended at least one service on census Sunday.[1] Since Nottinghamshire was very much an average county, with reported attendances just marginally above the national average, it is likely that the average percentage of church-goers in the adult population was in the vicinity of 40 per cent. Of course, the census was held on a single Sunday, when some church-goers must have been kept at home by illness, family commitments, or other reasons, and some must have been working. The proportion of the adult population attending services with some degree of frequency must have been somewhat higher.

The purposes of this chapter will be, first, to examine in turn each of the seven groups mentioned above, estimating their numbers, analysing their distribution, describing their characteristics, and evoking something of their distinctive ethos; and secondly, to examine the national pattern of church-going, in terms of social class, gender, regional distribution, and differences between town and countryside.

Church

In thousands of English villages the dominant building was the parish church, and this was an accurate reflection of the central place the church still held in the life of most rural communities. In towns and cities, the parish church had impressive competitors – Nonconformist and Catholic chapels, town halls, museums, factories and warehouses. But it still held its own. Not only in small market towns, such as Ludlow, Warwick or Oakham, or in places like Norwich or Bristol with a great medieval past, but in modern industrial cities, such as Birmingham or Leeds, the parish church was a formidable presence. Similarly with the position of the clergy in the social landscape: in most villages the vicar was the most powerful individual, or the most powerful individual next to the squire; in the town the vicar was part of a much larger and more variegated elite, but he still enjoyed a great deal of prestige and influence. The clergy of leading urban parishes were often outstanding personalities, who exercised a wide-ranging influence on the city's life, such as J. C. Miller of St Martin's, Birmingham, or D. J. Vaughan of St Martin's, Leicester. The personal and sacerdotal authority enjoyed by Anglican clergymen was also considerably enhanced in many cases by their social standing and their personal connections with other members of the elite.

The great expansion in the numbers of the clergy during the Victorian period was made possible by a gradual increase in the numbers of non-graduate clergy, typically recruited from a lower middle-class background. Of men ordained in the years 1834–43, 11 per cent were non-graduates, but by 1902–6 the proportion had risen to 35 per cent. They were mainly concentrated in poorly endowed parishes in the rural north or in industrial towns. They were relatively rare in London and in the rural south. Right through this period, the majority of clergy were graduates of Oxford and Cambridge Universities.[2]

Something of the wide-ranging social role of the clergy can be appreciated from replies to questions in the Essex University oral history project. These included one about the clergy. The comments of a Guildford man, born in 1900, whose father was a master tailor, indicate something of the strategic position occupied by the clergy in the local community:

Well they were very helpful to people – they played a big part in the lives of people. You went to them with your troubles, you went to them for references if you wanted a reference, you see – you went to them for

14

advice, they gave you advice – the poor man's lawyer was the parson I suppose, you see, advice on what to do if you got notice to quit your house ... you go to the parson and say that and he's very likely know a lady that perhaps got a house, and would advise 'em to go and see Mrs So-and-so and I'll put in a good word for you. Or you have a letter – the parsons used to write letters like for the hospital ... a letter of introduction you see. If you wanted to go as a patient you see. If you wanted a job, you see, and you didn't know the people, you go the parson and he would give you a letter of introduction.[3]

Apart from the indirect power that the clergy exercised as a result of their numerous connections, they also wielded considerable direct power through their role in the administration of charity. In a society where a large proportion of the people were struggling to obtain the most basic necessities of life, this role was crucially important. The famous surveys by Booth and Rowntree at the end of the nineteenth century found that 31 per cent of Londoners and 27 per cent of those living in York were living in poverty. Ellen Ross's research on London shows that for such families charity, often provided by religious agencies, made a vital addition to their income. Such charity could come with a price-tag: a Norfolk man whose father was secretary of the local branch of the farm labourers' union recalls that on Christmas morning the vicar told the choir to stay behind, and then 'He gave all the men five bob, he give the boys half a crown, and he give me sixpence.'[4]

The clergy were perceived as men of power – especially in the rural and small-town environment, but to a considerable extent in the city too. Another question in the Essex survey asked who were the most important people in the locality, and again and again the vicar is among those mentioned. Feelings towards such powerful figures were inevitably sometimes ambivalent. Clergymen were usually respected, often admired. A Devon farm labourer's daughter, whose parents were Methodists, recalls that 'The Vicar was the most important person in our village. We always looked on him as being the head of the village.' He visited everyone, especially the sick, and once saved her father's life by providing emergency medical treatment. A London docker's son, when asked who were the most important people in Wapping, replied: 'Well, of course, we used to take more notice of the vicar than anyone else.' He too put the main stress on the fact that the vicar did a lot of visiting. A Suffolk farm labourer's daughter recalls that they had 'a very nice clergyman when I was young. He'd go and visit his parishioners and they'd go and collect in the church on certain Sundays for the poor of the village you see, and he'd often slip my mother half a crown. Oh she was thrilled to death, oh yes, she was.'[5] Regular visiting, kindness, and treating everyone alike seem to have been the qualities most appreciated. Clergymen could also be feared. Some of this intermingling of contradictory feelings is hinted at in the answer by a London docker's son to a question as to who the most important people were in the East End where he grew up. He remarked that 'The church was always looked up to', and then went on to say that clergy and doctors were 'the two number ones. The two number one frighteners then.'[6] Of course paternal solicitude and authoritarian rule were often two sides of the same coin. Alun Howkins questioned two men from the same Norfolk village about the clergyman who had held the living in the early part of the twentieth century: he was remembered 'with great affection by one man as a giver of charity who looked after the poor. Yet by another man this same vicar was remembered as a tyrant whose paternalism found a corollary in violent opposition to trades unions, allotments and smallholdings.'[7]

And quite frequently there was a feeling that there was some incongruity between the status of the clergy as local bigwigs and their position as preachers of Christianity.

This view was put fairly forcibly in one of the most famous accounts from the inside of Victorian working-class life, published in 1868. Thomas Wright, 'The Journeyman Engineer', argued that the Church of England's greatest weakness was 'its own want of conformity between its preaching and its practice'. He admitted that 'many of the working clergy are Christians in the highest and purest sense', and respected accordingly by their working-class parishioners. But they tended to be so poorly paid that they had to depend on cast-off clothing from their more affluent colleagues:

> It may be depended upon that the working classes will never be brought to believe in the purity or earnestness of a church which leaves many of its best and truest servants to struggle through life on miserably insufficient incomes, while it passes all kinds of incompetents over their heads to the loaves and fishes at its disposal, simply because the incompetents have political or family influence.[8]

Similar points were made in a study of rural life published in 1913 by a former Liberal MP of High Church sympathies. He contrasted the limited influence of the rural clergy in England with the situation in Ireland, Belgium or Italy, where the clergy were often leaders of the rural community, enjoying the confidence of the majority of the population. He blamed this situation on the fact that the clergy were so closely tied to the rural elite: 'the Church remains out of touch with the spiritual needs of the labourer. Many of the clergy have earned his respect, but few his confidence. Few of them have taken his side in the questions which touch him most closely. To him they seem remote; a part of the world in which the landlord moves; prominent in the conservative party; dwellers in large houses.'[9]

While these authors may have drawn on stereotyped images for polemical effect, similar points were often made

17

on the basis of personal experience. According to a Preston factory worker, born in 1884:

From where I lived I could have thrown a stone into the yard of Christchurch church. You never saw in the whole time I lived there, probably getting on for twenty years, the Vicar of the parish in the street. The Salvation Army or the Church Army used to come down. Captain Smith of the Church Army. Or the Salvation Army would come round and, of course, the Vicar would go to the better class areas. Like Westcliffe, for instance, where it wouldn't be beer, it would be wine and the rest of it. One of the things that struck me was that we weren't good enough for the rich man's Christianity, but we were good enough for the poor man's. It was one of the things that made me think about religion and religious people.[10]

In the 1880s and 1890s a new style of clergyman was emerging, especially in urban working-class parishes, who was trying to get away from the image of clergymen as 'gentlemen' and who cultivated a democratic style. One of the most famous of these democratic parsons was the Reverend Stewart Headlam, who as curate of St Matthew's, Bethnal Green, in the East End of London, founded the Guild of St Matthew, the first of several groups set up by radical and socialist clergy around the end of the nineteenth century. Headlam was described by Bernard Shaw as belonging to 'a type of clergy peculiar to the latter half of the nineteenth century. . . . They wanted the clergyman to be able to go to the theatre, to say damn if he wished to do so, to take a large interest in political and social questions, to have dancing in the house if he chose, and to affirm the joyousness and freedom and catholicity of the church at every turn.'[11]

This was also the era of the 'slum priest', who devoted his life to work in an urban working-class parish and tried to identify himself totally with the life of its people. The most famous of these were often celibate high Anglicans, and preferred to be known as 'Father', such as Robert Dolling (1851–1902) of St Mary, Portsea, and St Saviour, Poplar; Lincoln Stanhope Wainright (1847–1924) of St Peter's, London Docks; or G. C. Ommanney (1850–1936) of St Matthew's, Sheffield, who 'survived rows, riots, obdurate churchwardens, Evangelical secessions, and thirty years of archiepiscopal discipline to turn St Matthew's into "one of the most famous churches of the Catholic revival in England", with sung mass, confession, the reserved sacrament, incense', as well as 'an admirable tradition of social work'.[12]

Celibacy and the cultivation of a distinctly priestly image no doubt helped in the attempt to get away from a privileged life-style – though it could provoke new kinds of resentment. But in spite of the efforts of those like Headlam, the prevailing image of the clergyman in the early twentieth century was still that of a highly educated gentleman, who mixed more readily with the elite than with ordinary parishioners. A woman born in an Oxfordshire village in 1895, and whose father was a carpenter, commented that although the rector was an active Liberal, and in some ways seems to have related quite well to his parishioners: 'everybody had to sort of – the men touch their hat and the girls had to curtsey. Oh he demanded all this you know.' She also commented:

And of course when you come to think of it, in their stumbling way, a lot of the villagers were very religious . . . [but] the parson, the one that we had, he was above their heads you know. . . . You see with all these poor frozen people, and half-starved and half-asleep a lot of them, he would be saying 'And of course, as Hegel said, as Kant said, and so and so said,' quoting from the great scholars. What did they know? They couldn't even read or write, a lot of them.[13]

The 1851 religious census showed that 51 per cent of

reported church attendances were at Anglican services. If we work on the assumption that approximately 40 per cent of the adult population attended some kind of service on census Sunday, this would suggest that about 20 per cent of adults attended an Anglican service. So, if the majority of the population had some kind of connection with the Church of England and would have regarded themselves as 'church' people, no more than about a third of 'church' people came to church on any given Sunday. The distribution of these active 'church' people was socially and geographically uneven.[14] In geographical terms they were heavily concentrated south of the Trent, with the very highest levels being reached in the southern rural counties of Hampshire, Dorset and Wiltshire. The Victorian era inherited a parish system which reflected the distribution of population and wealth in the early middle ages. Large areas of lowland southern England were densely filled with well-endowed parishes and impressive parish churches, while northern England, the Welsh Borders and Cornwall suffered from over-large parishes, poorly endowed, with small churches at a distance from much of the population. The church reforms of the 1830s and 1840s led to a reorganisation of church finances, the formation of many new parishes and a huge church-building programme.[15] But, throughout the nineteenth century, the Church of England remained considerably stronger in the south than in the north. The church was also considerably stronger in rural than in urban areas. There were some cities and large towns where Anglicanism was relatively well-supported in 1851 – mainly those such as Bristol or York with a long history and where nineteenth-century growth had been relatively gradual, or the new resort towns like Brighton and Bath. But in Liverpool, Manchester, Birmingham, Leeds and Sheffield, and many smaller industrial centres, Anglican attendance was well below the national average. Within the cities Anglican attendance patterns were socially highly skewed. Here the best figures are provided by the religious censuses of London in 1886–7 and 1902–3. In 1902–3, the percentage of adults attending an Anglican service on the day of the census rose with each step up the social hierarchy, from 4 per cent in the poorest districts to 22 per cent in the aristocratic West End.[16]

At the top of the social hierarchy 'everyone' belonged to the church, and most people at least maintained a façade of Anglican observance, certainly including regular attendance at services and some degree of Sunday observance, and often including the saying of family prayers – though by the end of the nineteenth century these were going out of fashion, Sunday observance was becoming more relaxed, and even church-going was less of a must than it had been twenty or thirty years earlier.[17] A woman born in 1892, the daughter of a duke, recalled that although she did not think her father had any religious belief, he 'led a conventional religious life and definitely went to church'. When she was asked if she had been christened and confirmed, she replied: 'Oh yes. Because that was conventional. No question not. No!'[18]

Queen Victoria was an Anglican while in England and a member of the Church of Scotland when in Scotland. In fact her religious preferences seem to have been Presbyterian, but she took a keen interest in the affairs of the Church of England, including the appointment of bishops.[19] This was a somewhat delicate constitutional issue, as although bishops were nominally chosen by the monarch, it had long been accepted that the final decision was made by the Prime Minister. In practice, Prime Ministers would listen to what the Queen had to say, but her views were only one among many factors which they took into account in making their choice. She disliked extreme evangelicals, and disliked extreme high churchmen even more. Her preference usually was for moderate liberals – those who were termed 'Broad Church'. In spite of her dislike of pietistic extremes, Queen Victoria was a devout and practising churchwoman. Edward VII, if scarcely very devout, was in his own way a practising churchman too, and in the later years of his mother's reign, when his

21

influence over aristocratic society was considerable, he threw the weight of his prestige behind a particular religious style which included a regularly practising though unostentatious Anglicanism, and a relatively friendly attitude towards Roman Catholics and Jews. (Nonconformists remained socially beyond the pale.) In the 1880s a guide to London Society noted that 'most of the smart people' went to church, 'to the Chapel Royal, or to St Margaret's, Westminster, if they belong to the political set; and many other shrines are specially set apart for Society's elect'.[20]

The aristocracy and gentry were overwhelmingly Anglican, with a small admixture of Roman Catholics. At every other social level, there was more of a mixture of different religious groups. However, Anglicanism was very strong in the upper middle class – among, for instance, successful business and professional men and their wives. Both Anglicanism and various forms of Dissent were strong in this social milieu, and the religious census of London in 1902–3 suggests that this was where church-going reached its maximum level. Wealthy suburbs like Hampstead and Blackheath in London, Edgbaston in Birmingham, or Clifton in Bristol all had large numbers of prosperous Anglican churches, whose tall spires thrust through the surrounding trees.[21] Many members of this class were active church members devoting much of their wealth to supporting religious causes, and much of their free time to good works. This was particularly true for upper middle-class women, who often escaped from a rather narrow existence and found a meaning to their life in visiting the poor.[22] By the end of the nineteenth century a certain proportion of middle-class women were beginning to go to university and to enter careers. But up till that time almost the only alternative to an entirely domestic life was involvement in church or charitable work of some kind – and most charitable work had a religious basis. But religious work also involved many upper middle-class men. The most famous example would be paternalist employers, who recognised some kind of responsibility for the physical and moral welfare of their workers. Many of these were Nonconformists, but there were also Anglicans such as the Birley and Houldsworth cotton-spinning dynasties in Manchester and Stockport. David Jeremy's analysis of the religious affiliations of English and Welsh business-men included in the *Dictionary of Business Biography* shows that 42 per cent of those whose affiliation is known were Anglicans. This was slightly less than the combined Non-conformist total, but far more than the numbers from any other denomination. The most notable point was the tendency for successful businessmen brought up in other denominations to convert to Anglicanism.[23]

The lower middle class included what was known in Germany as the 'old middle class' and the 'new middle class'. The former comprised shopkeepers and owners of smaller businesses; the latter comprised the many white-collar occupational groups, including clerks of all kinds, shop assistants, commercial travellers and teachers. This was the fastest growing section of the population in the late Victorian and Edwardian periods. It was also an area where increasing numbers of women were finding employment by the early twentieth century. The 'old middle class' tended, especially in small towns and country areas, to be deeply enmeshed in the system of conflict between church and chapel. In the small town in the Eastern Counties described in W. Hale White's novel *The Auto-biography of Mark Rutherford*, each branch of trade would have a church shop and a chapel shop.[24] In poor districts like the East End of London, shopkeepers and small businessmen made up a large part of the leadership of church and chapel. Family tradition often played an important role, as families maintained connections with a particular place of worship over several generations.[25]

The 'new' middle class, on the other hand, as a class without traditions, growing very rapidly in the later nineteenth and early twentieth centuries, and recruited from many different social backgrounds, pointed forward to the twentieth century in its anarchy of individual religious or non-religious commitments.[26] It was in lower middle-class suburbs that churches and chapels were particularly important as social centres: church organisations multiplied, and often provided important places for meeting members of the opposite sex. Mutual Improvement Societies, Church Drama Clubs, and cricket teams all flourished in the years around 1900. These areas include relatively high numbers both of strongly committed church-members and of the totally uncommitted. The London census of 1902–3 showed that church-going was slightly higher in lower middle-class suburbs than in districts where the skilled working class lived, but well below the level in wealthier suburbs. In terms of denominational split, there were slightly more Nonconformists than Anglicans, but very few Roman Catholics.

Up to about 1840 Anglican churches were conspicuously lacking from many working-class areas. For instance, Bethnal Green in the East End of London had, in 1837, a population of 70,000 and only two Anglican churches. However, ten churches were then built in as many years with funds provided by the Metropolis Churches Fund.[27] This was one example of a much wider phenomenon. Between about 1840 and 1890 the Anglican Church undertook a massive church-building programme, which filled previously neglected working-class districts, as well as new suburbs and remote country districts, with a dense network of parish churches. By 1890, when parishes of 60,000, or even 100,000, were common in Paris, Berlin and Vienna, few London parishes contained more than 20,000 people, and parishes of 10,000 people were more common.

In poorer working-class districts the parish church was supplemented by a 'mission', directed at those too poor to afford the 'decent' clothes which attendance at the main church would require. The mission often provided free breakfasts, cheap clothing, and other kinds of charitable assistance. There was a deep divide among working-class church-goers between those who accepted such help, and those whose 'pride' led them to refuse it, even when they were in dire straits. Most of those working-class people who were committed members of a congregation belonged to the latter category, and frequently they were fiercely independent, and bitterly contemptuous of anything involving charity. Pawning, gambling, and any kind of dirt or untidiness were often condemned for similar reasons, as reflecting an inability to stand on one's own two feet, or lack of control over one's situation.

'Respectability' was a key concept in Victorian England, and one that had great resonance for many working-class church-goers. Working-class and middle-class concepts of respectability overlapped, yet in some important aspects they were different. For instance, most middle-class people assumed that there was something intrinsically unrespectable about working with one's hands, and in middle-class usage a 'respectable' neighbourhood was one where middle-class people lived. On the other hand, it was a crucial part of the working-class understanding of the term that manual work was as honourable as any other, and that a working-class family who worked hard, lived 'decently', were independent, and brought up their children to be good citizens, were entitled to the same respect as the member of any other class who did these things.[28] The prevailing ethos in families of this kind is conveyed by a Bolton man, born in 1895, whose father was a moulder, active in his union, the co-op, the Liberal Party and his Anglican parish:

> We were called the respectable working class. And we were taught to make the best use of every halfpenny and penny that came into the house. My mother had that ingrained in her, and we had it ingrained in us.

His parents' aim was to produce 'God-fearing, respectable, law-abiding citizens. Respect for the law and respect for your parents. We were taught the Ten Commandments, and they were pretty well drilled into us.'[29]

A woman born also into an Anglican family and in the same year, in an Oxfordshire village, recalls that 'if you were very humble and very poor and really starving' you could get money for food or fuel from the Parish Fund, 'But mother wouldn't, she was rather a proud woman, you know, and she wouldn't do that. So I was rather weakly as a child . . .'.[30]

Clergy in urban working-class parishes tried to solve the problem of keeping in contact with a population of several thousand by employing one or more curates, and by recruiting a team of lay church workers, who might include middle-class women acting as voluntary district visitors, and paid working-class Bible Women and Scripture Readers, who would dispense charity, visit the sick, persuade people to attend church or join church organisations, and so on. Many non-church-going families, who seldom met the vicar, kept some kind of contact with the church through these various lay agents. In some cases, quite intimate and friendly relationships developed, particularly, it seems, with the Bible Women, whose social background was not too far distant from that of the families whom they visited, and who were often able to provide much-valued moral support in times of sickness or bereavement.[31] In rural parishes, populations tended to be in the hundreds rather than the thousands and it was usually possible for the vicar to have some degree of acquaintance with all of his parishioners. Personal factors could therefore play an important part in the rural parish, but social factors often had an even bigger role. In many rural parishes, the social hierarchy was very sharply defined, and by working with the local elite, the clergyman could ensure that they supported the church, the church school and church charities, both by providing money and by encouraging their dependants to attend services. In villages with a resident squire who was a keen churchman, the Anglican church was likely to be full. For instance, Michael Watts analysed patterns of church attendance in 1851 in 198 Nottinghamshire villages. In the

44 villages where all the land was owned by a single pro-
prietor, an estimated 40 per cent of the adult population
attended an Anglican service on census Sunday. In the
various other categories of village, Anglican attendance
varied between 20 per cent and 25 per cent.[32] Farmers
too sometimes insisted on the men who worked for them
attending their church or chapel.[33] But in larger villages
and those with a scattered population – which was the
situation in most parts of the north – there tended to be
a pluralistic religious situation akin to that in the towns,
with several Dissenting chapels and considerable numbers
of non-church-goers. Here the personal qualities of the
clergyman could have a determinative influence on his
ability to attract a good congregation.

Chapel

The religious census of 1851 showed that 44 per cent of
reported attendances were at Nonconformist services.[34] By
the later nineteenth century, the proportion of Nonconformists in the church-going population probably exceeded
50 per cent. Anglican attendances had declined somewhat
since 1851, while some branches of Nonconformity, particularly the more plebeian varieties, had grown. More
important, however, was the massive demographic shift
that had taken place during this period. In 1851 half the
population had lived in urban areas; by 1901 four-fifths
did so. Already in 1851 Nonconformists made up a majority of the church-going population in most of the larger
towns, and by the 1880s and 1890s this predominance was
even more marked. Robin Gill's research on church-going
patterns in 28 large towns in the 1880s shows that Nonconformists averaged 58 per cent of all church-goers.[35] In Liverpool, Catholics were the largest denomination, and in London,
Birmingham and Portsmouth, Anglicans and Nonconformists were neck and neck. But in most other cities Nonconformists made up over 50 per cent of church-goers –

for instance, in Bristol, Sheffield, Bradford, Hull, Leicester, Nottingham, Wolverhampton and the Potteries. The Nonconformist share of the church-going population probably peaked in the early twentieth century.

The 1851 census, as well as showing that chapel-goers outnumbered church-goers in most of the large towns, indicated that there was a marked regional pattern of rural religious practice. Church was far ahead in most of southern England from east Devon to Kent, in most of the south and west midlands, in west Lancashire and Cumbria. Chapel was dominant in Cornwall, in a narrow belt running through Bedfordshire, Huntingdonshire and the Isle of Ely to the Wash, in much of the north midlands, east Lancashire, Yorkshire and the north-east. Church and chapel were neck and neck in much of East Anglia and the east midlands, in parts of the north midlands and in the industrialised areas of north Somerset, north Wiltshire and south Gloucestershire (see Map 1).

Chapel people were divided into numerous denominations, of which four attracted congregations totalling over 100,000 in 1851, five had congregations totalling between 50,000 and 100,000, and a further six attracted between 10,000 and 50,000 (see Appendix, Table 1). There were also many other smaller bodies. The big four were the Wesleyan Methodists (14 per cent of all worshippers), the Independents or Congregationalists (10 per cent), the Baptists (consisting of autonomous congregations organised in several separate denominations) (8 per cent), and the Primitive Methodists (5 per cent). Each of these had its regional strongholds, and was the leading Nonconformist denomination in a considerable number of districts. The next group comprised the Presbyterians, and four smaller Methodist bodies (the Bible Christians, Methodist New Connexion, Wesleyan Reformers and Wesleyan Methodist Association). These also had major local strongholds, and each was the leading Nonconformist denomination in at least one district, but they did not have the nationwide presence of the big four. The third group comprised the

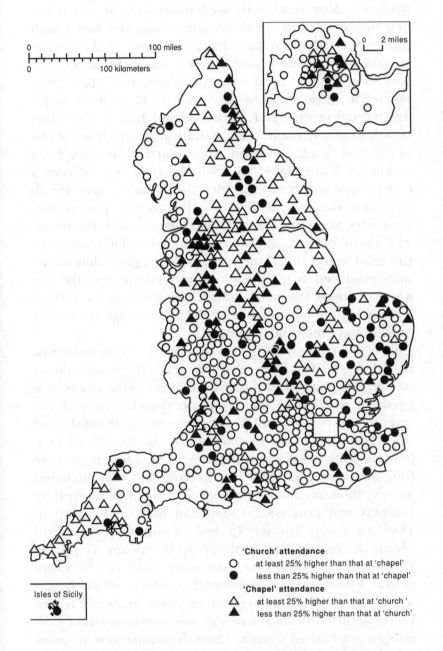

Map 1   1851 religious census: church and chapel

Unitarians, Quakers, Countess of Huntingdon's Connexion, Brethren, Moravians and Swedenborgians, of which the first two were scattered thinly but widely, and had a high profile because of the prominence of many of their members in business and local politics, while the latter four had some bigger local concentrations, but made little impact in most areas of the country. One other major denomination emerged in the second half of the nineteenth century, namely the Salvation Army. It grew out of the East London Mission, which started operating from a tent in Whitechapel in 1865. In 1877, the Mission's constitution was revised to give the former 'superintendent', now 'General', William Booth autocratic powers and, soon after, supporters started marching through the streets with music playing and wearing uniforms. Thus was born the most colourful of the many new religious denominations produced by nineteenth-century Britain, and the one which enjoyed the most dramatic expansion: by 1900 it had risen to a membership of 100,000, though thereafter growth was much more gradual.

In terms of their historical origins, the Nonconformist churches fell into three categories. First there were those, namely the Congregationalists, Baptists, Unitarians and Quakers, which had their roots in the civil wars of the seventeenth century and in the persecutions that followed the restoration of the monarchy and the Church of England. In spite of the many differences between them these four denominations had in common that they included among their members a significant element of wealthy business and professional men and that (at least up to 1886) they were strongly Liberal in politics. The second group, including the Methodists, Moravians and Lady Huntingdon's Connexion, had their roots in the Evangelical Revival of the eighteenth century, which began within the Church of England and only gradually led to the crystallisation of a series of new denominations outside the established church. These denominations included a higher proportion of Tories and of the apolitical than the older Dissenting groups, though by the mid-nineteenth century all branches of Methodism were moving in a strongly Liberal direction. The proportion of wealthy members in these denominations was smaller. The Methodists were in fact the most socially heterogeneous of the branches of nineteenth-century Nonconformity, ranging as they did from some very successful businessmen, through many shopkeepers, farmers, clerks and foremen, to a very large number of working-class people. The third category of churches founded in the nineteenth century was more heterogeneous. The Presbyterians were a bit different from the others in that they drew mainly on immigrants from Scotland and Ulster, and that they were not new except in the sense that they did not have a separate English organisation until the nineteenth century. The new churches founded in the nineteenth century included, beside the Salvation Army, the Brethren and the Churches of Christ. They had little in common apart from the fact that they reached relatively far down the social hierarchy, and that they tended to be apolitical – though in the case of the Churches of Christ the apolitical phase did not last for very long.[36]

In doctrinal terms, the main distinction in the mid-nineteenth century was between Calvinists (Congregationalists, Presbyterians, Lady Huntingdon, and most Baptists), Arminian evangelicals (Methodists, some Baptists, many Quakers), and those with a more idiosyncratic theology (Unitarians, many Quakers, Swedenborgians). These doctrinal distinctions became less important in the second half of the nineteenth century, as Calvinism was very much in decline, in spite of the popularity of its leading exponent, the Baptist preacher Charles Spurgeon. The larger denominations, most notably the Congregationalists, were increasingly influenced by liberal theology.[37] Organisational differences continued to be important. Here the main difference was between those denominations (Baptists, Congregationalists, Unitarians, Church of Christ) which had a congregational structure, and those such as the various branches of Methodism, the Presbyterians or the Quakers which were more centralised, being, in the case of the Methodists, under the control of an all-powerful Conference. A further distinction was between those denominations (the great majority) which had a professional ministry, and those (such as the Quakers and Brethren) which did not – though there was a further distinction between the Brethren, where all male members could preach, expound the Bible, or pray, but where the women could not, and the Quakers, who allowed all participants in their meetings to minister. In an intermediate position were the Methodists, among whom local preachers had a crucial role in making possible a vast network of village chapels and cottage meetings, often with tiny congregations, which could not possibly have supported a paid minister. There was a further distinction between the Wesleyans, who emphasised the prerogatives of the ministry, and until 1878 excluded laypeople from the Conference, and the other branches of Methodism, which made much less distinction between ministers and local preachers. The tension between local preachers and the 'travelling preachers' (later known as ministers), and the demand for more democracy within the church, was the principal reason for the numerous schisms which beset Wesleyan Methodism in the period from 1797 to 1850.

There were marked differences in regional distribution between the various branches of Dissent (see Map 2). It used to be thought that the main distinction was that the Old Dissent implanted itself in areas where the Church of England was strong, while the New Dissent entered the religious vacuum that had formed in areas where both Anglicanism and Old Dissent were weak.[38] Recent research suggests that the pattern is much more complicated. In regional terms the traditional distinction is still broadly valid. Thus the Baptists and Congregationalists were the predominant form of Dissent through most of the south and east of England, while Methodism predominated in the north, the west and north midlands, and Cornwall.

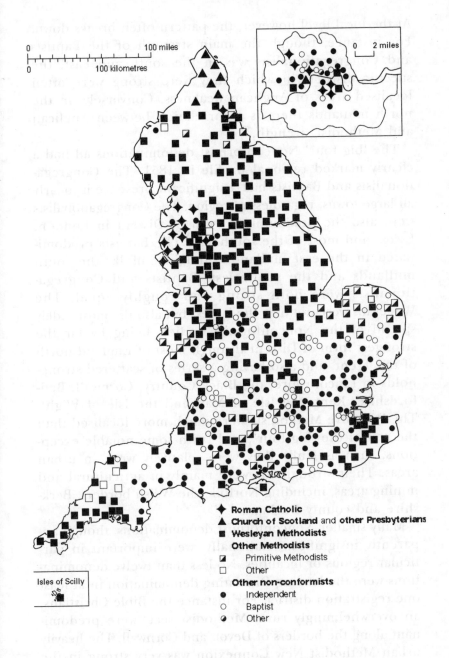

Map 2 1851 religious census: largest non-established denomination

Roman Catholic
Church of Scotland and other Presbyterians
Wesleyan Methodists
Other Methodists
Primitive Methodists
Other
Other non-conformists
Independent
Baptist
Other

Isles of Scilly

At the local level however, the pattern often breaks down. For instance, though the main strength of the Baptists and Congregationalists was in the south and east, the specific districts in which they were strong were often localised areas of Anglican weakness. Conversely, in the north midlands there is a correlation between Anglican and Methodist strength.[39]

The 'big four' Nonconformist denominations all had a clearly marked regional profile in 1851. The Congregationalists and Baptists had a significant presence in nearly all large towns, regardless of region. The Congregationalists were also the predominant form of Dissent in London, Essex, and most of the south-east. The Baptists predominated in the east midlands. And in Suffolk, the south midlands and the south-west, Baptists and Congregationalists were both strong and roughly equal. The Wesleyans were not only the largest but also the most widely spread of the Nonconformist bodies, being by far the strongest form of Dissent through most of England north of the Trent, and also having a series of scattered strongholds in Lincolnshire, the Black Country, Cornwall, Bedfordshire, Kent, the Isle of Man and the Isle of Wight. The Primitive Methodists were much more localised than the rest of the 'big four', and (with some notable exceptions, such as Hull) they were relatively weak in urban areas. Their strongholds were mainly in agricultural and mining areas, including Norfolk, the Welsh borders, Berkshire and county Durham.

Many smaller Nonconformist denominations, though apparently insignificant nationally, were important in particular regions or localities. No less than twelve denominations were the leading Dissenting denomination in at least one registration district. For instance the Bible Christians, an overwhelmingly rural Methodist sect, were predominant along the borders of Devon and Cornwall. The heavily urban Methodist New Connexion was very strong in the Potteries. The Presbyterians outnumbered Anglicans along much of the English side of the border with Scotland.

The Brethren had their stronghold in Plymouth. And even very small Nonconformist bodies had local pockets of strength, such as the Countess of Huntingdon's Connexion in Worcester, the Swedenborgians in Manchester or the Moravians in Pudsey.

The chapel embraced many different kinds of social milieu. At the top of the hierarchy, the most prestigious Unitarian, Congregationalist or Baptist chapels or Quaker meeting houses counted among their members MPs, mayors, industrialists, prominent journalists. Every town of any size would have included at least one prestigious Dissenting congregation, and in many cities there were several. One such was Horton Lane Congregational chapel in Bradford, described by Koditschek as 'a cathedral of Nonconformity'. In the early years of the nineteenth century it had a relatively humble membership. But in the 1830s and 1840s it became the chief stronghold of a newly emerging elite of self-made businessmen, who were challenging the older Tory-Anglican elite of men who had inherited their wealth and social position. In the 1840s, Horton Lane was attended by the editor of the town's leading Liberal paper, by four out of Bradford's first five mayors, and by the Liberal MP, factory-owner and philanthropist, Sir Titus Salt.[40] In the second half of the nineteenth century, chapels like Horton Lane were becoming places of established wealth, and there were many industrial towns dominated by Nonconformist business dynasties – the Congregationalist Crossleys of Halifax with their carpet business, the Quaker Palmers in the 'biscuitopolis' of Reading, the Baptist Colmans, 'Mustard kings' of Norwich, and so on.[41]

At the opposite end of the social spectrum were the many chapels that preserved a precarious existence because of the poverty of their members – or sometimes the hostility of the local elite. In the Nottinghamshire mining town of Eastwood, around the turn of the century, the colliery officials and the butties (sub-contractors) attended the Congregational chapel, whereas the Baptist church was mainly supported by miners and their families. They could not afford their own chapel, so they held services in the Sunday School, and they could not afford to pay a minister, so the running of the church was entirely in the hands of the deacons.[42] In churches of this kind one or two families could come to play a crucial role, and the church might collapse if one of them moved away.

In some small one-industry communities the Nonconformist chapel was the dominant religious institution, attracting most of the church-going population and acting as a community centre for many of those who seldom attended services. This was the situation in some of the Black Country nailing areas, in the fishing villages along the Yorkshire coast, and in many Durham mining villages. In the Deerness Valley, for instance, around the end of the nineteenth century the local leaders of the miners' union were also Primitive Methodist local preachers, officials of the village co-op, and leaders of local Liberalism. Many miners and their wives seldom attended services, but none the less sent their children to Methodist Sunday School, and themselves turned up for big occasions like the chapel anniversary.[43]

There were also many chapels where the prevailing tone was lower middle-class. Grocers, drapers, ironmongers, all included large numbers of Nonconformists. The milieu was described in fairly unsympathetic terms in Arnold Bennett's novel *Anna of the Five Towns* (Potteries Methodism), and William Hale White's 'Mark Rutherford' novels (Bedford Congregationalism). Historians of Nonconformity have tended to be attracted either by the cottage meetings and 'tin tabernacles', or by the 'pulpit princes' and their wealthy lay patrons: the equally important middle stratum of Dissent lacks the romance of either extreme, and has accordingly been neglected. On the whole the accounts of this milieu were written by those who were glad to have escaped from it, and those who remained within the milieu seldom wrote about it. One outsider's account fails to avoid the habitual patronising tone, but succeeds in showing

that the familiar clichés do not tell the whole story. It is
by Arthur Baxter who, in the 1890s, was one of Charles
Booth's assistants in the research that led to his monu-
mental *Life and Labour of the People in London.* Inevitably
the account tells as much about the upper middle-class
Anglican agnostic interviewer as about the lower middle-
class Nonconformist interviewee. Baxter described as follows his interview with William George, a 60-year-old deacon
at Victoria Park Congregational Church in east London.
George, who worked as a clerk at Somerset House, lived
in South Hackney, a lower middle-class area on the fringes
of the East End. The report begins predictably enough:

> I had never before met a Deacon in the flesh, but Mr
> G. was almost to a button what I had pictured the typi-
> cal Deacon: medium height, gray hair and full, but
> trimmed beard and whiskers, plain but not unpleasant
> face; inclined to be stout; dressed in a frock-coat of
> shiny black broad-cloth, with waist-coat opening rather
> low and showing two gilt studs; black bootlace tie tied
> in bow. He saw me at his home in Church Crescent,
> Hackney: everything very hideous and very philistinish:
> large portrait of Spurgeon on the wall.

But there is a surprise at the end. Eventually the conver-
sation got round to George's greatest passion, the Christian Instruction and Benevolent Society, which attempted
to provide 'practical Christ-like sympathy with distress in
whatever form it is found'. And 'as he talked about the
Society the elderly and commonplace Deacon became to
some extent transfigured and glowed in what I felt was a
genuine enthusiasm for philanthropy'.[44]

Roman Catholics

In 1851 only 4 per cent of the worshippers counted in
the religious census were Roman Catholics. But in some

37

parts of Lancashire, Cheshire, Staffordshire and London, the proportion was much higher. The high point of 38 per cent was reached in Liverpool. The Strand district of central London followed with 36 per cent. After that came Preston with 31 per cent, St George's, Southwark, in south London with 30 per cent, Manchester with 27 per cent. On the other hand, there were many rural districts of southern and eastern England where the number of Catholics was minimal.

The English Catholic community fell into three main groups. There were those who came from old Catholic families which had survived the long years of persecution, during which the proportion of Catholics in the population fell to about 1 per cent. Most of them originated from areas where there were concentrations of Catholic gentry families, who had their own chaplain trained at Douai, and who held services in their manor house. In parts of west Lancashire there were villages where everyone was a Catholic, and there were also concentrations of rural Catholics in Staffordshire and Yorkshire. While most of the Catholic gentry were relatively obscure, living in remote parts of the country on fairly modest incomes, there were a number of prominent Catholic aristocratic families, including most notably the Howards, from which came the Dukes of Norfolk. By the early nineteenth century there was a Catholic middle class in most Lancashire towns and in Birmingham, which was ready to take over from the gentry the role of lay patrons of the church.[45]

However, this was also the period in which English Catholicism was being transformed by a massive influx of Irish Catholics.[46] In the second half of the nineteenth century, Irish immigrants and their descendants comprised the great majority of English Catholics. Lancashire was already the most strongly Catholic county in England long before the massive Irish immigration of the 1830s, 1840s and 1850s, and towns such as Liverpool, Preston and Wigan already had some of the highest proportions of Catholics in their population. The fact that Lancashire attracted a far higher proportion of Irish immigrants than any other country meant that this Catholic character became even more pronounced, though for a long time some distinctions remained between the two categories of Catholic. For instance some churches attracted mainly English congregations, while others remained overwhelmingly Irish.[47]

The third major category of Catholics consisted of converts from Protestantism. Many, perhaps most, of these were working-class converts who, in the terminology of the time, 'turned' or 'perverted' as a result of marrying a Catholic. However, the main concern both of Catholic and of Protestant observers was with middle and upper-class converts, including a considerable number of High Church Anglican clergy. Some Catholics took a very close interest in these conversions, believing that they were signs that the reconversion of England to Roman Catholicism was imminent. The biggest catches of all were two very prominent Anglican clergymen, John Henry Newman and Henry Manning, who converted in 1845 and 1851 respectively, and went on to become Cardinals. But many other more obscure Anglican clergymen converted in the period from the start of the Oxford Movement in 1833 up to the First World War.

The principal Catholic recruiting-ground was among High Anglicans, both clerical and lay, who had become convinced that the Church of England was irredeemably Protestant, and that the efforts to convert Anglicans to a 'high' view of the church, the sacraments and episcopacy, to a sense of continuity with the medieval and early Christian past, to more Catholic forms of worship, and to a serious commitment to such Catholic doctrines as the apostolic succession, were all doomed to failure. But Catholicism also had an appeal for those in revolt against the puritanism and aesthetic poverty of a Protestant upbringing. This included many writers, artists, theatre people and bohemians. Right through this period, and beyond, Catholicism seems to have had a marked appeal for those in this social milieu. Notable converts in the Victorian and Edwardian period included the poet Gerard Manley Hopkins, the dramatist Oscar Wilde, the artist Aubrey Beardsley, and Catherine 'Skittles' Walters, who became a celebrity in high political circles in the late Victorian period by virtue of having been the mistress of several prominent politicians.

The importance attached to each of these categories of Catholic depended on one's angle of vision. In terms of position in the Catholic hierarchy the first and third groups for long remained more important than the second. The four Archbishops of Westminster in this period comprised three members of old Catholic families (Wiseman, Vaughan and Bourne) and one convert (Manning). Even in less prestigious sees, bishops of Irish descent remained the exception.[48] At the level of the parish clergy, the Irish element, including many priests who had been born in Ireland, was much more numerous. But perhaps the most notable point is that even in parishes where the laity were overwhelmingly Irish, a considerably proportion of the clergy were English or, indeed, European Catholics. The same applied to nuns, who played a big part in the Catholic education system, and a considerable proportion of whom were recruited from such countries as France and Belgium.[49] Whereas English Protestantism's overseas links were overwhelmingly with the United States – then as now a vigorous exporter both of evangelists and of new religious movements – English Catholicism had something of a European flavour, and of course most of the theological and devotional novelties of the century were imported from the continent. In terms of the laity, English Catholicism in the second half of the nineteenth century was overwhelmingly an urban and Irish phenomenon.

This meant, for a start, that Catholicism was to quite a large extent a religion of the slums, because the Irish were heavily over-represented in the poorest sections of the English working class. Early nineteenth-century Irish immigrants included a considerable proportions of skilled artisans. But the famine generation who came over in the 1840s and 1850s consisted predominantly of unskilled labourers. In spite of gradual processes of upward social mobility, at the turn of the century the heaviest concentrations of Catholics were still to be found in areas such as the dockland districts of London and Liverpool.[50] In 1897 one of Charles Booth's researchers spent an afternoon with a group of priests in Bermondsey in south London. When he showed the priests Booth's social map of London, in which areas of severe poverty were marked in blue, they commented that blue might equally be taken to represent the areas where Catholics lived.[51]

In the 1840s and 1850s the Catholic Church was overwhelmed by the flood of immigrants, and it was some time before priests were found and churches built to provide for the needs of the impoverished newcomers. Sheridan Gilley suggests that in London thousands of Catholic immigrants were losing touch with the church in this period, and in respect of Lancashire Connolly contrasts the very high rates of Catholic practice among the native Catholic population with the much lower levels prevailing among Irish immigrants.[52] There were several reasons for this. One was the fact that immigrants from the west of Ireland often came from areas where the modern Irish pattern of regular attendance at mass and confession had not yet been established, and where devotion focused on such natural features as holy wells and on the occasional visits of priests to remote farms. Immigrants who never went to mass, and had little contact with the clergy, but regularly prayed before a picture of Mary, hanging on the wall at home, were continuing patterns of observance well established in the country of their birth.[53] An additional problem for the church authorities in making contact with immigrants from the west was the lack of Irish-speaking priests. But perhaps most important of all were the effects of sheer poverty. In the 1840s and 1850s many Irish immigrants were struggling for survival, and had little time or energy, and even less in the way of material resources, to devote either to the church, or to anything else that did not relate directly to the business of making a living.[54]

In the second half of the century the Catholic Church gradually established its presence in the immigrant districts, and integrated a considerable proportion of the Irish-born and their descendants into the Catholic parishes and the network of associated institutions, which became increasingly visible and potent elements of Irish life in England.[55] Catholic priests went from door to door in the Irish districts, rebuilding contact with those who had long lost touch with the church; parish missions were held in which blood-curdling hell-fire sermons often proved very effective in persuading the lapsed to resume the practice of their religious duties; gradually a network of Catholic institutions, including schools and orphanages, was built up. Some priests played an extraordinary personal role in the life of their parishes, wearing themselves out in a constant round of visiting the sick, hearing confessions, and battling on behalf of Catholic and Irish interests on such bodies as the Board of Guardians or the School Board.

As the authority of the clergy grew, they were increasingly able to use authoritarian means of building up the church and reforming individual behaviour. Families who did not contribute to church funds could find themselves under heavy pressure, and so could drunken and brutal husbands, or youngsters who wanted to marry a Protestant.[56] If many priests of the years around 1900 had the air of 'benevolent tyrants' (to quote Charles Booth's description of Fr Whelahan of Woolwich)[57] some of them also had great reputations as peace-makers. They were known for their ability to stop fights in pubs, and they were also called in to mediate in family quarrels.

In the context of the religious culture of Victorian and Edwardian England, there were many respects in which the Catholics were unique. First, they were part of an international community, whose beliefs and practices were authoritatively defined by their leader in Rome. Indeed, loyalty to the Pope reached unprecedented heights in this period, which included the First Vatican Council and its definition of the dogma of papal infallibility (1870), as well as a succession of often highly controversial papal pronouncements, including the promulgation of the dogma of the Immaculate Conception (1854); publication of the Syllabus of Errors (1864); the encyclical Rerum Novarum (1891), which condemned socialism and laid out an alternative programme for social reform; and the decree Ne Temere (1908), which tightened the rules regarding marriage with non-Catholics.[58]

Secondly, in an age when sectarian tensions were endemic, Catholics were subjected to a degree of prejudice that was exceptional. There were two kinds of anti-Catholicism current in Victorian England, and both merged with a third kind of prejudice.[59] The first form of critique was rooted in Evangelical Protestantism. It was part of a continuous tradition going back to the Reformation, which saw Catholicism as idolatrous, as teaching a false faith in the possibility of human beings saving themselves through good works, and as downgrading the true Word of God, the Bible. In its most extreme form, 'No Popery' included the claim that the Pope was the anti-Christ. The second kind of critique was rooted in religious and political liberalism, and was propounded both by many Protestants and also by secularists. It focused on the Catholic Church's authoritarian structure and the denial of freedom of conscience, and rejected Catholicism as a stronghold of superstition and obscurantism. These two kinds of critique were not mutually exclusive, though they represent two alternative kinds of emphasis. Anti-Catholics of both schools liked to point to the economic backwardness of many Catholic nations (the prosperity of Catholic Belgium being conveniently overlooked), and to argue that Protestantism was synonymous with progress in the economic, as well as the religious and moral spheres.

At this point, anti-Catholicism tended to merge with anti-Irishism, and faults that were deemed to be characteristic of the Irish, whether in Ireland or in England, were taken as being characteristically Catholic. Charles Booth, commenting in 1903 on the London Irish, conveniently summarised several points of the hostile stereotype:

> The Irish Catholics form a class apart, being as a rule devout and willing to contribute to the upkeep of their church . . . but at the same time they are great beggars as well as heavy drinkers, and there is no sign that the form that practical religion takes in their case helps to make them in these respects either more self-reliant or more self-restrained.[60]

Catholicism was thus seen as a bogus form of religion which took to excess the externals, but failed to produce the moral fruits in terms of which the true worth of a religion could be judged.

Thirdly, Catholic styles of devotion were entirely strange in the eyes of most Protestants – though in the later nineteenth century they were finding their Anglican imitators. Photographs of Catholic streets in the East End of London at the time of the annual street processions in the early twentieth century convey something of the distinctive flavour of popular Catholicism. The photographs show the narrow streets of two-storey cottages, with banners hanging across declaring 'Hail, Queen of Heaven' or 'God Bless our Pope'. On the pavements in front of many of the houses stand shrines erected by the residents. Photographs of the processions show considerable crowds watching from the pavements or from windows.[61]

Those living in these 'Catholic streets' had a sense of collective identity, in which fidelity to the church was understood in terms of loyalty. This was why the Pope was so important: he was the supreme symbol of the Catholic community, and precisely because he was so much hated and derided by Protestants, Catholics felt bound to declare all the more loudly their loyalty to him. The shrines generally focused on Mary, and she had a place in Catholic life that was in some ways analogous to that of the Pope. She too had an emblematic quality and, next to obedience to the Pope, it was devotion to Mary that was the most criticised aspect of Catholic religion. But far beyond such considerations, Mary was also seen as the universal mother, who understood human suffering and human frailties, and who was always ready to come to the aid of her devotees. In particular, Catholics believed in the possibility of miraculous healings, brought about through appeals to Mary.[62]

Jews

Expelled from England by Edward I in 1290, the Jews were readmitted by Cromwell in 1656. A period of slow but steady growth in the numbers of English Jews in the eighteenth century and the first half of the nineteenth (mainly as a result of immigration from Germany) was followed between 1881 and 1905 by a large immigration of eastern European Jews, escaping the pogroms in the Russian Empire. In 1850 there were about 35,000 Jews in the United Kingdom. By 1881 there were about 60,000 British Jews, of whom about half were middle-class. Their level of prosperity was thus considerably above the average for the population as a whole. By far the most important Jewish community was in London, but there were also significant numbers in the large provincial cities, notably Manchester. By 1914 the Jewish population had risen to around 280,000, of whom the overwhelming majority lived in the three cities of London (180,000), Manchester (30,000) and Leeds (25,000), where they became prominent in all areas of the clothing industry, and where working-class Jews rapidly gained a reputation for trade union activism and political radicalism.[63]

Religiously the Jews were deeply divided. Historically the main distinction was between the relatively small Sephardic community of Spanish and Portuguese origin, and Azhkenazim from northern and eastern Europe. By the later nineteenth century the more important distinctions were between Jews of varying degrees of orthodoxy. The central religious institution of the Jewish community was the United Synagogue,[64] formed in 1871, to which many synagogues in London and the provinces were affiliated. It sponsored the Jews' College for the training of rabbis, and it was led by the Chief Rabbi, Nathan Adler, who was eventually succeeded in office by his son Hermann, so that the Adler dynasty remained at the helm for forty years. The United Synagogue retained the loyalty of the great majority of the Jewish elite and was even stronger among middle-class Jews. It stood for a moderate Orthodoxy, which was prepared to make minor modifications to the forms of worship, and which was less stringent than some would have liked in the observance of the sabbath and of the dietary laws. It was also emphatically British, and indeed patriotic. The Liberals had been the chief supporters of the political emancipation of British Jewry, enacted in 1858, and for some time after that most Jews remained Liberals. But by the 1880s and 1890s many of the wealthier Jews had become Conservatives or Liberal Unionists, and indeed several had become Conservative MPs. The Chief Rabbi was a strong supporter of the British cause during the Boer War.[65]

The opposition to the United Synagogue came from at least three directions. First, a large section of the east European immigrants who came to Britain in the 1880s and 1890s were rigorously Orthodox, and some of them saw the Chief Rabbi as a traitor. In areas such as the East End of London numerous small synagogues (*chevrot*) were formed, often by groups of immigrants from the same town in Lithuania or in Poland. In 1887 many of these small synagogues banded together to form the Federation of Synagogues, which represented the working-class and lower middle-class immigrant and for a time had more affiliated members than the United Synagogue.[66] In 1891 two of the *chevrot* formed the *Machzike Hadath* (Upholders of Religion) and explicitly repudiated the authority of the Chief Rabbi because of the alleged laxity of his supervision of the supply of kosher meat.[67] These bodies were supported by Yiddish-speakers, many of them largely or totally unadapted to British mores, and many of them active trade unionists and socialist in their political sympathies. So the conflict between the United Synagogue and the various upstart bodies from the East End had many dimensions.

Secondly, there was a section of British-born middle-class Jews who considered the United Synagogue too orthodox. The pioneer in the direction of more radical innovations in worship was the West London Synagogue of British Jews (1842).[68] In 1902 the Jewish Religious Union was formed, which provided the basis for the development of Liberal Judaism. The supporters of these movements remained, however, relatively few in number: many of the less religiously-minded middle-class Jews were content to remain affiliated to an Orthodox synagogue, while ignoring many of the requirements of Orthodox observance.[69]

Thirdly, there were those who had been brought up as Jews, but in later life deliberately rejected all Jewish observances. Again, these were in two groups. There was a small section of wealthy Jews, many of them men educated at public schools, or women married to Anglicans, who converted to Anglicanism.[70] On the other hand, there was a larger section of working-class Jewish radicals who, by the early twentieth century, had abandoned the Jewish faith and adopted socialism or anarchism as a secular creed.[71] While the first group often moved outside the Jewish community altogether, the latter tended to marry Jews and to remain in an overwhelmingly Jewish environment.[72]

Secularists and Agnostics

Those who rejected all kinds of organised religion were a small minority in Victorian and Edwardian England, but they none the less had considerable influence, and they were growing in numbers during this period. They were agreed in the fact that they did not believe the kind of religion taught by the orthodox churches, but they differed considerably among themselves as to what they did believe.[73] For instance, there is a distinction to be made between deists, agnostics and atheists. The atheists, of whom the most famous was Charles Bradlaugh, President of the National Secular Society from 1866 until 1891, simply said 'There is no God.' But they were a minority within a minority. More typical were the deists and agnostics. Deism, which had been the most common form of scepticism in the eighteenth and early nineteenth centuries, but was declining by the Victorian period, asserted that there is a Creator God, who can be known through the evidence of nature and through the use of our reason, but rejected all purported specific revelations of God, arguing that all of them contained false and unnecessary doctrines, and had led to a spirit of intolerance and fanaticism. The most influential exponent of deism was Tom Paine, whose *Age of Reason* (1794) for long remained the most widely read critique of Christianity in the English language.

In the later nineteenth century the vogue among religious doubters was for agnosticism. This term was coined by the scientist T. H. Huxley, in 1869, to denote the belief that the existence of God can neither be proved nor disproved – if there is a Supreme Being, it is by its nature unknowable, and human beings should not commit themselves to any belief that is not scientifically demonstrable. In 1893 the new doctrine received its fullest exposition in *An Agnostic's Apology*, by Leslie Stephen, who in 1862 had abandoned his Anglican orders and his Cambridge fellowship, after concluding that he no longer believed and, indeed, that he never really had believed.[74] To some extent the differences between these different categories of unbeliever were as much a matter of temperament or social position as belief. A Lancashire working-class secularist was credited with the observation that 'Agnostic is nowt but atheist with top hat.'[75]

Broadly speaking, it is possible to distinguish between two main streams of religious scepticism in the Victorian period, one with its roots in popular radicalism, and the other drawing on ideas developed by sections of the scientific and literary intelligentsia. In mid-nineteenth-century England, religious doubt was widely regarded as disreputable – partly because of a suspicion that it provided a philosophical smokescreen for those whose main objective was to free themselves of the moral restraints imposed by religion. So doubters were faced with a constant battle to demonstrate their moral credentials, and all sorts of euphemisms were devised to make scepticism more socially acceptable. In England, as elsewhere, it was common for non-believers to refer to themselves as 'freethinkers', freedom being generally recognised as a valuable quality; and if someone was referred to as an 'advanced' thinker, it usually meant that they rejected religion. Tennyson devised the new category of 'honest doubt', which he placed on a higher moral plain not only than 'dishonest doubt' but also than belief, because it meant a painful and courageous acceptance of uncertainties in areas where one would prefer to have certainties.[76]

Popular scepticism tended to be practical, political and organised. It found its main expression in the various secular societies, which in 1866 came together in the National Secular Society, and which reached their numerical peak in the 1880s during Bradlaugh's campaign to take his seat in Parliament.[77] Bradlaugh had been elected Liberal MP for Northampton in 1880, but was prevented from taking his seat on the grounds that as an atheist he was unable to take the oath. Bradlaugh wanted to be allowed to affirm instead, but only in 1886 was a Bill passed giving MPs this right. Even in the peak year of 1883, there were only 110 freethought societies in England, with a combined membership of a few thousand – which might be expanded to a maximum constituency of 60,000 if the many sympathisers were counted, who came to hear famous speakers, but never became paid-up members. The great majority were concentrated in three regions of the country: London, south-east Lancashire and west Yorkshire, and the north-east. Most were drawn from the upper working class or lower middle class.[78] In strictly numerical terms they were insignificant, even by comparison with many relatively small Nonconformist denominations. But their significance lay not so much in numbers as in the influence exercised by activists, many of whom were prominent in Liberal and later Labour politics, in trade unionism, or in radical campaigns of all kinds. Bradlaugh, for instance, was a prominent popular public speaker, not only in support of secularism, but in support of such causes as republicanism, anti-imperialism and opposition to coercion in Ireland. He also drew huge crowds for public debates with Christian champions. These events would last for several nights running, and in some respects resembled modern football matches, in that both the Christian and the Secularist champions would have teams of supporters in the audience ready to heckle the opposition, and fights sometimes broke out between the rival groups of fans.[79]

The secularist ethos is well brought out by a family history of the Davies family from Ancoats in Manchester. They had come to Manchester from north Wales in the 1840s, and many of them had skilled jobs in the textile and engineering industries. All of them seem to have been secularists, apart from one Primitive Methodist. Over several generations they had supported the radical causes of the day, beginning with Chartism, and moving through support for birth control to socialism. 'They held firmly that "religion is the opium of the people" – propaganda to keep the workers docile in the hope of a reward hereafter.' One member of the family, a cotton-spinner blacklisted by the employers, was remembered for his enthusiastic reading of Darwin and Marx and for a library that included Plato, Aristotle and Voltaire: 'Pa Holt was what was then called a Determinist, he believed that people were what their heredity and environment made them.

He denied "free will" and held that actions followed from a balance of desires.'[80]

Pa Holt was part of a relatively coherent and homogeneous tradition, firmly rooted in a distinctive social milieu. Middle and upper-class agnosticism was a more inchoate phenomenon. In so far as it had a home it was in the north-west London suburb of St John's Wood, which was already by the 1850s established as the characteristic place of residence of the more heterodox elements of the intelligentsia, including such luminaries as the novelist George Eliot. Later, this district was home to the scientist T. H. Huxley and the sociologist Herbert Spencer, and indeed Bradlaugh himself eventually found a home in St John's Wood – at some distance from his supporters in such artisan districts as Clerkenwell. In the 1850s the main organ of 'advanced' thought was the *Westminster Review* – contributors to which included not only unbelievers such as George Eliot or Frederic Harrison, but some very liberal Unitarians and Broad Church Anglicans.[81]

At this stage avowed unbelievers were a tiny minority in the middle and upper classes, and a lot of their intellectual sustinence came from Germany, where the 1830s and 1840s had seen the rise of the Tübingen School of radical biblical critics and the materialistic philosophy of Feuerbach. Throughout the nineteenth century, the German-speaking countries were the front-runners in the development of atheistic ideas, and the English-speaking world lagged far behind. Not until the 1870s and 1880s was there a relatively large body of agnostics and atheists in the middle and upper classes – mainly men, though by the 1890s journalists had devised the concept of the 'New Woman' to describe a new kind of young middle-class woman who, besides being a feminist, desiring the fullest possible education followed by a career, and being willing to talk freely and openly about sex, was very often an agnostic as well.[82]

Other Religious Groups

While the great majority of Victorians and Edwardians fell into one of the five religious or anti-religious categories so far described, there were a number of small religious groups completely outside the mainstream, of which the most important were the Mormons, the Spiritualists and the Theosophists. The Mormons grew rapidly in the 1840s, especially among the working class in Lancashire, but then declined with equal rapidity in the 1850s and 1860s because of emigration to Utah.[83] Theosophy, another American import, reached Britain in 1878. Its appeal was mainly to members of the middle class, who saw Christianity as too narrow, and who favoured an undogmatic mysticism, drawing especially on ideas drawn from Hinduism and Buddhism. It grew in the early twentieth century, when the churches were declining, and reached a peak of 5000 members in 160 lodges in 1927. So membership was scattered thinly but widely.[84]

Spiritualism was a more permanent and widely diffused presence in the Victorian and Edwardian religious scene. The movement took a variety of forms, including Spiritualist churches, famous mediums with a following in London Society, and those with a localised following. All had in common the central belief that it is possible to communicate with the spirits of those who have died. It had an obvious attraction for those who had suffered tragic bereavement, and the First World War, in particular, saw an upsurge of interest.[85] Mediums were also sought out by those with pressing problems to which they could not find any answer. But Spiritualism as an ideology appealed mainly to those who wanted a middle path between Christian orthodoxy and atheism. These included Christians in revolt against the harshness of certain orthodox tenets, especially the doctrine of hell, and secularists, who had rejected the churches, but refused to accept a strictly materialist view of the world. Organised Spiritualism was a mainly working-class and lower middle-class phenomenon, with its original stronghold in the Yorkshire textile town of Keighley, where a group was formed in 1853, the original converts being mainly Owenites and secularists – indeed, in his last years, Robert Owen himself was converted to Spiritualism.[86] West Yorkshire remained a stronghold of the movement: 'In Bradford, Bingley and other Yorkshire towns,' claimed the *Westminster Review* in 1862, 'there are [secularists], once notorious for believing nothing, now equally notorious for believing everything.'[87]

The links with political radicalism remained important. Like many other small religious denominations with a plebeian membership they produced far more than their fair share of labour movement activists, including particularly many members of the Independent Labour Party, whose 'ethical socialism' tended to be more attractive to Spiritualists than the Marxism of the Social Democratic Federation. The other important link within working-class communities was between Spiritualism and unorthodox healing. For instance, Logie Barrow has identified a network of mediums operating in the Manchester area in the 1880s including J. W. Owen, 'qualified Medical Herbalist', who also practised mesmerism; W. Johnson, 'the well-known trance medium'; and E. Gallagher 'Medical Clairvoyant'.[88] No doubt those seeking physical or psychological healing from these practitioners included a much wider circle than those who were actively involved in the Spiritualist movement.

There was also a more middle-class or aristocratic form of Spiritualism, which was in vogue from about the 1870s onwards and which, likewise, received a boost during the First World War. This branch of Spiritualism did not form an organised movement, but it had a very considerable following around the end of the nineteenth and the beginning of the twentieth century, including among its devotees, Sir Arthur Conan Doyle, creator of Sherlock Holmes; Sir Edward Marshall Hall, the great defence lawyer; and Sir Oliver Lodge, the scientist. This form of Spiritualism tended to lack the social–political dimension that was so important to its plebeian counterpart. Its significance was primarily intellectual. It appealed to those who wanted a free-ranging and unprejudiced investigation of bizarre psychic phenomena, untramelled by the dogmas either of orthodox Christianity or of orthodox science. It fitted well with the ethos of experimentation and of moral and intellectual individualism that was particularly characteristic of the 1890s.[89]

Neutrality

Finally there were some who were so completely uninterested in religion that they neither identified themselves with any denomination nor declared themselves to be secularists or agnostics. There is no doubt that most such people came from the poorer sections of the urban working class, or from other socially marginal groups such as smallholders, fishermen, miners or brickmakers living in remote settlements. George Bourne, in his account of a Surrey heathland hamlet, described the kind of community which could for a long time remain largely outside the competing worlds of church and chapel:

In estimating the influence of the Church (Dissent has but a small following here), it should be remembered that until some time after the enclosure of the common the village held no place of worship of any denomination. Moreover the comparatively few inhabitants of that time were free from interference by rich people or by resident employers. They had the valley to themselves; they had always lived as they liked and been as rough as they liked. . . . We may therefore surmise that when the church was built a sprinkling at least of the villagers were none too pleased. This may explain the sullen hostility of which the clergy are still the objects in certain quarters of the village. . . .

The same causes may have something to do with the

fact that the majority of the labouring men appear to take no interest at all in religion.[90]

But it is much less clear how widespread such total neutrality was, even in communities of this kind. Middle-class observers – usually in a spirit of anxiety or horrified condemnation, but occasionally with some degree of envy or admiration – sometimes made sweeping claims about the 'heathenism' or 'indifference' of the poor. For instance, an analysis of voting patterns in the Lancashire factory districts showed that religious affiliation was the principal influence – Anglicans being mainly Tory, while Dissenters, Methodists, Catholics and Secularists were mainly Liberal. However, the author concluded that the key group were 'the indifferents', who had no such predetermined loyalties, and whom he estimated as comprising half of the factory population.[91] But it all depends on how one defines the 'indifferent'. If the criterion was formal membership or regular attendance at a church, chapel or freethought society, the claim that half or more of the population were 'indifferent' would no doubt be valid. On the other hand it is clear that many people felt themselves as belonging to a particular religious denomination – even if they allowed themselves to be represented at church by their children. Moreover, many people who seldom or never attended services still had strongly held religious beliefs.

It is clear that in adopting regular church attendance as the main evidence as to whether a person was 'religious' or not, historians have adopted the criteria of the clergy of the time, rather than those of the working-class people themselves, whose criteria were often quite different.[92] In this area of popular religious belief and allegiance, oral history has revolutionised historians' understanding during the last few years. Interviews with those brought up in the late Victorian and Edwardian period indicate that there were very few households which did not have associations with one or more religious denomination. (In some households, of course, there were tensions caused by competing religious loyalties.) The overwhelming majority of children were sent to a church or Sunday School. In some cases, the choice of denomination seems to have been random and the parents took no apparent interest in the religious education received by their children. But such total indifference seems to have been the exception rather than the rule. In most cases the parents (or sometimes the mother) selected for the child the denomination which they themselves belonged to. The oral evidence also provides a wealth of information about the religious beliefs of non-church-goers. Sometimes, such people were simply indifferent or hostile (this was more often the case with men than with women). But very often they had their own forms of belief, which may have been different from those of clergy or regular church-goers, but were none the less firmly held, and important in shaping their view of the world and the way they related to other people.

Relations Between Religious Groups

These seven categories of belief or unbelief were not entirely mutually exclusive. In particular there was some degree of overlap between church and chapel. Among the Wesleyan Methodists there had, until about 1830, been a large element of 'Church Methodists', who continued to receive the sacraments at their parish church while also being members of a Methodist circuit. By 1850 denominational identities had become more sharply defined following the tensions of the 1830s and 1840s, caused both by the rise of the Oxford Movement and by the educational policies of Peel's Conservative government, which were seen as biased towards the Church of England. The development of ritualism in the second half of the nineteenth century led to further alienation of Wesleyans from the Church of England, and political tensions also increased as more and more Methodists came to share the Liberalism of the Old Dissent.[93] But there were still many people, especially in rural areas, who did not feel fully committed either to the Church of England or to the Methodists, and would happily attend services of either kind. One Lincolnshire curate was told by a parishioner: 'We comes to church in the morning to please you, Sir, and goes to chapel at night to save our souls.'[94]

The nearest thing to a universally recognisable symbol of the gulf between church and chapel was the different attitudes to alcoholic drink. In 1850 total abstinence had not yet won general acceptance among Nonconformists. Its most fervent advocates were found at the plebeian end of the Dissenting world. There was still resistance on the part of many Wesleyans, who saw it as a fad of ranters and radicals, and from more middle-class Dissenters who saw their glass of wine as a normal and harmless part of a cultivated life-style. But with each new generation of Nonconformists the teetotal shibboleth gained wider acceptance, until its authority stood at a peak in the years around the end of the nineteenth and the beginning of the twentieth centuries, when temperance campaigning fitted well with the strong social-reforming and progress-oriented emphasis of much Nonconformist preaching. It is estimated that between 1879 and 1904, the proportion of Congregational ministers who were total abstainers rose from 35 per cent to 83 per cent, and that by 1907, 98 per cent of Baptist theological students were teetotallers.[95]

On the Anglican side, there was certainly a considerable minority of teetotallers, including by the end of the century an Archbishop of Canterbury, Frederick Temple. Yet in the eyes of most Anglicans, it was Nonconformist temperance enthusiasm that best symbolised their puritanism and fanaticism. Satirists repeatedly portrayed Nonconformists as obsessively earnest, narrow-minded killjoys. Generations of Anglicans saw Nonconformity personified in such Dickensian caricatures as the Reverends Chadband and Stiggins. By contrast, Anglicans claimed to stand for a wider culture, where the arts were appreciated, and God's

good gifts enjoyed without a sore conscience. As one indication of the difference, Douglas Reid has shown that
in the period from the 1850s to the 1880s Anglican
churches in Birmingham were much readier than their
Nonconformist counterparts to provide recreational facilities.[96]

Meanwhile, Nonconformists shared with many secular
radicals the conviction that beer was the opium of the
people, and that total abstinence was the first step towards a future of companionate marriages, happy and well-
fed children, well-furnished homes, and evenings spent
listening to lectures on science or poetry, and attending
religious or political meetings.[97] Some Nonconformists held
that temperance was itself the universal panacea, while
many more saw it as just one essential ingredient in a
varied mixture of social and moral reforms. Temperance
provided common ground between Nonconformity's many
divergent parties and sects. This was especially important
in the period around the turn of the century when chapels
were often deeply divided in politics and theology.

Lines between Protestant and Catholic were more clearly
defined. The Catholic Church regarded attendance at a
Protestant service as a sin; and though discipline was less
tight in most Protestant denominations, Protestants usually
diapproved of Catholicism every bit as strongly as the
Catholics objected to Protestantism. But even here the
two compartments were not completely watertight. Some
Anglicans were strongly attracted by Roman Catholicism,
attended Catholic services from time to time, and attempted
to introduce Roman practices into the Church of England. Conversely, poor Catholics were sometimes attracted
by the greater charitable resources at the disposal of the
Protestant churches. In one poor Preston family a bitter
dispute was caused by the mother's decision to send one
of the children to live with a Protestant family, who sent
her to a Protestant school. The father was furious, but
the mother replied 'Religion won't keep you when all's
said and done.'[98] There were also, especially in Lancashire, considerable numbers of people who had some kind

of mixed identity in that one parent was a Catholic and the other a Protestant. In most cases, however, the parents made a decision to bring the children up in one faith or the other – or in some cases to bring the boys up in one and the girls in the other. So that most individuals saw themselves either as a Protestant or as a Catholic, even if there was a mixture within their family.

There was some overlap between the most liberal end of the range of church and chapel and the more moderate wing of secularism. This applied particularly to Unitarianism, the most liberal of the Christian denominations, which to some extent provided a haven for those whose unorthodox views would have made them unacceptable anywhere else. For instance, the Leicester Secular Society, which was one of the longest-lived, and also one of the least militant, included among its leading members several who also belonged to the Unitarian church.[99] While this situation was the exception among Secularists, who tended to be aggressively opposed to churches of any kind, it was quite common among agnostics, many of whom retained some kind of link with their church and continued to see things of value in the specific religious tradition from which they had come, even if they had lost their faith in God. A notable example would be Thomas Hardy: in his early 20s he became an agnostic and abandoned his plans to enter the Anglican ministry, but he remained deeply attached to the Bible and the Prayer Book and continued throughout his life to attend Anglican services.[100]

Patterns of Religious Practice

As a result of evidence collected by the government, by newspapers, and by the church authorities, and also through examining unpublished church records, it is possible to build up a fairly detailed picture of those involved in organised religion in the Victorian and Edwardian periods. The most familiar source is the national religious census of 1851, carried out in conjunction with the decennial population census, which included information on church attendance and on the accommodation provided by religious bodies. There were also numerous censuses of church attendance conducted by newspapers, most notably in the year 1881, though there were also a number of counts carried out in the years 1902–4. Many denominations, most notably the various branches of Methodism, published annual statistics of membership, which make it possible to plot the regional distribution of the various churches. These sources were all published, and so are fairly easily accessible. However, many forms of church records remain in local history libraries or in church cupboards. These include registers of baptisms and marriages, often listing the occupations of the child's father or of the couple marrying, or membership rolls. Where membership lists give addresses, it is sometimes possible to identify the members in censuses and thus build up a picture of the ages, occupations and gender of members (and sometimes of adherents). Broadly speaking, middle-class people were more likely to attend church or to be church members than working-class people, rural-dwellers more than those living in cities, and women more than men. There were also considerable regional differences. Inevitably, however, the picture was much more complicated than this bald summary might suggest.

Both the highest and the lowest levels of attendance were found in small towns and rural areas. At the top of the list was St Ives (Huntingdonshire), with an Index of Attendance (IA) of 116, and at the bottom was Longtown (Cumberland), with 16. Some other rural areas – mainly in the far north, near the border with Scotland, or the far west, near the border with Wales – had attendance levels far below the national average. But generally, rural and small-town attendances, at IA 71, were somewhat above the national average (of 59) and urban attendances somewhat below the average, at 49. There was thus a clear though not dramatically wide difference. Inevitably the averages concealed considerable variations. In particular, both rural areas and industrial villages varied very widely in their levels of church-going. In the cities the range was narrower. In the pluralistic urban environment there was always a considerable non-church-going population, and there was also a wide range of different religious denominations available. By contrast, smaller communities sometimes had very high levels of church-going, and were often dominated by the Church of England, or by the Church of England together with one branch of Dissent. Registration Districts with very high levels of attendance (IA of over 75) included many with substantial populations of industrial workers or miners, for instance, Haslingden (cotton workers), Nuneaton (silk), Hinckley (hosiery), Melksham (wool), Truro (miners), but very few large towns. On the other hand there was no simple correlation between urbanisation and a decline in church-going. For instance, many of the Black Country towns had a higher level of church-going than the surrounding countryside,[101] and in the northern counties of Cumberland, Durham and Northumberland attendance was higher in the towns than in the countryside.

The pattern of urban/rural differentiation was complicated by regional differences.[102] Towns situated in areas of high rural church-going (such as Bristol) tended to have higher levels of church-going than those situated within regions of low rural attendance (for example Carlisle). Since migration to the towns was generally over short distances, it is hardly surprising that towns took on some of the colouring of the surrounding countryside; conversely, cultural influences emanating from the towns may have helped to shape the culture of particular rural regions. Most of the larger towns were situated within regions of relatively low rural church-going, and this influenced their patterns of religious practice as much as any factor that was common to cities in general. The belt of high rural church-going ran from Cornwall and Devon, along the south coast as far as Hampshire and the Isle of

Wight, and up through Somerset, Gloucestershire and Wiltshire, across the south and east midlands to East Anglia. Rural church-going was around the national average in Kent, most of the north midlands and Yorkshire. It was below average in Sussex, Surrey and Middlesex, in the west midlands, in Lancashire, and in the north. Cities which fell within the belt of high rural attendance, such as Plymouth, Bristol and Leicester, had levels of attendance above the urban average, but most cities fell outside this belt (see Map 3).

Two kinds of evidence throw light on the class pattern of church-going: the religious censuses (which by 1881 can be broken down by district, in order to correlate attendance patterns with social composition), and membership records. The first type of evidence indicates a clear pattern whereby church-going was generally significantly higher in middle-class than in working-class districts. In Birmingham, for instance, attendance on a given Sunday peaked at around 40 per cent of the total population in upper middle-class districts such as Edgbaston and Moseley; it was 33 per cent in the middle-class district of Handsworth; 20 per cent in Balsall Heath, a typical working-class district; and about 10 per cent in the poor districts immediately to the north and east of the city centre. A very similar pattern was shown in London. In more church-going towns, such as Bristol or Leicester, both middle-class and working-class attendance levels were higher, but the same basic pattern was repeated. The only city to be to some extent out of line was Liverpool, where the high church-going levels in Catholic working-class districts exceeded those in some middle-class districts.[103]

However, analysis of Nonconformist membership records shows that nearly every church included a substantial working-class element among its membership. Here the most thorough study is that by Rosemary Chadwick on Nonconformist congregations in Bradford towards the end of the nineteenth century. She found that working-class people were somewhat under-represented among the

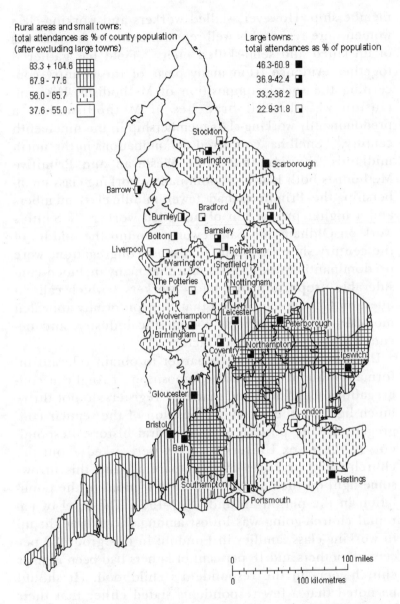

Rural areas and small towns:
total attendances as % of county population
(after excluding large towns)

83.3 + 104.6
67.9 - 77.6
56.0 - 65.7
37.6 - 55.0

Large towns:
total attendances as % of population

46.3-60.9
36.9-42.4
33.2-36.2
22.9-31.8

Stockton
Darlington
Scarborough
Barrow
Bradford
Hull
Burnley
Bolton
Barnsley
Liverpool
Rotherham
Warrington
Sheffield
The Potteries
Nottingham
Wolverhampton
Leicester
Birmingham
Peterborough
Coventry
Northampton
Ipswich
Gloucester
London
Bristol
Bath
Hastings
Southampton
Portsmouth

0   100 miles
0   100 kilometres

*Map 3   Church attendance in rural areas in 1851 compared
with attendance in large towns in the 1880s*

Note: The 1851 census included Sunday School children,
whereas the census in the 1880s did not

63

membership. However, skilled workers and working-class women were reasonably well-represented: the shortfall was of unskilled and semi-skilled men.[104] Field has gathered together evidence from many parts of the country concerning the social composition of Methodism. His conclusion was that all branches of Methodism had a predominantly working-class membership in the nineteenth century.[105] Snell has compared denominations in the north midlands, showing that while Wesleyan and Primitive Methodists both had a predominantly working-class membership, the Primitives had fewer middle-class members and a higher proportion of unskilled workers.[106] Smith's work on Oldham and Saddleworth around the middle of the century shows not only that most congregations were predominantly working-class, but that many included considerable proportions of factory workers – which calls in question Gilbert's argument that Nonconformity appealed most strongly to workers in domestic industry, and declined with the rise of the factory.[107]

Unfortunately, it is much harder to obtain relevant information about the social composition of Anglican congregations. Baptismal and marriage registers do not throw much light on the social composition of the regular congregation. One possible source is oral history. Respondents in the Essex University survey were asked about the church-going practices of their parents, and this throws some light on the habits of different sections of the population in the period around 1890–1914. The level of parental church-going was lowest among those brought up in working-class families in London: in this group 22 per cent of mothers and 18 per cent of fathers had been regular church-goers in the respondent's childhood. (It should be noted that a few respondents stated either that their parents had formerly been church-goers but had given it up, or else that they started going to church after their children had grown up: such people are excluded from the present calculations.) The level was somewhat higher among those brought up in working-class families in Lancashire: in this group 40 per cent of mothers and 32 per cent of fathers were regular church-goers. It was higher still for those brought up in agricultural working-class families: here the figures were 58 per cent of mothers and 50 per cent of fathers. And it was highest of all for middle-class families, where the figures were 75 per cent of mothers and 60 per cent of fathers. In all cases there was a mixture of Anglicans and Nonconformists, plus a few Roman Catholics.

In view of the small number of cases involved, these figures must not be taken too literally. In any case, they refer to no precise point in time, since the respondents' memories refer to a variety of different points within a period of about twenty-five years. However, it is interesting to note that Elizabeth Roberts's interviews with those brought up in working-class families in north Lancashire produced very similar results to those in the Essex survey from south Lancashire. Some general conclusions may be drawn. First, church-going by mothers was consistently higher than that by fathers, though the difference was not as great as some contemporary observers claimed. Secondly, church-going by the urban working class was a minority activity, but even in London the minority was far from negligible, and in Lancashire the numbers involved appear to have been very considerable. Working-class church-going seems to have been considerably higher than was recognised by some middle-class observers, such as Horace Mann, the author of the famous official commentary on the 1851 census.[108] It was also somewhat higher than was suggested by the censuses, which counted attendance on a single day, and so missed some of those who attended regularly, but not every Sunday.

These figures confirm the importance of class. Middle-class church involvement in this period was certainly high – though not quite as high as some historians have claimed (Patrick Joyce even goes so far as to assume that all middle-class families in Lancashire industrial towns went to church at the time of the 1851 census).[109] The figures also suggest that rural/urban differences need to be taken seriously, though the evidence is inconclusive.[110] The patterns of church-going in the rural working class remain exceptionally unclear, because of both regional and occupational variations, but it would seem that at least in some regions (for example Essex and Suffolk, where a lot of the interviewing was done) the level of attendance was rather high.

The main analysis of the gender composition of church membership has been done by Rosemary Chadwick (in respect of Bradford Nonconformity) and by Clive Field (who has looked at evidence concerning Baptists and Congregationalists from all parts of the country).[111] The great majority of the congregations analysed had a female majority, the proportion of women generally falling between 60 per cent and 70 per cent. The major exception was the Bradford Quakers, where the sexes were more or less equally balanced. Generally speaking the proportion of women was higher in congregations with a large working-class membership than in those that were mainly middle-class. For instance, at one Congregational chapel women made up 58 per cent of middle-class members, but 78 per cent of working-class members, and at another the proportions were 65 per cent and 82 per cent.[112] Bradford's working-class families, Chadwick argues, frequently saw religion as 'women's work', and thus falling within the women's sphere of responsibility,[113] whereas middle-class families frequently favoured companionate marriages in which husband and wife spent a large part of their free hours together. A few church-attendance censuses, notably that held in London in 1902–3, separately counted men, women, and children.[114]

While women attended church in somewhat greater numbers than men, the differential was much less than in the case of church membership. In the County of London the attendance rate upon a single Sunday was 24 per cent for women and 18 per cent for men. It would seem that there were many men who attended services, but were reluctant to enter the deeper commitment associated with applying for membership.

There were significant denominational differences in the relative proportion of male and female attendances. Oral history suggests that there may also be regional differences. The 1902–3 census of London showed that 61 per cent of church-goers aged 15 and over were female, whereas only 54 per cent of the population were female. The Christian denominations fell into three clear categories. The highest proportion of females were found in services of the Church of England (66%) and Roman Catholics (64%). Then bunched together in the middle were most of the larger Nonconformist denominations, including the Baptists (60%), Brethren and Presbyterians (59%), Free Methodists, Congregationalists, Wesleyans and Salvation Army (all 57%). Finally there were two denominations where males were slightly over-represented, namely the Quakers and Primitive Methodists (both 52%). Meanwhile the Jews had a completely different patterns of synagogue attendance, with only 22 per cent being female. A number of counts made in smaller towns in the years 1901–6 produced similar results. In every case the proportion of women in Anglican congregations was higher than in Nonconformist services, whereas the high proportions of women in Catholic congregations in some towns contrasted with low proportions in others – possibly because of demographic differences between the Catholic communities.[115]

There seem to be four factors which influenced the degree to which services of a particular denomination were attended with much greater frequency by members of one sex than of the other. For reasons already mentioned, the first factor favouring such a disparity was a high proportion of working-class members. A second factor was the existence of sharp distinctions between lay and clerical roles. This seems to be because clericalism provoked a corresponding anti-clericalism which, in this period, was a predominantly male phenomenon, probably because women were accustomed to the idea of the public sphere being dominated by men, and so resented clerical pretensions less than men did.

A third factor was the degree to which the denomination posited essential differences between the qualities of women and men, and thus separated male from female roles both within the church and in society generally. This was done most explicitly by Orthodox Judaism, which distinguished between public religious observances, which were a male responsibility, and those within the home, which were a female responsibility.[116] In practice, Anglicans and Roman Catholics, and to a lesser extent mainstream Nonconformists, often took the view that religious matters belonged to women's sphere of responsibility, although this particular separation of spheres was not any part of the official teaching of their churches.[117] The fact that preaching and administration of the sacraments were male monopolies, and that positions of lay leadership were exclusively male, helped to promote the idea that women and men were essentially different, and thus to legitimate the idea, widely current throughout society, that churchgoing was a highly appropriate activity for women, but less so for men. On the other hand, denominations such as the Quakers and the Salvation Army where, by the early 1900s, all offices were open to members of either sex, or the Primitive Methodists, where women were local preachers, helped to subvert such assumptions.[118]

Finally, the disparity tended to be lower in the more sectarian denominations. This reflected the fact that sectarian families had made a commitment to a way of life which to some extent set them apart, and made them partly immune to many of the assumptions prevailing in the wider society. Since the Quakers scored high on all the factors associated with an even balance between the sexes, and low on all those associated with a disparity, it is not surprising that they come nearest to reproducing in their meetings the gender distribution found in the general population. The other denominations mixed characteristics pointing in one direction with those that pointed in the other.

While patterns of male and female involvement were influenced by the teachings, structures and ethos of the various denominations, and by class differences, they may also have been affected by the nature of the local economy. Respondents in the Essex University oral history survey, which interviewed a socially and regionally representative sample of men and women born between 1872 and 1909, were asked about the church-going habits of their parents. Taking those respondents who were brought up in working-class families in English cities and industrial districts, we find that about 35 per cent replied that their mother attended church with some degree of frequency during their childhood and that about 25 per cent replied that their father did so. In Lancashire and West Yorkshire the gap was fairly narrow, attendance by both mothers and fathers being high; in the north-east and the north midlands, the gap was wide, attendance by mothers being high and by fathers being low; and in London the gap was narrow again, with attendance by both being low.

One possible clue to the explanation for these differences is offered by Elizabeth Roberts's comment that the sexual division of labour within the family was much less rigidly defined in textile towns, where a high proportion of married women worked in factories, than in towns dominated by engineering, where women tended to be limited to such home-based jobs as taking in washing.[119] It is particularly interesting to note that whereas church-going by women was no lower in Lancashire than in other regions of England, that by men was higher. The greater interchangeability of roles included, for instance, the possibility that the husband would take the children to church while the wife stayed at home – something that does not seem to have happened in any of the north-eastern families whose habits were recorded in the Essex interviews.

In areas such as the north-east, where the economy was dominated by heavy engineering and mining, the pattern seems to have been for a more sharply defined division between male and female worlds. The relatively high earnings enjoyed by a section of the male workforce opened the way for two possibilities: first, the development of a strong culture of exclusively male institutions, including trade unions, friendly societies and pubs; and secondly, wives who were not required to earn money, and who thus had more time to devote not only to their children, but also to the church and/or the Women's Co-op Guild.[120]

In London the combination of a large middle and upper-class presence with the prevalence of industries where earnings were low and/or irregular, including building, docking and tailoring, meant that there were both plenty of opportunities for part-time female employment, and often an acute need for women to supplement the inadequate earnings of their husbands. Working-class London women were accustomed to spend a large part of their time at the sewing-machine or the wash-tub, and there were large numbers of them who had little life outside the home.[121] On the other hand, for those who did get out, churches and chapels were in competition with the numerous music-halls and theatres. While mothers' meetings, in particular, attracted large numbers in London too,[122] churches and chapels did not enjoy the degree of cultural dominance that they had in many parts of the north, where they were the only alternative to the pubs.

2

A CHRISTIAN COUNTRY?

Victorians liked to refer to England as a 'Christian country'. In doing so, they could point to the existence of the established church, whose supreme governor was the reigning monarch, to the facts that in the coronation ceremony the new sovereign was crowned by the Archbishop of Canterbury, that Anglican bishops sat in the House of Lords, and that Christianity was legally protected through the blasphemy laws. Yet all of this was rather superficial. In the twentieth century there have been several countries, England among them, which have undergone considerable secularisation while the superstructure of unity between church and state has remained largely in place. More significant, therefore, was the massive presence of Christianity in so many areas of daily life. The first part of this chapter will explore some of the dimensions of this Christian presence. In the latter part of the chapter I shall look at some of the limits of this pervasive Christianity.

Pervasive Christianity

The most obvious symbols of this Christian presence were the religious buildings which filled most townscapes and many landscapes. In some counties, such as Norfolk, and some ancient cities, like Norwich and York, the super-abundance of churches was a legacy of medieval piety and prosperity, and actually exceeded nineteenth-century requirements. But in most parts of the country that century saw a massive increase in the number of religious structures. Many villages were given an Anglican church for the first time, and in many more the old parish church was joined by a Dissenting chapel or even by several chapels. In the larger towns, most denominations wanted their own prestigious city-centre church or chapel. Simon Green has found that in the West Riding of Yorkshire 1840–60 was a crucial period: the larger Nonconformist denominations would demonstrate that they had arrived by building a large central chapel to rival the parish church, and the Anglicans hit back by enlarging and improving the parish church. Middle-class suburbs also attracted large and imposing churches, while religious buildings in working-class areas made up in number what they lacked in size: almost ever street had a church, chapel, mission hall, Sunday School, parish hall or institute. The period of most extensive building was the last third of the nineteenth century, and indeed Green concludes that 'probably about two-thirds of all those churches, chapels and mission-churches *ever built* in Halifax and Keighley were constructed between the passing of the Second Reform Act and the death of Queen Victoria'. Halifax had 7 churches in 1801, 25 in 1851, 99 in 1901, 104 in 1914 – and then by 1939 the total had dropped to about 80. In 1901 the population of Halifax was 106,000, so that there was approximately one religious building for every 1000 people. As Green shows, one of the major motives for building was sectarian competition and one of its major consequences was a legacy of debt which bedevilled many congregations, especially from the 1890s onwards.[1] So the profusion of religious structures went beyond what most denominations could afford, and often beyond what the people could effectively use.[2] But it did mean that organised religion was highly visible and accessible, and available in a variety of forms suited to a wide range of tastes.

The great majority of the population began their relationship with the Christian churches in the first few months of life by receiving infant baptism. Figures are available for the years 1902–14 which show that the proportion of Anglican baptisms to live births oscillated between 66 per cent and 70 per cent.[3] Probably about 5 per cent of children were baptised as Catholics, and it is likely that a large proportion of the rest were baptised by one of the Nonconformist churches. Although the Prayer Book prescribed that baptism should take place within two weeks of birth, a delay of between one and two months seems to have been normal – though Obelkevich, in his study of rural Lincolnshire, notes that weak and sickly babies were baptised as soon as possible, which suggests that one motive for baptising children was still the fear of what might happen to them if they died a 'heathen'.[4] At least some of the clergy fostered such fears. For instance, a woman brought up in the 1880s in the outer suburbs of London recalls her sister running home screaming from their church school after the vicar had told her 'we wouldn't go to heaven because we weren't christened'.[5] In fact their parents were devout Christians, but believed that baptism should wait until the person concerned knew what he or she was taking on. This was very much a minority viewpoint, confined to Baptists and some independent-minded members of other Nonconformist bodies. However, the motives that guided the conforming majority of parents to the font are less clear.

The greatest degree of light on this subject has been thrown by two studies of working-class south London, by Alan Bartlett and Sarah Williams, based substantially on oral history. Alan Bartlett, on the basis of his study of Bermondsey around the turn of the century, suggests that the meanings given were 'varied and multi-dimensional' and included 'naming, luck, gaining a christian identity, thanksgiving to God'.[6] Two quotations from interviews reflect different aspects of the phenomenon. A Bermondsey woman, when asked why children were always baptised, replied 'just rules and regulations', and a Southwark woman, when asked whether her mother went to church, replied:

> She believed, and I mean, when any of us were born, she'd go to church, before she went out anywhere, to be blessed, and she's make sure we was all christened.[7]

The first quotation suggests that having your children christened had become a matter of respectable behaviour. The second suggests that it meant that you were a Christian, and that your child was a Christian, even if you seldom went to church at other times. This latter interpretation is also suggested by another of Sarah Williams's interviewees, who expressed approval of a vicar who had regarded all those families whose children were baptised at his church as members of his congregation and, in particular, visited them when they were sick; she was very indignant at another vicar who paid attention only to those who regularly attended services.[8]

In Bermondsey it was only fairly late in the nineteenth century that a pattern of very high levels of baptism was achieved. Ratios of baptisms to live births were still rising in the 1880s and 1890s, and may have reached a peak in the early twentieth century. Up to that time, there were significant numbers of working-class families who did not baptise their children, either because they did not think it important, or because they had lost contact with all churches or chapels, or because they had no 'respectable' clothes to wear during the ceremony. The rising proportion of baptisms seems to have been associated with the processes by which the Church of England put down roots in a relatively newly-formed working-class community, and whereby, as rates of in-migration slowed down, an increasing proportion of the population had kin living locally, had intimate relations with neighbours, and were personally acquainted with local clergy or other church workers.[9]

The next stage in a person's religious upbringing was likely to be the learning of prayers – usually with mother, though sometimes with father, an elder sister, a grand-parent or, in more exalted circles, a nurse. In the early years of the twentieth century, it would seem that the large majority of children brought up in middle-class or rural families were taught their prayers as children, though in London working-class families the proportion was lower – about a half.[10] A woman brought up in an Essex vil-lage, where her father was a gardener at the big house, described a typical procedure: 'Oh yes, I had to fall on me knees and say me prayers before I went to sleep, yes. "God bless daddy, mummy, granddad, grandma, aunts, uncles, cousins, and ... all unkind friends and all good friends. For Jesus Christ's sake, amen". I think that's what it was.'[11] One London working-class woman who was *not* taught her prayers by her mother, felt deprived of a moment of peculiar intimacy between mother and child – she made sure she did better by her own children.[12]

Implicit, of course, in the prayers was belief in God, and many parents told their young children about God in a more explicit way. The Bristol Oral History Project asked interviewees whether as a child they had believed in God. In a sample of twenty-one working-class Bristolians born between 1885 and 1905, thirteen stated that they had and three stated that they had not, while in five cases this question seems to have been omitted. Though this is seldom explicitly stated, it would seem that parents, day schools, and Sundays Schools contributed in about equal measure to the development of people's religious ideas. A few admitted to having had some doubts, but most seem to have taken their belief in God more or less for granted.

The main stress in parental teaching seems to have been that God expected them to be good. As one example, a docker's daughter, born 1897, when asked if she believed in God at the age of 12 or 13, replied: 'Oh, yes we were made to, I mean to say our parents was only poor, but we were made to know there was a God and if you done anything wrong you would be punished. So I remember saying once to my father, he was going to give me a good hiding for something . . . and I said "God wouldn't punish me like that".[13] A woman born in 1895, whose parents were Baptists, and whose father was a boot checker, recalls that she once stole when young, as a result of which she and her mother knelt together and prayed to God for forgiveness: she never stole again.[14] The same emphasis on the moral consequences of belief occurs in the memories of a docker's daughter, born in 1904, who does not seem to have learnt much about religion from her parents, and who regarded religious teaching at her day school as just 'a matter of form', but who became 'a confirmed Christian' as a result of the teaching at Sunday School: 'I knew then that I knew right from wrong and lived a respectable life.'[15] A woman born in 1886, whose parents were respectively a carpenter and a shop assistant, and who 'loved' her Church of England school, remembers having a very vivid sense of God's presence:

I thought God was there. They told us he was and we believed it. I believed it. I always felt that when I went to bed at night, look down over the staircase to see if I could see that eye watching me. Yes it was as near as that, I believed it.

In spite of this emphasis on a God who was 'watching' you, and who would punish wrong-doing, there is little evidence that religious belief became morbid or obsessive. One man admitted to having had an interest in cemeteries, and one women claimed that prolonged attendance at the Shaftesbury mission led to her father contracting 'religious mania'. On the whole, however, the main emphasis of the religion both of the respondents and of their parents seems to have been practical and relatively low-key. Respondents were asked if they thought a lot about heaven and hell as a child. A few explicitly stated that they believed in heaven, and two who had lost close rela-

tives when young said that they believed the loved one
had gone to heaven. One explicitly stated that she believed in hell, but no-one claimed to have thought a lot
about it.[16] There were also a number of respondents who
said that though they believed in God, their religious belief
had not been of great importance to them.

In very poor families, religion meant, above all, charity. As soon as they could walk and talk, poor children
were likely to learn where the best free meals were to be
found. Back-street missions, in particular, often established
a local reputation as places where those in need could
obtain help. For one Preston woman, born into a poor
Irish family in 1898, her earliest happy memories were of
pea soup at a Protestant mission: 'Shepherd Street Mission used to be a grand place for people who were very
poor. Mr Williams never sent anyone away.'[17] The memoirs of an east London criminal, Arthur Harding, provide a vivid description of the place of church charities
in the economy of the very poor. He was born in 1886
and brought up in the Nichol, a district of such notoriety that it was the focus of the London County Council's
first slum-clearance scheme. On weekdays he got his breakfast from the Shaftesbury Mission:

> It was a good breakfast. You got a great big bowl of
> milk. And you had as much bread as you could eat,
> dipped into the milk. The mission was an enormous
> place, with long tables and great murals round the wall,
> pictures of the Crucifixion, feeding the five thousand
> and all that. We used to have a hymn and a 'Thank
> God from whom all blessings flow' and then they'd say,
> 'Now, children, don't be late for school'. . . . Apart from
> breakfast you had to trust for luck for your meals. It
> was no good going home for lunch when you came out
> of school, because your mother wouldn't have time
> to cook anything, even if there was anything to cook.
> You went to Father Jay's, by Holy Trinity. The old Irish
> housekeeper there, she used to make great big jam

puddings. . . . You got a big lump of jam pudding, but if Father Jay was out of puddings you had to go and forage. At that time many people had more empty days than dinner days.[18]

By about the age of 5, children would be ready for Sunday School. By the late Victorian period the overwhelming majority of working-class children went to Sunday School up to the age of about 13. Many middle-class children attended Sunday School too, though church-going middle-class parents might take their children with them, rather than sending them to the more plebeian Sunday School. Sunday Schools were such an established part of working-class life that, beginning in Glasgow in 1892, Socialist Sunday Schools were established, so that the children of non-church-going socialist parents could receive the same kind of training in the parental faith that other children received in Christian Sunday Schools. For instance, a London working-class woman recalls her father coming home from the First World War disillusioned with religion, and immediately telling her that she was switching from an Anglican to a Socialist Sunday School.[19] This was a continuation of an older radical tradition – in the 1840s there had been Chartist Sunday Schools. But these alternatives were very much a minority option.[20]

Some observers were cynical about the motives that prompted parents to send their children, or the degree of thought that went into the choice of school. One London vicar suggested that parents were keen to get their children out of the house, because Sunday afternoon was a favourite time for marital sex. The famous Edwardian journalist and Liberal politician C. F. G. Masterman thought that parents gave so little thought to the nature of the education provided, that schools run by 'mild-mannered and generous Buddhists (provided they were white)' might do as well as those of the Anglicans and Methodists.[21] However, parents varied greatly in the seriousness with which they took their children's religious education.

Masterman and the London vicar probably accurately described the situation at one end of the spectrum, where parents simply recognised that Sunday School was the accepted custom – and one that might have certain advantages. At the other end of the spectrum, there were parents who took a close interest in what their children learnt, and reinforced the lessons with teaching of their own. An east London man recalled his office-cleaner mother reading to him from the Bible every Sunday evening, and saw his own religious upbringing and that which he gave his children as the main reason for the fact that both he and they had grown up as upright citizens.[22] Between the extremes of strong religious commitment and complete uninterest, there were large numbers of parents whose beliefs may not have been so clearly articulated, but who were still conscious of belonging to a particular religious denomination, and of wanting their children brought up in the same way.

By the later nineteenth century, Sunday Schools were so much taken for granted that only parents who either had very strong anti-religious convictions, or were completely indifferent to considerations of respectability, were likely to keep their children away. Even among the former, there were some who let their children go, because they did not want them to feel too different from everybody else; and among the latter three were some whose children insisted on going, even without any parental prompting. The great rise in Sunday School enrolments had taken place during the first half of the nineteenth century. Enrolments as a proportion of the population aged under 15 rose very fast between 1801 and 1851, and more slowly between 1851 and 1881. The peak of around 50 per cent was reached in the period from about 1880 to the First World War. There was then a slow decline in the inter-war years and a much more rapid decline after the Second World War.[23] Clearly a major factor in the early growth of Sunday Schools was their importance as places for the secular education of children who were working all through the week. But by 1880, with compulsory elementary schooling, following on many laws limiting or prohibiting child labour, this motive was no longer important in inducing parents to send their younger children to Sunday School, though some teenagers stayed on at Sunday School after starting work because of the educational facilities.

In this latter period four other kinds of consideration were more important. First there was the child-minding function already mentioned, which was certainly important, especially considering the conditions of severe crowding in which the working-class families, who were the Schools' main customers, frequently lived. Secondly, the importance attached to Sunday Schools as a place of religious and/or moral education certainly should not be under-estimated. For parents who themselves had strong religious convictions, it was more or less a matter of course that they wanted their children brought up to know about the life of Jesus, to hear Bible stories, to sing hymns and to learn about Christian moral teachings – and such parents certainly included many who were not themselves regular church-goers. But other parents who were less certain of their own religion still tended to think that learning about religion was a necessary part of growing up into a decent adult. Robert Tressell, in his caustic novel of Edwardian working-class life, *The Ragged Trousered Philanthropists*, observed that all his characters, however slight their own religious convictions, agreed that 'Religion was a nice thing to teach children.' Thirdly, attendance at Sunday School could lead, directly or indirectly to material benefits. Arthur Harding's mother, who was 'a forager', was well aware of the connections. Arthur was only able to enjoy so many free breakfasts because he picked up tickets at Sunday School. Sunday Schools also played an essential role in establishing her credentials as a member of the 'deserving poor' vis-à-vis the various charities from which she sought help. 'They were always asking whether we was good children or not, and whether we were clean, and whether we went to Sunday School.'[24] Finally, many of the children seem to have enjoyed Sunday School. This was principally because of the treats, which were a major event in the calendar.

Many Sunday School outings seem to have started as counter-attractions to big fairs or race-meetings, but by the later part of the century they had become big events in their own right. There was the sense of adventure associated with going to the seaside, or Epping Forest, or a big country house, after months confined to the city streets. There was the exhilaration of being part of a crowd. There was a partial release of inhibition. There was the food, the games and the prizes. And on the journey back, there was the singing. One satisfied customer summed it all up in the words: 'Do you know it was a lovely afternoon, and it didn't cost us anything.'[25] The treats tend to take pride of place in memories of Sunday School, but they could make an impact in other ways too. One rather unexpected testimony comes from Arthur Harding:

> Everybody in the Nichol went to Sunday School. Morning and afternoon. Twice in the day. The hymns didn't make much impression on me, but the Bible did. 'Jesus loved little children.' They was all very kindly people the teachers, men and women. When I look back I wonder why they done it – there must have been something in it for them. The thing that made a vivid impression on me was the great pictures that were around the wall – Christ feeding the five thousand and all the rest of it; coming up to Jerusalem for the Passover. They were not ordinary pictures but great big murals, half the size of the wall.[26]

Harding was precisely the kind of product which secularists liked to mention, when arguing for the ineffectiveness or even the harmfulness of Sunday School education. But since most of the population passed through Sunday School, supporters of the institution could easily point to philanthropic businessmen, tribunes of the people, or heroic missionaries as counter-examples. Harding was only one of many graduates who made favourable comments about the teachers, and in some other cases the latter seem to have exercised a more formative influence on their pupils. Laqueur, in discussing the development of Sunday Schools in the earlier part of the century, notes that 'Teachers were ... encouraged to develop a highly personal relationship with the children in their class, to get to know their homes, and most importantly to let love and kindness guide their dealings with their classes.'[27] While this no doubt described an ideal that was seldom fully achieved, it was clear that the religious objectives of the Sunday School could only be achieved by persuasion rather than coercion. At its best the Sunday School offered a vision of a better way of life, and the teachers offered attractive role-models to a certain proportion of the pupils. A good example of what Sunday Schools meant to at least some of their pupils is offered by the memoirs of 'An Old Potter', who had grown up in the 1830s and 1840s in Burslem and Tunstall, and who later became a Methodist local preacher. He acquired a passion for reading – and also an old Bible, given as a reward for good reading at Sunday School. In his teens, his Methodist New Connexion Sunday School teacher was a major influence on him; the Sunday School library was his main source of books; and a Young Men's Mutual Improvement Society, based on the Sunday School, was his main intellectual forum; he also developed an enthusiasm for Milton – as a result of which his preaching 'had less of dogma in it than imagination and rhetoric'.[28]

The overwhelming majority of day schools provided some kind of religious education, and a high proportion were attached to a specific religious denomination. Most Roman Catholic and Anglican parishes sponsored an elementary school for working-class and lower middle-class children. There were also considerable numbers of Methodist schools. The British and Foreign Society, founded by Nonconformists in 1808, and later the non-sectarian Board Schools set up as a result of the 1870 Education Act, provided non-denominational religious teaching. At Roman Catholic schools the children were likely to be in trouble on Monday if they had not been seen in church on Sunday.[29] Anglo-Catholic clergy often saw their parish schools as presenting a unique opportunity to inculcate the rising generation with a genuinely 'Catholic' way of looking at the world, and of rising about the pervasive Protestantism of their environment. In Board Schools the main emphasis would be on teaching knowledge of the Bible, though religious teaching was a smaller element in the curriculum and the style of teaching was likely to be more low-key.

The grammar schools (attended by children of the middle class) and public schools (attended by children of the upper middle and upper classes) were generally Anglican, though independent of any church control. Clergymen were regarded as the most suitable headmasters for the boys' grammar and public schools. Indeed, throughout the Victorian period the most prestigious boys' boarding schools, attended by future members of parliament, senior civil servants, colonial administrators, military leaders, and members of the aristocracy and gentry, would only appoint clergymen. Roman Catholics and Nonconformists, recognising the pull of the great schools and the conversion to the established church of young men from wealthy non-Anglican families, established their own rival institutions – though only in the twentieth century, as denominational distinctions have lost a large part of their significance, have such schools as the Catholic Ampleforth or the Nonconformist Mill Hill won recognition as equals by their Anglican counterparts.[30]

By the time a child left school he or she was likely to have some sense of sectarian identity, whether acquired through school, through the influence of parents, or a mixture of both. This sense of sectarian identity was strongest where the main division was between Catholics and

Protestants, or between Christians and Jews. It was somewhat weaker in areas where the main division was between
church and chapel, sincè some people quite happily attended both Anglican and Nonconformist services, and
there was no stigma on intermarriage. The cleavage between Catholics and Protestants was profound, especially
in Lancashire, where the huge Catholic presence meant
that Protestant consciousness was more fully developed
than elsewhere. Children were brought up from an early
age to be aware of the symbols of their own religion, and
to regard adherents of the rival faith in terms of a series
of hostile stereotypes. These preconceptions were often
revealed more or less unconsciously, as by the Barrow
Protestant who had once worked in a convent, and was
impressed by the fact that 'it was spotlessly clean although
they were Catholics', or the Preston Catholic who mentioned that his mother always went to 'a Catholic doctor'.[31] On St Patrick's day in Preston, Protestant schools
traditionally fought with Catholic schools. On Whit Monday
the children of each sect paraded through the streets with
their Bibles or their statues of the Virgin Mary, while friends
cheered and enemies booed. Every large town had its
Catholic neighbourhoods. Even in London, where sectarian
divisions were much less pervasive than in Preston, local
boundaries could be defined in terms of adherence to
different churches: 'Our part of Wapping, in our little
sector, was more or less the Church of England crowd,
and as you got over the bridge you run into the St Patrick's
crowd.' In Liverpool, where the religious make-up of every
street was well known to locals, the sectarian riots of 1909
included the eviction of hundreds of Catholic families living
in mainly Protestant streets, and Protestant families living in mainly Catholic streets.[32]

A large folklore grew up concerning the supposed characteristics of the rival community. In Preston, for instance,
Protestants would claim that the local custom whereby
Catholics concentrated in particular places of work applied even to the town's brothels, the prostitutes being,

of course, all Catholics, which could be told from the fact that they turned out to kneel on the pavement when a religious procession passed down the Manchester Road.[33] Meanwhile in Bristol, Protestant children followed nuns in the street, chanting:

Catholic, Catholic, quack, quack, quack,
Go to the devil and never come back.[34]

The memories of a woman brought up around the turn of the century in a strongly Nonconformist family in Dewsbury throw some light on how sectarian differences were perceived. She regarded the Anglican clergy as part of the upper class of the town, and 'on the whole the people going to the Anglican church were the wealthier people'. Her father was in fact a convert from Anglicanism – a fervent radical, in revolt against the forelock-tugging of the village from which he had come, and apparently attracted to Congregationalism partly by its democratic ethos, and partly by its association with the temperance cause. The family had a permanent guest in the form of an ex-Catholic priest, who was being hounded by local Catholics (but continued to say mass every morning in his room). At one stage they had to ward off some 'rough-looking men', who came demanding to see the ex-priest. She regarded the town's Catholics as 'absolutely scruffy'. They lived in an area called Dawes Green 'that we were forbidden to go near. It was very rough.' Her view of Catholicism changed somewhat when her sister fell ill with smallpox. Their minister did not visit, because he had a family and was afraid of infection; but her sister was regularly visited by a Catholic priest.[35]

The generally hostile perceptions of the rival faith could thus be modified by personal experience, and, in particular, many Protestants had some respect for the Catholic clergy as pastors – though their reputation for devotion was often modified by suspicion of what were seen as their tyrannical methods. However, few people were so broad-minded as to accept with any degree of equanimity the prospect of a member of their family marrying someone from the other side. In 1923, an Anglican clergyman, whose daughter had announced that she intended to marry an Irishman, was said to be greatly relieved to discover that his future son-in-law was not a Catholic but an atheist.[36] Many Catholics saw 'mixed marriages' as treachery; Protestants often regarded marriage with a Catholic as degrading. Although such marriages were in fact quite frequent, opposition from one or both families, often reinforced by clergy or nuns, was inevitable, and in some cases one partner or both would continue to be shunned by relatives for several years afterwards.[37]

When, at 12 or 13, a working-class boy or girl left school, religion might well have an influence on where they found work. In rural Lincolnshire in the mid-nineteenth century there was 'a wide-ranging network of co-religionists who reinforced religious ties with economic interest, social intercourse, and kinship'.[38] Wesleyan farmers frequently employed Wesleyan labourers, patronised Wesleyan craftsmen and shopkeepers, and did business with Wesleyan corn merchants. Sectarianism could also operate in a negative way. In the countryside, where every local family was likely to be known, it was a simple matter to decree that work would only be given to members of 'church' families, and many landlords had such a policy.

In towns and cities religious screening was harder to apply with complete effectiveness, but having the right religious connections might well be an advantage. In Bristol, the big tobacco factories, where jobs were much sought after, required applicants for jobs to provide references from their Sunday School. Foremen would often recruit workers for their department through a church or chapel network, so that within a large firm there were local concentrations of people of a given denomination. In the early years of the twentieth century, stories of sectarian preferentialism in the allocation of jobs were rife, though the stories may exaggerate the degree to which religious affiliation was given priority over other criteria. In Preston at the time of the First World War it was said that the only way to get a job on the station was 'to say that you went to such a church'. From the same period there are also stories of Catholics being preferred in the London docks and Methodists being preferred in some Durham mines.[39] In some areas municipal patronage was alleged to have a sectarian character. In Tory Liverpool it was claimed that Protestants got preference in the allocation of city jobs. And in the London dockland boroughs of Bermondsey and Poplar in the 1920s, some Labour councillors were said to have established a system of jobs for Catholics. Allegations of this kind were of course frequently made by those who failed to get jobs what should have been rightfully their's. For instance a Bristol man claimed that he had been turned 'into a Red' by the experience of being rejected for a job as a printer, and seeing the foreman give it to a lad who belonged to his Bible class.[40] It is not often that anyone actually admitted to having got a job through belonging to the right church.

In less tangible ways, belonging to the right church or chapel could provide connections, and evidence of respectability and integrity, for those who were at the early stages of a business career. In the 1890s, 'A steady young man commencing life in Liverpool without capital or good friends' could not do better for his own future 'than by joining and becoming active, useful and respected in a large dissenting congregation'. One who followed these precepts was Joseph Chamberlain, who in later life very seldom went to church, but on his arrival in Birmingham, aged 18, had immediately joined the Unitarian Church of the Messiah. He taught an evening class there, and later took charge of the accounts, and many of his business and political associates were fellow Unitarians. On his first Sunday at the church he had been very struck by a well-dressed family who had swept in without a word to anyone at the beginning of the service, and swept out without a word at the end. They proved to be a branch of the Kenrick hollow-ware dynasty. As a young man with an eye to 'his own future', he decided that these were just the sort of people he wanted to know. It was a slow business, but seven years later he married the daughter.[41]

Religion might also determine where people spent their free hours, as so many leisure facilities were provided by churches or chapels. This role was particularly important in small towns and rural areas, where the range of alternatives was likely to be relatively narrow. In the Cornish fishing village of Mousehole, for instance, recreation

> was all centred round your place where you went to worship on Sunday. If you were church, well you went to church activities, and we had a strong Salvation Army in the village at that time, and the Salvation Army folk had their various things carrying on, you see, and the band could be playing different parts of the village Sundays and in the week, and then of course the Methodists they had their own activities, and between the concerts getting up and the Band of Hope meetings and then choir practice you know, I never had a dull moment.[42]

And a man from the Barrow Island district of Barrow in Furness mentioned: 'Friendly Societies, Boys' Clubs, Boys' Brigade, Mothers' Union, Women's Meetings and they were all well attended. That was the social life of the Island, around the church, because there was very little else, no telly, no radio, and people got linked up with the church, and they attended all the functions that took place.'[43] But even in larger cities, facilities provided by church and chapel tended to have the advantage of being cheap and convenient, quite apart from any preference a person might have for spending their leisure hours with people they knew, and who shared the same religion.

In London, church clubs seem to have made an important contribution to the working-class amateur boxing boom of the 1880s and 1890s. In this instance, the churches concerned seem to have been largely Anglican, together with a few Roman Catholic – Nonconformists, with their pacifist tendencies, seldom seem to have succumbed to the mystique of the ring. On the other hand, many secularists were boxing enthusiasts (fights were staged at Bradlaugh's Hall of Science), and in the early twentieth century boxing was very popular among Jewish immigrants in the East End of London – though here it seems to have been an alternative to, rather than a complement to synagogue-attendance.[44] Around the turn of the century, a wide range of other kinds of amusement were provided by churches and chapels, whether for their own members, or for anyone who was interested. As Elizabeth Roberts notes in respect of Barrow and Lancaster: 'for young people and children there was something to do every evening: indeed the enterprising went from church to chapel to mission depending on what social activity was offered'. Meanwhile 'Older children and adults went to the Girls' Friendly Society, concert parties, gymnastic clubs held in church halls, played games like tennis and badminton in church clubs and enthusiastically supported socials and dances.'[45]

The period from about the 1880s to the First World War marked a peak in a build-up of church-based leisure facilities that had been gathering force since about the middle of the century. Doug Reid's research on Birmingham shows that the front-runners were the Anglicans and that the growth in church-based provision started in the 1850s with the formation of a Working Men's Association, based on St Martin's Church in the Bull Ring – before the beginnings of the boom in commercial provision in the 1870s. Rather than being merely imitative, this was an innovative response to a variety of perceived problems. It was an attempt to steer working men away from less desirable alternatives, whether Chartism or alcohol, and it was also a potential recruiting-ground for future church members. Equally important, however, was that it reflected a new and more positive evaluation of leisure.[46]

The attempt to use leisure facilities as a recruiting-ground for the church seems never to have been very successful.

Many people seem to have been quite consciously selective – going to the church in the evening because it had an excellent gymnasium, but not going at other times. They may also have had ideas of what they wanted from their leisure which clashed seriously with the ideas of the clerical sponsors. For instance in 1902, the Anglican University Club, which was a leading centre for amateur boxing in the East End of London, was closed down and later re-opened with a largely new membership, because the managers objected to gambling; and in Lancashire, clergy felt impelled to intervene in church dances where the styles of dancing became excessively intimate.[47]

Sometimes, subsidiary institutions would develop a distinct esprit de corps over against the main congregation. Clergymen who actually tried to persuade members of these groups to attend services often met resistance. Sometimes the reluctance was mainly on social grounds. For instance, in the 1920s one of the Anglican churches in Preston had a Young Men's Bible Class, which flourished until the vicar tried to close it down and persuade the members to go to the main services instead. This idea fell completely flat, as the mill workers who felt at home in the Bible Class had no wish to join 'the doctors' at church. In Hackney Wick, however, a very poor district in east London, there was said in the 1890s to be a positive antagonism between the religiously-minded men and women who attended the church and the members of the Men's Club, where the tone was positively sceptical.[48]

On the other hand, football, amateur dramatics, etc., do seem to have played a part in confirming the loyalty of those who were already involved. In the years around 1900 there were many people – middle-class, working-class, and perhaps most of all, lower middle-class – whose social life centred on their place of worship. 'We used to live there nearly,' said a Co-op grocery worker, describing the full programme of religious, educational, musical and sporting activities provided by his Primitive Methodist chapel in Barrow.[49]

Religious issues played a major part in politics throughout this period, and religious affiliation was a major influence on voting. For instance, the survival of poll-books from the period before the introduction of the secret ballot in 1872 makes it possible to link party preference with occupation. Nonconformist ministers and Roman Catholic priests showed an overwhelming preference for Liberal, Whig or Radical candidates. Anglican clergymen were more likely to vote Conservative than the members of any secular profession.[50] At the local level, many of the new borough councils elected after the Municipal Reform Act of 1835 were dominated by Dissenters. In Leeds, for instance, over half the new council were Dissenters and the first mayor was a Baptist. In Leicester, more than two thirds of the council elected in 1836 were Dissenters, and the first mayor under the new regime was a Unitarian, as also in Manchester.[51] For several decades after this, MPs of both parties sitting for English and Welsh constituencies remained overwhelmingly Anglican, though the few Nonconformist MPs were nearly all Liberal. Only in the 1880s did non-Anglicans begin to be elected in large numbers. An analysis of the religious affiliations of candidates in the 1900, 1906 and 1910 elections shows that 64 per cent of Anglicans were standing as Conservatives or Liberal Unionists and that 91 per cent of Nonconformists were standing for the Liberals or for Labour.[52] There were some denominational variations. Baptists were unanimously Liberal or Labour, and Congregationalists, Quakers and non-Wesleyan Methodists overwhelmingly so, whereas the Wesleyans, Unitarians and Presbyterians included a somewhat larger minority of Unionists. There is no doubt that the same pattern broadly holds true in respect of the ordinary voter. Most Anglicans voted Conservative, though there was a substantial minority who went the other way. Most Nonconformists, Roman Catholics and Secularists, and probably most Jews,[53] voted Liberal or Labour, though there was a fairly small minority of Tories.

It is much harder, however, to determine just *how*

important the religious factor was, and how it compared with other significant variables, such as class. The most thorough study of this question has been made by Kenneth Wald. His statistical analysis of elections between 1885 and 1910 suggests that in every general election held in this period the strength of religious Nonconformity provides the best predictor of the result in any given constituency. Only in 1918 did class supplant religion as the key variable – a major reason for this probably being the extension of the franchise in that year, which considerably increased the proportion of working-class voters in the electorate.[54] There is much evidence to suggest that class was a growing influence on voting patterns in the pre-1914 period, but Wald's analysis detects no such pattern.

The correlation between religion and politics had several dimensions. Most obviously, the two main parties directly appealed to a sectarian constituency. The position of the Church of England as the established church of England and Wales, and the various disadvantages suffered by those outside the establishment, meant that the Whigs and later the Liberals were able to attract the support of most Dissenters, Catholics, Jews and Secularists by promising religious equality. Equality came slowly, and even in 1914 it had not been fully achieved. So members of the various religious minorities always had a motive for voting Liberal. Conversely, the Conservatives attracted Anglican votes by promising to defend the church and its privileges.[55] Sectarianism as a political issue reached a highpoint in the Parliament of 1868–74. The principal election issue had been the Disestablishment of the Church of Ireland, which Gladstone's victorious Liberals proceeded to carry through. These years also saw the abolition of compulsory church rates and of the application of religious tests at Oxford and Cambridge Universities. Most important of all, it saw the Education Act of 1870, which was angrily condemned by many Nonconformists for falling far short of what they wanted, but which none the less marked an important stage in the establishment of a religiously pluralist society. The biggest political issue of the 1880s was Ireland, which kept religious issues in the forefront, but led to some degree of realignment after Gladstone's espousal of Irish Home Rule in 1886. The effect was to confirm the support of most Catholics for the Liberals, but to cause the defection to Liberal Unionism of some Nonconformists, including most notably the Unitarian and leader of the radicals, Joseph Chamberlain, and the 'pulpit princes' Charles Spurgeon and R. W. Dale. However, just as the old battles between church and chapel seemed to be losing some of their relevance, Balfour's Education Act of 1902, with its promise of rate-aid to Anglican and Catholic schools ('Rome on the Rates'), led to furious Nonconformist protests, while the Liberals' abortive Education Bill of 1906 was equally strongly opposed by Anglicans and Catholics. For many Anglicans and Nonconformists, voting Conservative or voting Liberal was thus simply a matter of loyalty to their own community. For Catholics, admittedly, matters were more complicated since Irish issues drove them one way, while education drove them in the other. For the laity it appears that Irish issues took precedence, whereas quite a lot of clergy disagreed.[56]

Both parties also became associated with causes which were generally attractive to certain religious constituencies and unpopular with others. For instance, the Licensing Act of 1872 confirmed the Liberal reputation as the party of temperance, a cause dear to the hearts of many Nonconformists, and also confirmed the support for the Tories of brewers and licensees. Conservative propaganda certainly tried to attract the beer-drinkers' vote,[57] though there is no evidence that this vote was ever of much electoral significance. More important was the Tory campaign to annex the Protestant vote, which in Lancashire proved to be a major force. From the 1830s onwards the Orange Order and militantly anti-Catholic evangelical clergy were highly influential in Liverpool. They gave their support to the Conservatives, thus laying the basis for an often-troubled alliance, but one which led to Tory domination of the city's politics for over a century.[58] By the 1860s they were successfully presenting themselves as the Protestant party in many other parts of Lancashire, where large-scale Irish Catholic immigration in the later 1840s and 1850s had led to the formation of numerous Orange Lodges and Protestant Working Men's Associations. Defence of the Church of England and its schools and opposition to Irish Catholic nationalism was often combined with a form of Tory populism, which championed the rights of the Protestant worker, not only against Catholic workers, but also against Liberal Nonconformist employers. Meanwhile ritualists in the Church of England became surrogate victims for the Roman Catholics, who lay beyond Parliament's control: a good deal of 'Protestant' energy was thrown into campaigning for legislation that would preserve the Anglican Church from crypto-papist infiltrators.[59] In Disraeli's Public Worship Regulation Act of 1874 they had their one great (Pyrrhic) victory – Pyrrhic because the consequent imprisonment of several ritualist clergy provided the cause with just the aura of martyrdom which best served to gain public respect and large numbers of converts.[60]

There were also broader affinities between the ethos of particular denominations and particular kinds of politics. The attachment of most Catholics and Jews to the Liberal Party seems to have been relatively superficial, and caused by a temporary identity of interests. The link between Nonconformity and Liberalism seems to reflect a deeper affinity, though there were at least three forms of Nonconformist Liberalism.

There was the Liberalism of the new urban elite of successful businessmen, which emerged in the 1830s and 1840s to challenge what they saw as an antiquated establishment of Tory Anglicans, standing in the way of necessary reforms. Their Liberalism and their Nonconformity were two aspects of their nineteenth-century modernity, their belief in opportunity, efficiency, and a healthy atmosphere of free competition. In Bradford, for instance, this group tended to be closely involved in the Congregational or Baptist churches. They were self-made men, with little education, who had risen from modest lower middle-class backgrounds. They had a passion for self-education, which they later promoted through Mechanics Institutes, and the virtues they most admired were summed up in the concept of 'character'. Koditschek points out that this concept was two-edged: it implied a criticism of the old elite, who owed their position to mere heredity; but it was equally critical of those who remained at the bottom of the social pile, and whose failure could be attributed to the lack of such sterling moral qualities. The rhetoric of 'character' was used to justify the existence of a new elite, who had gained their position by superior merit.[61]

There was a working class Liberalism, embodied in figures such as Joseph Arch, the agricultural workers' leader, or John Wilson, the Durham miners' leader, both Primitive Methodist preachers, believing that Nonconformist religion and Liberal politics were two different but complementary expressions of the ideals of democracy and equality. Education, temperance and trade unionism were the three pillars of working-class emancipation. Di Drummond's work on the railway town of Crewe provides a vivid portrait of this milieu. When, in 1885 and again in 1889, large groups of 'trouble-makers' were dismissed from their jobs at the railway engineering works, most were said to be Liberals and Nonconformists, who lambasted the tyranny of Chief Mechanical Engineer Webb, 'the uncrowned king of Crewe', with a rhetoric drawn half from the Bible and half from modern Liberalism. Most of them were craftsmen, very proud of their skills, and many belonged to the Blue Riband temperance organisation.[62]

There was also a Nonconformist version of the New Liberalism of the late Victorian and Edwardian period. The main social base of this movement was in the lower middle class, among groups such as teachers, white-collar workers, and some small businessmen. Their political programme received eloquent support from many Nonconformist pulpits. It rested on an optimistic vision of the moral and material progress which might result from the reforming energies of a local and national government, with a sense of responsibility for all citizens, and a willingness to intervene in every area of life. In practice, this meant a mixture of puritanism and social reform. These ideas found characteristic expression in the policies of the Lib-Lab Progressive Party, which ran the London County Council from 1889 to 1907, combining ambitious housing and educational schemes, extensive regulation of small shopkeepers and street traders, and measures to stamp out alleged obscenity in the music-halls. Jeffrey Cox, in his study of the south London borough of Lambeth, has provided a memorable account of the Nonconformist local politicians of this era, and the preachers who supported them – figures like the Baptist minister who wrote in his church newsletter at the time of the LCC elections in 1907: 'The Progressives draw support from all followers of Jesus Christ – the Moderates [Conservatives] from company promoters, slum landlords, drinksellers, bookmakers, and brothelkeepers.'[63] Or Alderman Nathanael Hubbard, Free Methodist coal merchant, temperance enthusiast, pioneering campaigner for old age pensions, who, as a Lambeth vestry member, took a leading part in the building of public baths. Or Frank Briant, one of a large contingent of Congregationalists active in local politics, who, as a Guardian, favoured generous out-relief, and later became MP for the impoverished North Lambeth constituency.

The affinity between Anglicanism and Toryism had three characteristic dimensions. There was an old-fashioned paternalist Toryism, most characteristic of rural parishes, and declining, but far from dead in the late nineteenth century. Flora Thompson's account of a north Oxfordshire village church in the 1880s catches some of the flavour of this kind of Anglicanism:

The Squire's and clergyman's families had pews in the chancel, with backs to the wall on either side, and between them stood two long benches for the school-children, well under the eyes of authority. Below the steps down the nave stood the harmonium, played by the clergyman's daughter, and round it was ranged the choir of small school-girls. Then came the rank and file of the congregation, nicely graded, with the farmer's family in the front row, then the Squire's gardener and coachman, the schoolmistress, the maidservants, and the cottagers, with the Parish Clerk at the back to keep order. . . .

Mr Ellison in the pulpit was the Mr Ellison of the Scripture lessons, plus a white surplice. To him, his congregation were but children of a larger growth, and he preached as he taught. A . . . favourite subject was the supreme rightness of the social order as it then existed. God, in his infinite wisdom, had appointed a place for every man, woman and child on this earth, and it was their bounden duty to remain contentedly in their niches. A gentleman might seem to some of his listeners to have a pleasant, easy life, compared to theirs at field labour; but he had his duties and responsibilities, which would be far beyond their capabilities. He had to pay taxes, sit on the Bench of Magistrates, oversee his estate, and keep up his position by entertaining. Could they do these things? No. Of course they could not; and he did not suppose that a gentleman could cut as straight a furrow or mow or thatch a rick as expertly as they could.

On the Sunday following the 1886 election, Mr Ellison's composure was momentarily lost as he launched into a diatribe against those members of the congregation who had voted Liberal.[64] By the 1880s this style of Toryism was going out of fashion – and it was recorded mainly by those who, like Flora Thompson, regarded it as, at best, quaint, and at worst, a travesty of Christianity. But ideas of this kind were still quite widespread, especially in rural parishes. A north Lancashire woman claimed to have left the Anglican church in the 1920s after hearing a sermon on the text 'In my father's house are many mansions', in which the preacher argued that there would be class distinctions in heaven.[65]

A second kind of Tory Anglicanism, associated especially with Lancashire, was much more democratic in tone, and emphatically Protestant. Like its more traditionalist counterparts, it was fiercely opposed to Dissent, but its counterstrategy involved mobilising the Anglican masses, by identifying with some of their economic interests, by championing some of their leisure pursuits, and by presenting the Church of England as 'the church of the people'. Partly it was a matter of style: Patrick Joyce records that at a Tory meeting in 1868 a Mossley clergyman 'rolled up his sleeves, hitched up his robes and then to the delight of his audience sprang forward in clogs'. Partly it was a matter of identifying with the people and defending them from the attacks of moralists. Nonconformists were thus pilloried as 'scurrilous, psalm-singing, canting hypocrites' and the working man's right to his well-earned pint of beer was strenuously defended. This political programme was in fact seldom stated so clearly as it was by the maverick radical J. A. Roebuck, who successfully intervened with Conservative support in the Sheffield election of 1874 in order to defeat the young Joseph Chamberlain. His manifesto championed 'The Briton's Bible and the Briton's Beer: our National Church and our National Beverage'.[66] In the Sheffield context these slogans were directed against Chamberlain's particular form of Nonconformity (which included a preference for purely secular teaching in the Board Schools). But in Lancashire these slogans gained added potency because of the dual threat from Dissent and from Rome. In Lancashire more than in any other part of the country both working-class Toryism and working-class Anglicanism were major forces, and very often the two causes were supported by the same people. The Lancashire form of Tory Anglicanism was typically represented by figures like the Audenshaw vicar, Heffill, who wore clogs, championed the miners and chaired miners' galas, and also supported the 'no Popery' lecturer William Murphy, who toured the north of England in the late 1860s, leaving a trail of destruction in his wake as Protestants enflamed by his oratory marched into Catholic districts attacking houses and churches.[67]

A third kind of Tory Anglicanism focused on the nation and the Empire. The Empire was understood in terms of a God-given mission to propagate English Christianity and English culture. A representative figure here might be Arthur Winnington-Ingram, Bishop of London from 1901 to 1939, who during the First World War achieved immense popularity with one part of the nation, and notoriety in the eyes of another part, because of his famous recruiting-sermons, in which he declared that the United Kingdom was engaged in a 'Holy War'. Admittedly, the circumstances of war made expansive patriotism and bitter denunciations of enemy nations common currency, but Winnington-Ingram was largely repeating things that he had always believed. According to his biographer, 'There was for him a sacredness about England that was beyond argument', and 'he would never have any scruples about joining in "Land of Hope and Glory" with its refrain of "God, who made thee mighty, Make thee mightier yet"'. As a fervent imperialist, he believed as strongly in British rule in South Africa and Ireland as he later did in the national cause during the two world wars. It was partly a matter of defending 'the honour of their country', but he also believed that his country was fighting for 'the freedom of the world', and that Englishmen who were risking their lives in defence of this great cause were part of a great national tradition that linked them with their ancestors' who had fought at Agincourt, and who had resisted the Spanish Armada and Napoleon. He was equally fervent in his loyalty to Anglicanism, and he believed that the 'Mother Church of England', with its perfect balance of the Catholic and the Protestant, of orthodoxy and rationality, would one day play a central part in the reunification of Christendom.[68]

Christian Culture

Nineteenth-century English Christianity found typical expressions in three cultural features which, to a considerable extent, crossed the boundaries of class, politics and denomination: knowledge of and reference to the Bible as a final authority; the love of hymns; and the observance of Sunday as a day set apart.

To begin with the last of these: the 'quiet Sunday' was by no means limited to middle-class people, or even to those who were church-goers. In the later Victorian period it seems to have been accepted as normal by most families living above the level of poverty, although certainly households differed in the stringency with which the sabbath was observed. The idea of a quiet day seems to have been accepted as a matter of respectability even by families that were non-religious. While strongly Evangelical families might ban games of any kind on Sunday, even non-church-going families frequently banned noisy games or games in the street. And the ideal of a day where work was reduced to a necessary minimum seems to have been widely accepted – though there was no consensus at all as to what kinds of work were acceptable and which were not, on the sabbath. Strongly Evangelical families barred Sunday newspapers, but for many working-class families Sunday was the great newspaper-reading day: the most popular mass-circulation papers in the Victorian period were Sunday papers, like the radical *Reynolds News* or the sensationalist *Lloyd's Weekly News*, later supplanted by the *News of the World*.

The view of the Victorian Sunday as seen by its critics is very familiar. One of the best-known images is from *Little Dorrit*. Arthur Clennam returned to London on a dreary Sunday evening, when 'Everything was barred and bolted that could by possibility furnish relief to an over-worked people.' As he sat in a coffee-house, the sound of 'Maddening church bells of all degrees of dissonance, sharp and flat, cracked and clear, fast and slow', brought back to him memories of 'a legion of Sundays, all days of un-serviceable bitterness and mortification' – 'the dreary Sunday of his childhood', 'the sleepy Sunday of his boy-hood', 'the interminable Sunday of his nonage', 'the re-sentful Sunday of a little later'.[69] Dickens was writing in 1855 when sabbatarianism was near to its highest point. Nearly forty years later, when the sabbath had lost a little of its rigour, Gissing presented Sunday even more vividly as a symbol of the tyranny of meaningless conventions. Godwin Peak, the hero of his novel *Born in Exile*, is going for a Sunday afternoon walk, when he comes across a policeman who is stopping some children from playing in the street:

The youngsters fled, conscious of a shameful duty. There it was! There spoke the civic voice, the social rule, the public sentiment! Godwin felt that the policeman had rebuked him, and in so doing had severely indicated the cause of that isolation that he was condemned to suffer. Yes, all his life he had desired to play games on a Sunday; he had never been able to understand why games on a Sunday should be forbidden. And the angry laugh that escaped him as he went by the guardian of public morals, declared the impossibility of his ever being at one with communities which made this point the prime test of worthiness.[70]

There were clearly a lot of people who agreed with Godwin Peak, for by the 1890s growing numbers of the younger generation were insisting on 'playing games on Sundays'.

This hostile view has so much come to shape our con-ception of the Victorian Sunday that it has become diffi-cult to understand the viewpoint of the many people for whom Sunday had much more positive connotations. The Methodist potter, mentioned earlier, who had started work at the age of seven, remembered as he looked back to his childhood that 'Sunday brought sweetness into my life and lifted me out of the demoralising influences of the working days.'[71] Sunday then meant the Sunday School, where he found his circle of friends. Later he became a local preacher, and Sunday meant tramps out into the countryside to preach at village chapels. Apart from the drudgery of the long hours of work and the bullying of those in authority, he was also repelled by the heavy drinking of many of his workmates. Sunday by contrast offered a brief vision of a better life. Another view of what Sunday could mean is suggested by an account of a working-class Methodist household in Keighley, where 'me father used to try and keep the sabbath as the sabbath' in the early 1900s: in the morning father went to the working men's club and in the evening to the Wesleyan chapel. The children went to Sunday School. Mother only went to chapel for special events like anniversaries. In the evening the whole family would gather together, and big sister would play the organ – 'sing-songs, hymns, all sorts. Father's favourite was "The Rugged Cross" and as they sang it, tears would run down his face. Then each child had to do an individual turn you know, – and you'd always get to tell your dad what you'd learnt at Sunday School, and what you'd been talking about you know.'[72]

Several significant points emerge from this account. Critics of Sunday saw it as an aimless day, in which, like Godwin Peak, people did things mainly to relieve their boredom, rather than from any more positive motive, or like Arthur Clennam they were too depressed to consider doing anything at all. On the other hand, those who prided themselves on 'keeping Sunday as Sunday' treasured the ritualised character of their sabbaths. Each Sunday followed the pattern of hundreds of previous Sundays, and they would have felt deprived if any part of the ritual had been forgotten. But, as this example indicates, there was no standardised pattern – every household had its own way of observing Sunday, and while most had at least some taboos, there was no generally recognised code of what was acceptable and what was unacceptable. In this case, for example, going to the club, which many sabbatarians would have condemned, was as much a part of the ritual as going to chapel. The strictest sabbatarians barred cooking on Sundays, which had the advantage of reducing the burden on women, for whom the idea of a day of rest was often something of a mockery, because most of the morning was devoted to producing the main meal of the week. So most women cooked on Sunday, but they frequently made a point of barring other kinds of work, such as sewing. For many working-class women the closing of museums and the prohibition on football matches on Sundays were the least of their problems. Indeed, some of them would have liked more, rather than less, religion on that day.[73] They often had their sabbath on Monday evenings, sometimes called 'Mother's Day', when some would go to the pub with other women, and some would go to a Mothers' Meeting or Pleasant Monday Evening at a church.[74]

Sunday had eight characteristic ingredients: the absence of, or at least a diminution of, work; wearing special clothes; eating better food than on other days; spending time with family; meeting close friends; religious observance; music; and appreciation of the beauties of nature. The wearing of Sunday best was taken for granted by anyone who could afford it. Otherwise, each household mixed the ingredients in different ways. For those who were more strongly religious, each of these features was part of an interlocking whole. The bar on work made available the time in which the other things were possible; the wearing of special clothes showed proper respect for the meaning and dignity of the day; attending church together, eating together, and singing hymns together strengthened the bonds of family; church or chapel was the place where they met many of their closest friends; music was a means of praising God; and it was above all through nature that the greatness of God and the wonders of Creation could be experienced. Wigley, referring to evidence to a royal commission in the 1840s, offers a rival model, followed by many non-church-going working-class families, according to which Sunday was primarily 'a feast day'. On Saturday night they laid out their one set of non-working clothes, their Sunday best. For breakfast they prepared tea or coffee instead of gruel. At the middle of the day came the main meal of the week ('We always have a good dinner at one; it is very wicked to omit that'), and this was followed by a good tea and, if the weather were fine, a walk in the evening.[75] But there were many different ways of mixing the ingredients, or of adding extra quantities of one while leaving out others.

For the more strictly sabbatarian families music tended to have a very important recreational role, since religious music was one kind of amusement that was quite acceptable on Sundays. In the strongly Nonconformist fishing village of Mousehole, where all other forms of Sunday amusement were strictly taboo, the sabbath calm was broken by the playing of Salvation Army bands and the singing of Methodist choirs. Indeed, religious music also provided a justification for Sunday travel, as Methodist choirs would go to sing in the chapels of neighbouring villages. And for families in all parts of the country, in all social classes, and of every religious or non-religious persuasion, Sunday was the great day for playing the piano. In some households that meant Chopin, and in some it meant 'Boiled Beef and Carrots' and 'My ol' man said "Foller the van"'. But in the majority of cases it meant hymns. The most evocative symbol of what Sunday meant to those who believed in 'keeping Sunday as Sunday', was the family gathered round the piano after tea, singing hymns. In one non-church-going working-class family in Bristol in the early 1900s, sitting round the fire and drinking cocoa as they sang hymns added to the sense of cosy togetherness, and a little bit of mild self-indulgence. In a middle-class Congregationalist family in Tunbridge Wells, the mother's friends came round on Sunday evening to join the hymn-singing. In a Methodist rural labouring family in Devon, the father played the accordeon and mother the concertina. They all sang hymns together on Sundays, and sometimes on weekdays, if it were wet and the children could not play outside.[76] For D. H. Lawrence, looking back on his Nonconformist childhood, singing hymns together on Sunday meant warmth, intimacy and security. Hearing a woman singing in the dusk, he was reminded of 'a mother who smiles as she sings':

> In spite of myself, the insidious mastery of song
> Betrays me back, till the heart of me weeps to belong
> To the old Sunday evenings at home, with winter outside
> And hymns in the cosy parlour, the tinkling piano our
>   guide.[77]

In Victorian England hymns were the most universally popular art-form, and the nearest thing to a cultural inheritance common to women and men, working class and middle class, old and young, the sceptical and the devout. In the earlier part of the nineteenth century, women workers in the Yorkshire woollen industry were said to alternate between gossiping and singing hymns as they worked in the burling shed; and around the end of the century a Barrow woman remembers her non-church-going father returning from Saturday night drinking bouts to sit on the toilet singing 'all Sunday's hymns'.[78]

Hymns could express emotions of joy and sorrow, of gratitude or defiance, hope or longing, in an idiom that was acceptable to all but the relatively few convinced secularists. In 1813 when a group of Luddites were hanged at York, they had marched to the scaffold singing 'Behold the Saviour of mankind, Nail'd to the shameful tree'. Meetings of the farm labourers' union in the 1870 and 1880s sometimes began with hymns such as 'Hold the Fort' and 'Dare to be a Daniel'.[79] In the 1890s a south London woman would keep her spirits up by singing 'Tell me the old, old story', as she worked through the day on her sewing machine.[80] The 'Brides in the Bath' killer, George Joseph Smith, would follow up the murder of his victims by playing 'Nearer, my God, to thee' on the harmonium. Hymn-tunes were also widely familiar and could be adopted for other purposes: at the Norfolk village of Titchwell in 1921, striking farm labourers sang a song about their employer to the tune of 'The Church's One Foundation'.[81] Hymns often had immense nostalgic appeal for those who had become estranged from the church or had lost their religious faith. Helen Corke, who like D. H. Lawrence had been brought up in Congregationalism, and like him had rejected it, and was a close friend during the period when they were both teachers in Croydon, later recalled a Sunday walking on the Downs together, which ended with them irresistibly drawn by the sound of church bells – 'the church is warm, and we both like singing the evening hymns'.[82] In church and home, hymns established an emotional unity which might at least temporarily cover over internal divisions.

If hymns offered sentiment, nostalgia or a sense of togetherness, the Bible was much more divisive, and potentially more creative. In spite of the growth of Roman and Anglo-Catholicism in this period, English popular religion remained strongly Protestant, and its focal point was the Bible. Big 'Family' Bibles had a place of honour in large numbers of homes, recording with due formality the crucial dates in the family's history, and proclaiming by their size and weight, and by their thick black binding, the solemnity that surrounded the sacred book. An evangelical missionary working in a poor area of Birmingham in 1838 found that two-thirds of the households in one court had Bibles – including a few where no-one could read. Indeed the author of an account of working-class life in Lancashire in the depressed early 1840s claimed that 'In the houses of the needy and the afflicted I have often found the Bible the last piece of furniture remaining.'[83] The term 'furniture' may suggest that the Family Bible was intended to be seen, rather than to be opened, and there were no doubt many households where the function of the Bible was more symbolic than practical. But even those who never read the Bible inevitably had considerable experience of hearing it read. Education in Sunday Schools, church day schools or Board Schools ensured that almost everyone had at least some knowledge of the Bible. Church services almost always included readings from the Bible, and, even more important, the focal point of the Protestant service was a sermon based on a biblical text.

In many aristocratic and upper middle-class families, the practice developed, under the influence of the evangelical revival, of assembling the whole household at the beginning or the end of the day, or even at both the beginning and the end, to hear the head of the household read from the Bible. This custom does not seem to have spread very widely in other social classes. But for two or three generations it ranked almost as a matter of etiquette at the upper end of the social hierarchy. Bible-reading was widespread further down the hierarchy, though it tended to take a less formal character. In a south Devon labouring family, where the parents never read anything but the Bible, mother or father would sometimes read it to the children. A Bristol boot checker, who was a fervent reader, claimed that his favourites were the Bible and history books. In another Devon labouring household the father would tell Bible stories to the children. In the Keighley working-class family whose Sunday routines were described earlier, husband and wife would read the Bible together before going to bed.[84] A survey of 1906 which asked the newly-elected Labour MPs which books had influenced them most found that the Bible was the work most often cited. Indeed one early Labour MP, Ben Turner, who had been a Yorkshire textile worker, was said always to carry a Bible with him, and often to pull it out to quote passages during his parliamentary speeches.[85]

The whole-page illustrations in the huge Family Bibles captured the imagination of countless readers, as they depicted the many dramatic, mysterious, affecting or terrifying episodes with which the scriptures were filled: Belshazzar transfixed by the writing on the wall, or the Israelites escaping through the parted waters of the Red Sea; David slaying Goliath, or Samson shaking the pillars of the temple; Christ in the midst of the children or walking on the waters – each depicted in appropriate eastern settings, including camels, flat-roofed houses, dark-eyed women and bearded men. The Bible provided an inexhaustible supply of dramatic stories, colourful characters, and memorable sayings, to which keen readers repeatedly returned as their own experience provided parallels with what they had read. Many people turned to its pages for guidance in times of perplexity. And many people used the Bible to explain a course of action they had taken.

The secular societies recognised the key role of the Bible in popular religious thinking, and attacks on the credibility of the scriptures were a central plank of their propaganda. Bible-knockers were often in fact former Bible-punchers, who thus had a good knowledge of the book they were attacking. Indeed a survey of the books read by secularists found that they too named the Bible as the one that had most influenced their thinking – though in this case in a negative direction.[86] The second choice was Tom Paine's *Age of Reason*, an attack on the Bible in such crudely literalistic terms that it was only likely to impress those readers who believed that all parts of the Bible were inspired, that each part was consistent with every other part, and that all were to be understood literally. In the 1880s readers of the *Freethinker* were entertained to a series of cartoons entitled the 'Comic Bible', which resulted in a prison sentence for blasphemy for the editor, G. W. Foote. The comic effect was achieved partly by presenting biblical characters as Jewish stereotypes, and partly by presenting the events recorded as being absurd, implausible or morally dubious. The basic assumption, how-

ever, was that readers would be familiar with the personalities and the episodes lampooned, and that the 'comic'
presentation would amuse, shock, or both.[87]

Authority and Rebellion

In the early years of the twentieth century the Yorkshire
factory village of Oakworth was dominated by two mills,
owned respectively by the Liberal Clough family and the
Tory Haggas family. The end of the village round the
Clough mill was said to be largely Wesleyan, and round
the Haggas mill, Anglican. As in other parts of northern
England the members of the various Sunday Schools in
the village 'walked' at Whitsuntide, carrying banners and
other symbols of their institution or their denomination;
after the walks the Methodist children went to be entertained at Clough's mill and the Anglican children at
Haggas's. According to an Anglican (who may not have
been a totally unbiased observer), workers at Clough's 'were
more or less expected to go to the chapel because he
built the chapel, you see'.[88] There was also a third church,
which did not quite fit into this pattern – and which,
because it was smaller, could easily be overlooked. The
Congregational chapel was described by one of its members as a 'Free Speech place' and 'a working man's institution'. While the Wesleyans and Anglicans benefited from
the largesse of their patrons, the Congregationalists had
to pay for their chapel by interminable special events;
and after the Whit Walks, when the other children headed
for the big mills, the Congregationalists had their tea in
a field behind the chapel. The Congregationalist just
quoted noted that his family were all Labour, and that
they owed their religious and political independence to
the fact that his father was a gas works labourer, and so
independent of the big mills – and indeed his parents
insisted that each member of the family find a different
employer, so that they did not become dependent.[89]

Here we have a microcosm of the relationship between religion and the structures of authority in later Victorian and Edwardian England. The links between religion and the systems of authority and social control were very obvious. Those in positions of power supported religious institutions and cultivated close relations with their leaders. Compulsory or semi-compulsory religious observances were used to maintain the identity and cohesion of most public institutions, and many that were privately controlled. Religious authority was used to legitimate existing power structures. These relationships were so highly visible that it could easily be forgotten that religion was also one of the most important sources of alternative values, and that in a variety of ways, some quite evident, and others more subtle, it could sustain those who were trying to subvert the prevailing values and power structures. So any credible account of the social role of English religion in this period must do justice to this duality.

Anglicanism, as the established religion, supported by the state and by most of the nation's rulers, was the characteristic religion of authority. The example of Oakworth Congregationalism reflects the fact that there was often an intimate relationship between religious dissent and social or political dissent. Yet, as the example of Oakworth Wesleyanism indicates, a dissenting church might operate in very much the same way as the established church, and at the local level it might be very much part of 'the establishment', even if at the national level it was part of 'Dissent'. Moreover, the Anglican church was sufficiently decentralised to permit considerable variation at the local level. The control over appointments, and the disciplinary powers exercised by Roman Catholic bishops generally, and by Anglican bishops in some other countries, enabled them to place their stamp on a diocese and to weed out those clergy who were deemed too independent-minded. In the Church of England, by contrast, most appointments were in the hands of private patrons, and the 'Parson's Freehold' made it very difficult to remove an incumbent, except in cases of flagrant immorality or extreme unorthodoxy. As a result, the clergy of each diocese represented a variety of liturgical and theological tendencies, and each diocese had its share of eccentrics or rebels who went their own way, guided by their own consciences, or by what they believed to be the needs of their parishioners.

The relationship between Anglicanism and the system of authority was most visible in such 'total' institutions as public schools, prisons, workhouses or the army, which had their own chaplains and compulsory church parades. In fact the relationship was closest in the public schools, where the headmaster was generally a clergyman, and frequently acted as chaplain, preparing the boys for confirmation, and regularly preaching in the chapel. Sermons became a crucial means of defining and reinforcing the official line on any urgent issues of the day – from the evils of masturbation to the virtues of team-games – as well as inculcating, in a more general way, loyalty to the school and to the values approved by the school. Throughout this period it was normal for males of the upper and upper middle classes to spend the years from 8 to 18 at a preparatory school and then at a public school. A very high proportion of those who would go on to take leading positions in the government of the United Kingdom and of the Empire, in the armed forces, the law – and indeed the Church of England itself – would spend their formative years in institutions where authority was explicitly Anglican. For many of them, public school religion remained with them for the rest of their lives, and helped to shape the ways that they used the positions of power that they occupied. According to Honey, 'The sermons of Vaughan at Harrow, of Farrar and Cotton at Marlborough, of Benson at Wellington, created an indelible impression on generations of their pupils, who discussed them in letters home, in their diaries, and later in their memoirs.'[90]

There were of course other clerical headmasters who left less happy memories. Some were ferocious disciplinarians.

For instance, Roald Dahl claimed to have been turned off Christianity by the beatings administered by his head-master, the later Archbishop, Geoffrey Fisher.[91] Anglicanism remained important in a negative way even for those who rebelled against their public school upbringing: the rebellion tended to include a bitter rejection of the religion that had held it all together.

In the British Army, where religion seems to have played a rather limited role in the earlier part of the nineteenth century, the 1850s saw the beginnings of the attempt to establish a 'Christian Army', with a permanent corps of chaplains, initially Anglican, Roman Catholic or Presbyterian, but later including Wesleyans. The chaplains were to be officers, and after 1860 they wore uniforms. The big military encampments built in this period always included a large interdenominational chapel, and from 1864 the religious affiliation of new recruits was recorded, so that they could be supplied with Bibles or other religious literature of the right kind, and required to attend the appropriate church parades.[92]

The links between Anglicanism and authority were equally apparent in many agricultural villages or small towns, where the rector or vicar was unmistakably part of the local elite, and where holders of secular authority frequently held prominent positions in the Anglican parish. At its most extreme there was the situation in some 'close' or 'closed' parishes, where an all-powerful squire worked hand in hand with a clergyman whom he himself had chosen – and who might even be a member of his own family. In the Essex village of Shalford in the early years of the twentieth century every family in the village had their own pew in church – 'they had to sit in them pews each Sunday and then they could soon see which wasn't there and which was'. 'Squire Marriott used to go all round: "Why wasn't you in church?" and that. And "Oh, he wasn't very well", or something. "You be sure you'll be there next Sunday", you see. Church used to be full of people. More than they dare do was not go to church.'[93]

In larger towns and in industrial areas, the elite was likely to be religiously divided, the range of religious possibilities was likely to be much greater, and the social role of religion more complex. As the example of Oakworth illustrates, many employers established close links with a place of worship, and sometimes employees were encouraged to attend – but the church selected was as likely to be Nonconformist as Anglican, and denominations that had a privileged position in one town might be underdogs in another. By about the 1890s there were a number of Anglican clergymen in working-class districts of London who tried to act as tribunes – recognising, no doubt, that if the Church of England was to have any future in working-class areas it had to identify itself more closely with the aspirations of the people. An early example was the Reverend W. A. Morris, a curate and later a vicar in Lambeth, the workingmen's club at whose church was the headquarters of the London gas workers' strike in 1890, and who later became a trustee of the gas workers' union. In Bermondsey in 1909 a prominent local clergyman stood as an Independent Labour Party candidate for the borough council, styling himself 'The Workers' Champion', and arguing that his work as a clergyman brought him into daily contact with problems of unemployment and inadequate housing which the council was failing to confront. At the time of the 1912 dock strike, sixteen Anglican clergymen in the east London borough of Poplar, headed by the rector, signed a declaration of support for the strikers.[94] In suburban and rural areas (as well, of course, as in many parts of Lancashire), the Anglican clergy were still mainly Conservative, often strongly so: the increasing tendency was for the Anglican Church to take on the colour of the local environment.

The precise nature of the relationship between religion and the system of authority varied considerably from one town to another, but some points were applicable fairly generally. For instance, hierarchical seating arrangements were normal in those churches, chapels, and indeed synagogues, which had a substantial middle-class membership. As early as the 1840s, a series of Anglican churches had been built in the East End of London with entirely free seats. And in many of the poorer Nonconformist chapels, seat rents were charged, but at a low and standardised, or nearly standardised, rate.[95] But in churches or chapels with a more socially differentiated membership it was normal to charge the wealthier members more and, in return, to provide them with better seating.[96] Where exactly the 'best' seats were seems to have varied. Most often they were at the front, but in Dewsbury Congregational chapel they were at the back: 'The people who sat in the back pews of the chapel, well you hardly spoke to them, you certainly didn't unless they spoke to you. And they seldom spoke to you. They were very superior.' Many Victorian churches had galleries, and on the whole they tended to be occupied by those at the lower end of the social scale: for instance at Guildford parish church in the early 1900s the galleries were the preserve of the living-in shop assistants from the big High Street shops.[97] But occasionally the galleries would have a more exalted status – for instance, rural churches sometimes had a small but strategically placed gallery, where the squire and his family could have a place on their own. The general point, however, is that, at least in the larger churches, social distinctions were generally expressed in the seating, and thus received some degree of religious legitimation.

Close links with a church or chapel, often including the holding of lay office, also played a part in underpinning the authority of employers. For instance, Hugh Mason, millowner, Liberal MP for Ashton, was also a deacon of Albion Congregational chapel. An account of the chapel in the later nineteenth century noted that whenever a bazaar was planned for the purpose of reducing the chapel debt, the first step was to get the support of Mason (here referred to as 'Henry Stonor'). 'It was a definite enrichment of life to everybody in the task to be familiar with Mr Stonor, who in turn was distinctly though distantly known to Mr Gladstone.' The author later described the conservation caused by 'Stonor's' death and the huge funeral that followed.[98] In some of the north-eastern mining villages Methodist mine-owners or managers and Methodist trade union leaders seem to have established a rapport born out of a common way of looking at the world, and industrial relations retained a certain degree of harmony at a time when they were rapidly deteriorating in neighbouring villages.[99] It is doubtful whether many people would have respected an employer simply because he belonged to the same religious denomination as themselves. Indeed, if their conduct in some way fell short, they would be obvious targets for the accusations of 'hypocrisy' to which those who combined wealth with piety were always vulnerable. But if he were seen as a 'good' employer, and if his religious profession were combined with personal qualities that were admired, and an approved form of politics, the mixture could be a very potent one, and employers who scored on all these counts could enjoy immense loyalty.

If most forms of authority claimed a religious justification, religion was also among the most important sources of alternative values. It was certainly not the only source of alternative values, and sometimes secular or religiously neutral alternatives were more important, but it was among the most widespread, and potentially the most effective. As centres of radical or unorthodox thinking, many of the smaller Nonconformist denominations certainly had an importance out of all proportion to their numbers. This was true of the Quakers and Unitarians at the more middle-class end of Dissent, and at the more plebeian end it was true not only of the Primitive Methodists, but of many much smaller bodies, such as the Independent Methodists, Churches of Christ or Swedenborgians, who were significant in particular districts but were almost unknown elsewhere, or of the Spiritualists, who had a more widespread following, but whose unorthodoxy set them somewhat apart from the rest of Nonconformity.[100] However, within the mainstream denominations there were also alternative sources available. So far as Nonconformists were concerned, their ostensible principles and many of their traditions were democratic and egalitarian, and it was easy to see that the oligarchic practice of many chapels did not accord with what Nonconformity claimed to stand for. But even Anglicans and Roman Catholics, belonging to hierarchical and traditionally conservative churches, could turn to their Bibles and insist on taking literally the parts that many wealthier church members were trying to explain away.

The chief foundation of Victorian Christianity was the Bible, and a detailed knowledge of the Bible was general among those who made any claim to be religious. The orthodoxies of the time were therefore very vulnerable to criticisms derived from the Bible. Three types of such criticism were particularly common. Most notably, the Old Testament in particular, and to a lesser extent the New Testament, return repeatedly to the theme of social justice, to vindication of the rights of the poor, and to condemnation of the rich. These passages, especially from the prophets Amos and Micah, and from the epistle of James, were frequently cited by Chartists, radicals and socialists.[101] Secondly, the Sermon on the Mount, as well as various other passages in the gospels, provided powerful support for Christian pacifism.[102] And thirdly, the New Testament provided an inspiration for those who despised worldly success and worldly wisdom, choosing to devote their lives to some cause which they believed to have God's blessing, but which offered little chance of social acceptance or even of any evident success. Such causes might take any number of different forms, but the one thing that was certain was that there would always be idiosyncratic saints who interpreted their Christian calling in their own way, and would be immune to considerations of orthodoxy or respectability. One of the most famous examples was Josephine Butler (who will be discussed in the next chapter). Another was the London Anglican clergyman Stewart Headlam, whose friendships with ballet-dancers and with secularists got him into trouble with his bishop, and whose liking for extravagant ritual led to attacks by ultra-Protestants, but whose finest act of defiance of the conventionally religious was to befriend Oscar Wilde at the time of his trial and subsequent imprisonment for homosexuality.[103]

The importance, and also some of the limitations, of religion as a basis for challenges to existing power-structures was indicated by the example of the 'Revolt of the Field' in 1872–3. The role of Nonconformists, and especially of Primitive Methodists, in this movement is inescapable. Nigel Scotland's study of officials of the two main Agricultural Unions in Suffolk, Norfolk and Lincolnshire during the years 1872–96 shows that slightly over half can be identified as Methodists, and about 30 per cent of union officials actually held office in one of the branches of Methodism, most often as a local preacher.[104] These of course are minimum figures, since there were many individuals for whom little biographical information is available. In many rural areas the Nonconformist chapel had a uniquely important role as a place out of the reach of squire or parson, where independent thinking was possible, and where ordinary men and women could enjoy a sense of freedom, could exercise responsibility, and could be made aware of their own value and dignity.

Nonconformists were also likely to be among the most literate members of a substantially illiterate community, and the only ones with any experience of public speaking. They might have been brought up on stories of oppression or persecution by the rural elite – and a few of them might even have experienced such oppression. So it is hardly surprising that Nonconformist chapels were the principal recruiting grounds for rural radicals, nor that the most proletarian branch of Nonconformity, the Primitive Methodists, had a pre-eminent place.

Scotland's analysis of the rhetoric used by union speakers reveals the overwhelmingly important influence of the Bible. Argument in favour of union demands took one of three forms: 'Either an appeal was made to an innate sense of what was just, usually based on the justice of God or the expected standard of Christian behaviour. Or second, reference was made to the life and example of Jesus. Or third, quite frequently there was a direct quotation from a biblical passage.'[105] Union propaganda made heavy use of Old Testament texts such as 'Woe unto him that buildeth his house by unrighteousness and his chambers by wrong, that useth his neighbour's services without wages, and giveth him not for his work' (Jeremiah 22:13). Equally biblical were the hopes for the future that union orators offered, in which Moses, the escape from bondage, and a coming age of freedom, prosperity and social equality all featured prominently. They explicitly presented the movement as a religious crusade.

Meetings often began with hymns. Special services, conducted by one of the many Union leaders who was also a local preacher, were held on Sunday afternoons, sometimes in chapels, but often in the open air or even in a skittle alley. Union tactics were also influenced by the religion of a large part of the leadership. Violence and intimidation were strongly discouraged. Self-help was strongly encouraged. The emancipation of the labourer was to be achieved partly by better wages, shorter hours, and such measures as the provision of allotments, but equally important were temperance, the establishment of Co-operative stores and friendly societies. They would certainly have agreed with the Anglican Christian Socialist J. M. Ludlow who, according to E. R. Norman, saw 'severe limits to the proper sphere of political action':

Social transformation did not of itself make men free. What was needed was a change of heart, an inward cleansing of the sort which Christianity preached: then were men truly able to set themselves in the service of their brothers. But while social conditions degraded them men could not attain the prior internal change. Hence the dialectical relationship of religion and politics.[106]

In many parts of rural England at that time religious Nonconformity was uniquely placed to mobilise huge numbers of previously depressed and unorganised workers. But Nonconformist chapels also had some disadvantages as sources of leadership for the labourers. It has often been suggested that the millenarian rhetoric of many Union orators raised expectations unrealistically high, and thereby contributed to the subsequent disappointment, and the rapid decline suffered by many of the labourers' organisations in the later 1870s. Problems might also arise from the position of the chapels as parts of nation-wide organisations with many middle-class members. Class warfare and political radicalism clearly had enormous disruptive potential in such organisations, and there were always ministers and lay leaders who tried to contain this potential by imposing some kind of 'No politics' rule. There was frequent opposition to the expression of politically controversial views on chapel premises, and some chapels even objected to lay preachers engaging in political controversy off the premises. For instance, Scotland notes the case in 1876 of a Wesleyan local preacher who was told to stop his 'agitation work' for the labourers' Union – though he apparently ignored this advice, and continued both to preach and to agitate.[107] Howkins also shows how Nonconformist plebeian radicalism was continually in danger of erosion through the upward social mobility that often followed from the ethos of hard work, thrift, education and temperance. By the early 1900s, the links between rural unionism and Nonconformity in Norfolk were greatly weakened, and union meetings were often being held in pubs.[108]

Some of the same points can be made about the role of religious Nonconformity in the emergence of the Independent Labour Party (ILP) in the 1890s and in the early years of the twentieth century – though here the picture is much more complicated because of the religious pluralism of the independent labour movement. Indeed, the extreme variety of religious input into the ILP is suggested by E. P. Thompson's analysis of the religious backgrounds of eleven early leaders in west Yorkshire: four were Nonconformists, one a Roman Catholic, two were Secularists, one a disciple of Edward Carpenter, the 'new life' guru, and three he defined as 'happy pagans'.[109] Moreover, definition was not always easy: one of the Nonconformists, F. W. Jowett, later became prominent in the Labour Churches, and one of the Secularists, Ben Turner, later termed himself an 'undenominational Christian', and was an avid Bible-reader. Apart from the sheer variety of religious backgrounds here, perhaps the most interesting point is the absence of Anglicans. So Nonconformity was far from being the only religious influence on the ILP, or even the dominant influence, but it surely ranked as the most significant out of the many kinds of religious or irreligious influences on the party.

The number of individuals who had some kind of link with Nonconformity was certainly very large. And in some areas there were direct institutional links, with a particular chapel having played a major part in the formation of the first ILP branch, as with the Independent Methodist chapel in Nelson, Lancs, or the Primitive Methodist Bible Class in the Durham mining village of Quebec.[110] In the more pluralistic atmosphere of towns and industrial villages Christianity did not provide a common language to the same extent that it did in rural East Anglia. Yet, as Thompson points out, ILP speakers still tended to make a lot of references to the Bible – and in Wales, Keir Hardie would still open a meeting with a prayer and a hymn in the way that Joseph Arch had done in the 1870s.

Thompson argues that 'It is not a question of creed, belief or church, but a question of language, a question of moral texture' – and certainly the Labour Churches, to which many ILP pioneers belonged in the 1890s, coped with diversity of belief by playing down questions of doctrine.[111] But if the labour movement of the 1890s could not be as closely identified with any specific form of religion as the agricultural labourers' movement of the 1870s had been with Primitive Methodism, the formative influence of Nonconformist Christianity remained crucially important at the individual level. This was clearly shown by a study of 249 Labour MPs elected in 1929, the great majority of whom had been born between 1860 and 1890. Of these MPs 105 claimed to belong to one of the free churches. (In addition, there were certainly a considerable number who had lived nearly all their lives in Scottish Dissent, though this was obscured by the fact that the Church of Scotland had reunited in 1929.) Three points emerged continually from the autobiographical accounts. First, it is clear that active participation in religious organisations during adolescence or early adulthood had frequently had a formative effect, especially in encouraging independent and critical thinking about the world around them and in providing opportunities for discussion and sometimes for public speaking. This point would apply not only to those who continued to be active in church or chapel, but also to many of those who broke away. Secondly, socialism was repeatedly justified as a practical application of Christian teaching. Thirdly, it is noticeable how many had been Conscientious Objectors or declared a commitment to pacifism. While it would require some fairly thorough research to substantiate the point, I would suspect that this pacifist tendency arises out of the specifically Nonconformist roots of an important part of the British Labour Party of that period.[112]

The Limits of Christian Influence

Pervasive as the Christian influence was in Victorian England, and profound as was its influence in some respects, there none the less were important limits to this influence. Most obviously, there was a small but growing group of those who consciously rejected all forms of religion, and a much smaller group of those who adhered to religions other than Christianity. Both groups were mentioned in Chapter 1, and the former group will be considered again in Chapter 4. My concern here, however, will be with two other major limitations on the influence of Christianity and the churches: first the isolation from organised religion of many of the poor in both town and countryside; and secondly the tension between formal religious beliefs and other beliefs and loyalties, which sometimes affected people's thinking and behaviour at a deeper level.

At its simplest, the distance of many poorer people from religious organisations (or any other kind of organisation) was simply a function of a life where bare survival was the main priority. Many women in poorer working-class families were tied down by large families, and in addition to bringing up large numbers of children, they often took in washing or made up clothing. The men often had somewhat more free time, but little surplus energy for anything beyond a visit to the pub. For those in the most severe poverty, hunger dominated their thoughts. Those in more moderate poverty still had few spare resources to devote to subscriptions or to buying the respectable clothes that everyone expected of church-goers. This was often regarded as a pretext, but it was in fact a very serious point, as no-one wanted the humiliation of sitting in rags amid a crowd of people in their Sunday best. The churches, admittedly, tried to respond to this situation by establishing mission churches specifically for the poor, where respectable dress would not be required, and certainly some poor people took advantage of such initiatives.

But problems remained: many people were ashamed of their poverty and intended to be seen in public properly dressed or not at all; and some blamed God for their poverty, or rejected any belief in God because of their experience of suffering. It is interesting to note that in a sample of twenty-one people from working-class families interviewed in the Bristol Oral History Project there were only three who explicitly stated that they did not believe in God. All of the latter had experienced severe poverty, and two explicitly related their unbelief to their experience of suffering. One was born in Bristol in 1896, the daughter of a labourer and a sewing machinist. Her father was frequently unemployed and they went through long periods with very little food. At the age of twelve she was raped, which left her with lasting feelings of bitterness – she did not believe in God, because a God would not have allowed her to be raped, or her parents to treat her so badly. She always arrived late for school to avoid Religious Instruction, and told her teacher 'You make me sick talking about Jesus.'[113]

The religious views of the very poor were recorded in unparalleled detail by the missionaries who went from door to door in poor districts of Victorian cities with the aim of converting people to their form of Christianity. The missionaries were required to keep diaries in which they recorded the conversations they had, and these often provide a vivid record of life in the slums. Some people regarded the missionaries merely as intruders, and concentrated on getting them off their doorstep. But some came to regard them as friends, or at least people whom it was useful to know, because they could help in obtaining money, work, hospital letters, etc. And many people seem to have been quite ready to talk about their circumstances and/or their religious beliefs. Some of the most detailed records were left by missionaries attached to Carr's Lane Congregational Church in Birmingham in the 1830s and 1840s.[114] The entry for 26 January 1838 by Edward Derrington recorded a situation that would emerge time and time again in records of this sort. He referred to a Methodist woman who used to attend class, but was excluded when she failed to pay her subscription, and her Baptist husband, who used to attend an adult school, but gave up going when he had to pawn his Sunday clothes. He commented: 'The anxieties of the present life so incessantly occupy and fill the mind that [preaching the gospel] is like putting more in that which is already full.' Very much the same conclusion was reached by the

Salvation Army some fifty years later, and it provided a justification for their increasing involvement in work to ameliorate the conditions of the poor.[115] Interviews by oral historians with those brought up in poor families around the beginning of the twentieth century provide many examples of this sort of situation.

For instance, James Malone was born in 1904 in Highgate, north London. His father was a carpenter and his mother had been a factory worker, but in James's childhood she was fully occupied with looking after her four children. The family were frequently in poverty, and at one point they were evicted. When asked whether his father ever helped in the home, James replied: 'Help himself to pints of beer, that's what his favourite pastime was. . . . Great drinkers them days, you know, well, the homelife, they wanted to get out and escape from it. And the mother was – the mother with the children was – handcuffed. No emancipation at all, no.' James described his parents as 'apathetic'. They sent him to Sunday School: 'It was the accepted thing to do them days. The result of going – whether you became religious – never entered my father's mind, no. It was traditional and a kind of a must. "Now, go on, get dressed, go to Sunday School," you see.' Rather unusually, James did not even know what religious denominations his parents belonged to: 'I assume they were Protestants, but I don't know, as father never spoke about religion, or never spoke to me. There was never a Bible in the house.' (His parents took no overt interest in politics either, though James thinks his father was a Conservative.)[116]

While Mr Malone senior was somewhat unusual in the extent of his religious and political apathy, his enthusiasm for spending most of his free time in the pub was shared by very large numbers of working men. Moreover there was a good deal of rivalry between pub and church. On the part of the churches, and more especially the chapels, the rivalry was quite open and often outspoken. Publicans and pub-goers were seldom so openly hostile to the churches, but in practice the tensions were clear.

Among the occasional pub-goers were many who also went to church. But regular night-in night-out pub-going seems to have excluded regular church-going to a greater degree than anything else. The important thing seems to have been the degree to which the pub-goer was fully integrated into a pub-based sub-culture. Pub and church were competitors for the male worker's free time, but they also nourished opposing values. While the one brought men and women together and stressed the virtues of family life, the other tended to offer the attractions of an all-male environment; the one offered easy-going good fellowship, while the other encouraged an attitude of purposive self-improvement; the one tolerated or encouraged activities that were tabooed by the other, including gambling, poaching, swearing and 'broad' humour. In Norfolk villages the pub was, as Howkins says, 'a stronghold of the rough culture', providing a little island of freedom from the power of farmers and squire in which 'poached game could be sold or hidden, radical opinions expressed, and rumours about the qualities of different employers handed on'. It was also an alternative to the Methodism of many of the 'respectable working class', who disapproved of the pub-goers' dancing, singing and fighting.[117] The son of a Nottingham hosiery worker neatly summed up the rivalry like this: 'There was nothing else to do, only chapel or church or public houses, that's about all there was, and if you went to church or chapel you was a snob, and if you went to a pub you was a hail fellow well met.'[118]

Of course there were many people who emotionally had a foot in both camps, like the Darlington labourer who never went to mass himself, but ensured that his children did, taught them their prayers, and brought them up to revere the Catholic Sisters; or like A. J. Cook's father, who, as a keen drinking man, felt that he would not be welcome in chapel, but liked his daughter to read him religious books.[119] None the less some aspects of the pub sub-culture inspired horror in many church-goers. A Methodist farm labourer from Devon was said to regard

125

horse-racing as 'the devil's work'. The daughter of a Tyneside post office sorter gave a more comprehensive list of Methodist taboos: 'we didn't drink and we didn't gamble and we didn't buy on the never-never and we didn't swear'.[120] Taking all the interviews in the Essex University survey with respondents brought up in working-class families in the industrial districts of northern England and south Wales, we find that 33 per cent of non-church-going fathers were reported to spend most of their free time in the pub, as against 25 per cent of those who were occasional church-goers, and 7 per cent of those who were regular church-goers. Or, to put it differently, 12 per cent of regular pub-goers were also regular church-goers, but 45 per cent of those who went to pubs infrequently or not at all were regular church-goers.

While pubs might offer for some an effective antidote to the pervasive influence of church and chapel, some people living in isolated rural areas had little contact with any place of worship, and there were some rural communities where organised religion had never had much of a presence. Admittedly, the number of such places had sharply declined since the later eighteenth century. First the Methodists set up numerous cottage meetings in isolated settlements, some of which were later replaced by small chapels. Then the Anglican revival from the 1840s onwards resulted in the building of many new village churches, particularly in the north and the Welsh Marches, the regions hitherto most neglected.

However, James Obelkevich, in his study of religion in rural Lincolnshire, presents the challenging thesis that the influence of Christianity on the rural poor was relatively superficial, even in a county of flourishing Methodist chapels and with a reasonably strong Anglican presence. Citing the popularity of the various 'wise men', who were consulted in all kinds of difficulties and who were credited with gifts of prophecy, the numerous magical rituals whereby villagers protected their animals and crops, and the fundamentally pessimistic view of the world which he

detects in accounts of the mentality of the rural population, he argues that the outlook of most labourers, farm
servants and small farmers was more pagan than Christian. Indeed, he goes so far as to argue that if research
in other areas confirms his findings, 'the "ptolemaic" theory
of popular religion – with Christianity at its centre and
paganism at the fringes – will need to undergo a "copernican
revolution"'. Unfortunately, no major study has yet been
attempted which tests the validity of Obelkevich's arguments against the evidence of other areas. Keiner, in his
work on Buckinghamshire, criticised some aspects of
Obelkevich's treatment of the Church of England, but did
not attempt to explore the area of popular religion. Snape
comes closest to offering a critique. Analysing rather similar
sets of beliefs in north Lancashire in the eighteenth century, he questions their designation as 'pagan', arguing
that many of them could find justification within the Bible or Christian tradition, and that they represented an
interpretation of Christianity in the light of the situation
and mental world of the rural labourer – an interpretation necessarily different from, yet as valid as, that of the
clergyman, urban intellectual or businessman. Since, however, Snape's study stops at the end of the eighteenth
century, and refers to an area that was partly industrialised, it is not directly comparable to that by Obelkevich.[121]

Some working-class women (such complaints came less
often from men) regretted that their crowded weekly time-
table left little opportunity for going to church. In the
upper and upper middle classes there was a very different situation. Thanks to their servants, most of these people
had ample free time, and social conformity decreed that
some of this was spent in church or in other religious
observances. But there was often a tension between the
teachings of the churches and some of the accepted practices of everyday life. The most glaring example of this
was the 'Double Standard' of sexual morality, according
to which extra-marital sex by women was severely condemned, while in the case of men it was widely tolerated.[122]

This was not of course the view taken by feminists or by Christian preachers, both of whom fervently insisted on the fact that the same moral rules applied to both sexes. The inequality was probably less widely accepted in the working class or middle class than it was in the aristocracy. But there certainly were large numbers of men in all classes who felt that the double standard applied to themselves, and in the upper reaches of the social hierarchy there was a fairly widespread acceptance by men (and even by some women) that such a double standard existed, even if it could not be morally justified. Wealthy men frequently kept mistresses and sometimes had affairs with their servants, and there were many men in all classes who visited prostitutes.[123]

Politicians and members of the royal family did not face the press inquisitions that have brought down so many of their present-day counterparts – unless their extra-marital adventures landed them in a divorce court, in which case the press, and the public opinion of their own class, took a different view.[124] Divorce cases, like court cases of all kinds, were eagerly reported by the press and avidly consumed by the newspaper-reading public. The sexual peculiarities of prominent public personalities were widely known, and were favourite subjects of gossip among men (and to some extent women) of their own class. But to allow these to become widely known among the general public, and thus among social inferiors, was a form of indiscretion which could be severely punished. In the case of politicians it could mean the end of their career. The most famous example was Charles Stuart Parnell, leader of the Irish National Party, whose affair with the wife of a fellow MP was common knowledge in political circles – so much so that the fervently Anglican Liberal Prime Minister, Gladstone, addressed letters to Parnell, 'c/o Mrs O'Shea'. However, when in 1890 Parnell was cited by Captain O'Shea in an action for divorce, there was a public outcry, leading the Liberals and the majority of his own party to disown him. The Prince of Wales attracted unflat-

tering press publicity, both in the 1870s when he was
subpoenaed to give evidence in a divorce case, and in
the 1890s when he was called to give evidence in a libel
action involving cheating at cards. The first of these episodes gave a considerable boost to the republican movement, which was then at its height. As these incidents
indicate, there was not only a tension between the official
religion of the country and the actual behaviour of many
male members of the dominant classes, but also a conflict between what was permitted by the social code operating within the elite and what public opinion regarded
as acceptable.

The implicit acceptance of a double standard by many
of the nation's rulers found expression in the famous, or
infamous, Contagious Diseases Acts, passed between 1864
and 1869.[125] These attempted to deal with the prevalence
of venereal disease in the British armed forces by introducing a system of compulsory medical inspection for
women thought to be prostitutes and practising their profession in certain military towns such as Aldershot and
Plymouth. The first of these Acts was passed with very
little comment. Members of Parliament seem to have seen
it as a sensible way of dealing with the problem. Only
some years later did a group of women start to campaign
against the Acts on a mixture of Christian and feminist
grounds, finally securing their repeal in 1886. The repeal
crusaders almost immediately won the support of the
Nonconformist churches. But they had much bigger problems in persuading MPs to take them seriously, and for
years they faced ridicule at the hands of the press, and
opposition not only from a large section of the medical
profession and the military authorities, but even from many
of the Anglican clergy. The debate had several dimensions (which will be discussed a little more fully in Chapter 3), but the most relevant point at the moment was
the differing attitudes to prostitution which were revealed.
For the Christian and feminist campaigners for repeal, it
was simply evil. Supporters of the Acts included many who

took a pragmatic view, according to which prostitution was certainly an evil, but one that was likely to remain for the foreseeable future, so that the emphasis of legislation should be on mitigating its harmful effects. But there was also a segment of political and medical opinion which positively accepted prostitution, arguing that it provided a means of diverting the excessive sexual appetites of many men into relatively harmless channels.[126]

The ultimately successful campaign against the Contagious Diseases Act was one of the highpoints of the eruption into politics of a moral crusading style which had its main roots in provincial middle-class Nonconformity, and which was alien to most of the Anglican gentlemen who made up a large part of the membership of the two Houses of Parliament for most of the nineteenth century. In an analysis of the orientation of 456 men who were Liberal MPs for English constituencies between 1859 and 1874, John Vincent argues that the only ones with much interest in bringing about change were the 20 described as 'Radicals' and the 34 'militant businessmen', defined as those 'with a sense of mission'. They were far outnumbered by the 198 'large landowners'.[127]

And however moralistic these 'militant businessmen' may have been in the House of Commons, it does not necessarily follow that they applied such strict standards to the running of their business. The gap between the Sunday profession and the weekday practice of pious businessmen was a subject of endless complaint by working-class people, and a major source of working-class alienation from organised religion. A typical critique was that of Robert Tressell, who provided this account of the relations between the Shining Light Chapel and its caretaker:

In a seat at the back of the hall knelt a pale-faced, weary-looking little woman about thirty-six years of age, very shabbily dressed, who had come in during the singing. This was Mrs White, the caretaker Bert White's mother. When her husband died, the committee of the Chapel, out of charity, gave her this work, for which they paid her six shillings a week. Of course, they could not offer her full employment; the idea was that she could get other work as well, charing and things of that kind, and do the Chapel work in between. . . . An evil-minded, worldly or unconverted person might possibly sum up the matter thus: These people required this work to be done: they employed this woman to do it, taking advantage of her poverty to impose upon her conditions of price and labour that they would not have liked to endure themselves. Although she worked very hard, early and late, the money they paid her was insufficient to enable her to provide herself with the bare necessaries of life. Then her employers, being good, kind, generous, Christian people, came to the rescue and bestowed charity, in the form of cast-off clothing and broken victuals.[128]

Yet there clearly were businessmen who tried very hard to reconcile their religion with the need to make a profit. Indeed there were some who took their religion so seriously that they ultimately went out of business, like Sir Joseph Pease, the Quaker coal-owner, banker and railway magnate, who as a matter of principle pursued a policy of peaceful relations with the Durham Miners Association, even at times when more aggressive tactics by the owners could have smashed the union, and who refused to close down a chronically loss-making factory because 'it was his Christian duty as an employer to sustain those workers in employment who had served the family loyally'.[129] In boom times, it may have been relatively easy for those who seriously wished to apply their religious principles to the conduct of their business to do so – though there were always plenty of successful businessmen who made no attempt at all to close the gap between Sundays and week-days: as one farmer replied when told that his treatment of his workers defied 'common Christianity', 'If you want Christianity, you should go to church.'[130] In times of depression, however, the 'Christian businessman' walked a tightrope.

Beside the conscious hypocrisy of the many men who did what social custom required in terms of religious observance, but went their own way in matters of morality, there was an important section of educated middle and upper-class opinion which argued for moderation in matters of religion – which accepted the truth of Christian doctrine and insisted on the necessity for practical Christian virtues, but was highly suspicious of any exaggerated religious zeal or ostentatious piety. The religious ideal most commonly presented by such apostles of moderation was that of a middle-of-the-road Anglicanism, orthodox but undogmatic. On the other hand, Nonconformist ministers and Roman Catholic priests were suspected of being mostly fanatics, and the more militantly Evangelical or Tractarian Anglican clergy were possibly even worse. Throughout the 1850s, 1860s and 1870s, when the influence of these various forms of militancy was very high, the pages of *Punch* offered a vivid portrait-gallery of clerical stereotypes in which the cartoonists frequently managed to convey the message that clerical extremists, as well as being a nuisance, were not really gentlemen. Dickens was particularly explicit in contrasting true Christianity with religious bigotry. A striking example is *Little Dorrit* (1857), where the genuine piety of the heroine, which cannot be identified with any sect or party, was set against the backdrop of the repulsive, and identifiably evangelical, bogus piety of Mrs Clennam. Similarly in *Middlemarch* the strident evangelicalism of the crooked businessman Bulstrode contrasts with the sincere but undemonstrative religion of the liberal clergyman, Farebrother. Scandals involving apparently devout businessmen were sufficiently common in mid-Victorian Britain for this account to have a certain amount of verisimilitude.

By about 1890 there had been a considerable change in the moral and intellectual atmosphere. By this time, critics of bigotry and puritanism were readier to reject religion altogether, and were much more radical in their presentation of new alternatives. For instance, Grant Allen in 1894 was advocating a 'New Hedonism', and Edward Carpenter and Havelock Ellis emerged at about the same time as the most influential advocates of a revolution in attitudes to sexuality. At the same time Thomas Hardy and Bernard Shaw were, in their different ways, offering outspoken challenges to existing moral orthodoxies. Meanwhile, within the Christian churches, an increasingly wide range of doctrinal possibilities had been opened up, and many old taboos had been at least partly lifted. It was becoming increasingly easy for those with unconventional ideas simply to say what they meant. But for a large part of the Victorian period, those who were unhappy with the existing theological and moral orthodoxies seldom felt strong enough to challenge them directly.

3

SIGNS OF THE TIMES

This chapter will begin by looking at three individuals, each of them a middle-ranking celebrity and each, in her or his different way, a characteristic figure of the time.

Josephine Butler (1828–1906) was born into a Northumberland landowning family and was related to the Whig prime minister Lord Grey. She was brought up in an atmosphere of cultured liberal Anglicanism. At the age of 24 she married a clergyman, and she travelled round the country with him for some years before settling in Liverpool. She was convinced that she had a divine call to work for 'the moral elevation of her sex'. Her main early interest was in extending to women opportunities for higher education, but then she switched her attention to what she called 'the protection and reclamation of women subjected to vicious influences'.[1] In 1870 she became the Honorary Secretary of the Ladies' National Association for the Repeal of the Contagious Diseases Acts (LNA), and she soon emerged as the most prominent and widely influential leader of the campaign. The Ladies' Association worked alongside the male-dominated National Association, which included Members of Parliament and Nonconformist ministers among its most prominent members. The LNA in the 1870s was an organisation of middle-class women, predominantly Nonconformist, and including particularly large Quaker and Unitarian elements.[2] Butler gave the movement a strongly moralistic tone, an uncompromising style, and a rationale that was both Christian and feminist. There were two main planks to the repealers' platform. First, state regulation of prostitution amounted to state acceptance of an evil that no Christian society should be prepared to condone. And secondly, the fact that it was women who were subjected to compulsory medical inspection, although the soldiers were equally responsible for the spread of the diseases, was a blatant example of discrimination against women. Butler also pointed out that women turned to prostitution because of the low rates of pay in many of the trades filled by women, and that economic as well as moral and religious means were therefore needed to help women escape from the degrading and miserable business of prostitution. The Liberal MPs who supported the cause frequently stressed the fact that the Contagious Diseases Acts were an example of the over-mighty state at work, sending batallions of bullying policemen and officious doctors to interfere in the lives of the citizen – including, as a series of *causes célèbres* attested, many who had no connection at all with prostitution. The various objections to the Acts were neatly summarised in 1871 by the Conference of the United Methodist Free Churches, which declared that the Acts were 'immoral in tendency, contrary to the law of God, dangerous to the liberty of the subject and do not secure the sanitary and restraining effect for which they were professedly enacted'.[3] Butler would have agreed with all these points – indeed she believed that in condoning prostitution Britain risked the kind of divine judgement that had fallen on France in the Franco-Prussian War. She also saw the campaign as a feminist crusade:

> It is womanhood which has been wronged for generations, and even our best and truest friends among men are not to be permitted by God, for He will not permit it, to wipe out the wrong. The avenging angel must be one of the sex which has been outraged.[4]

The LNA was the first British political organisation conducted entirely by women. It encountered considerable ridicule from politicians and sections of the press as a result – though it also received a great deal of public attention, which might have eluded a more conventional campaign. Josephine Butler became its most effective speaker – and indeed the first Englishwoman to make a nationwide reputation as a public speaker. In one year she travelled 3,700 miles in support of the repeal campaign, speaking to 99 meetings and 4 conferences. According to one male colleague, she had 'a voice of great charm and softness and intense but subdued earnestness and perfect simplicity in her style of speaking such as only the most accomplished orator possesses'.[5] Her efforts were finally rewarded when, in 1883 and 1886, the Acts were repealed. In her later years she turned her attention to the continent, and in 1880 she became the leader of an international committee for the suppression of the white slave traffic.

She also had an important influence on our second figure, Hugh Price Hughes (1847–1902). Born in Carmarthen, the son of a doctor, and converted at 13, he became a boy preacher and then trained for the Wesleyan Ministry. He spent the rest of his life as a minister in and around London, and he was to become the most famous of the many Welshmen who occupied prominent English pulpits in the nineteenth and twentieth centuries. While in his first station, he went to hear Josephine Butler and was immediately converted to the repeal cause.[6] He came to prominence as editor of a repeal journal, and then went on to found the *Methodist Times*, through which he quickly became established as the leading voice of the younger Wesleyan generation, and one of the most prominent figures in the Nonconformist world.

He was typical of that generation in his combination of Liberal politics, a somewhat liberalised evangelical theology, and an insistence that Christians must preach a social gospel. As he declared in 1889: 'Jesus Christ came into this world to save human society as well as to save individuals, indeed, you cannot effectually save the one without saving the other.'[7] Like many of the Nonconformist ministers of his generation he was a fervent teetotaller, arguing that though drink might not be wrong in itself the misery and the social evils resulting from excessive drinking meant that everyone should be an abstainer in order to set an example to those who were incapable of moderation.[8]

As a democrat he felt that the free church ethos was in accord with the spirit of the age, and that their time had now come. Hughes was impressed by everything that was big, powerful and dynamic, and he felt sure that if the divided forces of Dissent could only learn to work together, they could claim the dominant position in national life that was rightfully theirs.[9] He therefore supported the early steps towards the reunification of Methodism and towards free church federation, and in 1896 he became the first president of the Free Church Council.

He was also a leading advocate of the Wesleyan Central Missions, which were set up in the centre of English cities from 1885 onwards, and which combined simple services and lively preaching with extensive social services. From 1887 he directed the West London Mission, which gave him a platform in the heart of the capital. Believing that the churches had a right and a duty to speak out on public issues, he became one of the best known exponents of what was termed the 'Nonconformist Conscience'. His most famous intervention was in 1890, when, in a sermon at his West London Mission, he denounced the Irish parliamentary leader Parnell for his adultery. Insisting that the Liberals shun their former ally, he declared that 'What is morally wrong can never be politically right.' As his daughter wrote: 'Undoubtedly by that Sunday he was at white heat, for he increasingly realised all that was involved in the issue of the moment. That public life should be animated by Christian ideals was one of the leading principles of his career.'[10]

In his later years he became a supporter of imperialism, and eagerly accepted the idea that the world's future lay with English-speaking Protestant nations. He believed that the British Empire had a place in the divine plan, and that Britain had a mission to spread the principles of democracy and good government to all parts of the world. He was impressed with the results of British rule in India, Egypt and elsewhere, and, much to the disgust of many of his former allies in the free churches, he supported the Boer War, on the grounds that Kruger's government in the Transvaal was undemocratic, that it favoured the drink traffic, and that it held the African population in conditions of 'practical slavery'.[11]

C. T. Studd (1862–1931) was one of three brothers (the others being J. E. K. and G. B.), sons of a retired planter, all of whom became enthusiastic sportsmen at Eton, and went on to captain the Cambridge cricket XI. C. T., who was an all-rounder, played against Australia in the famous Oval Test of 1882, where the 7-run Australian victory was said to have marked the death of English cricket. (After the match a tiny urn, containing the ashes of a bail, was presented to the Australian team as a symbol of the deceased English game – and ever since, Australian and English teams have competed for these 'Ashes'.) The following winter, while still allegedly studying for his degree at Cambridge, he joined the MCC tour of Australia, playing in several more Tests.

During his time at Cambridge, his previously passive Anglicanism changed into a fervent evangelical commitment (the trigger apparently being a serious illness suffered by his devout elder brother). He persuaded several members of the England team to go and hear Moody and Sankey, who were then in London, and when he left Cambridge he announced that he was going to China as a missionary. By the time he left England in 1885, several other Cambridge men had also volunteered to join Hudson Taylor's China Inland Mission, which combined an extremely conservative form of evangelical theology with a requirement that missionaries adopt the forms of dress and diet of the people to whom they were preaching. Studd and his colleagues became known as 'The Cambridge Seven', and the press was fascinated by the fact that they included, besides the celebrated cricketer, the Stroke of the Cambridge Eight, another talented oarsman, and two military men. Before leaving for China, they toured the country addressing meetings of students. After a particularly well-attended meeting in Edinburgh, one observer commented:

A wonderful work of grace has begun, and is going on in our University. The event that has precipitated the shower of blessing which has, and is, falling in our midst is the recent visit of two young Christian athletes from Cambridge, who are now on their way to preach Christ to the Chinese. Students, like other young men, are apt to regard professedly religious men of their own age as wanting in manliness, unfit for the river or cricket field, and only good for Psalm-singing and pulling a long face, but the big, muscular hands and long arms of the ex-Captain of the Cambridge Eight, stretched out in entreaty while he eloquently told out the story of Redeeming Love, capsized their theory; and when Mr C. T. Studd, a name to them familiar as a household word, and perhaps the greatest gentleman bowler in England, supplemented his brother athlete's words by quiet but intense and burning utterances of personal testimony to the love and power of a personal Saviour, opposition and criticism were alike disarmed, and professors and students together were seen in tears.[12]

Studd spent nine years in China, six years in India, and eighteen in Africa, with intervals in which ill health brought him back to England. He died in what was then the Belgian Congo. His biography, written shortly after his death, is written as an adventure story, with chapter titles like 'Among Cannibals', 'Perils and Hardships in China', and 'A Man's Man'.[13]

Contained in these three life-stories are a number of the themes that recur most often in the religious history of this period: the evangelistic imperative, the moral crusading style, the social gospel, the sense of an inter-relationship between Christian mission and a British national mission, a 'muscular Christianity' that defined itself in masculinist terms, and a Christian feminism, which believed that women had a unique role to play in the christianisation of society, and that women had a right and duty to claim their proper place in the church.

Evangelism

C. T. Studd's zest for evangelism was such that on a journey to the station he would try to convert the cab-driver, and when, during a country-house weekend, the butler brought a jug of hot water to Studd's bedroom, he was told to sit down and answer questions about the state of his soul – inevitably several members of the crew were converted as a result of Studd's efforts during the voyage to China.[14] Studd was an extreme example of a more general phenomenon – the emphatic evangelistic orientation of most churches. The later eighteenth and early nineteenth centuries had been the golden age of the itinerant preacher, going from village to village, preaching in market places.[15] In the Victorian period evangelism tended to be more localised. It included preaching at street corners and in parks, preaching in pubs, and perhaps most important, door-to-door evangelism. A lot of missionary activity was focused on specific groups whose occupations or recreations marked them out as in need of conversion. For instance, in the 1890s one Dewsbury chapel held a 'Midnight Mission', directed at those who were emerging from the town's pubs at that late hour. Members of the chapel marched through the streets, headed by the minister and the Sunday School teachers, with the senior scholars following, and they stopped outside pubs to sing hymns and invite the drinkers to a special service. They got quite big crowds, and some who came forward to the 'penitent form' (a specially designated bench at the front of the room) and claimed to have been converted.[16]

Already in the 1830s there was a tendency to claim that the working-class districts of the cities, and especially the poorer working-class districts, were one vast mission field.[17] Disturbed by low levels of church attendance, by examples they encountered of religious unbelief, and by what they regarded as symptoms of unbelief – ranging from drunkenness and illicit sex to political radicalism – many clergymen made sweeping claims for the prevalence of 'heathenism', 'godlessness', or at least complete religious apathy. The rector of Bethnal Green, in the East End of London, informed his bishop in 1862 that 'the greater part of the population consists of Radicals, Infidels, and persons who are to all good works reprobate'.[18] Published accounts, designed to secure the release of public or private funds for religions purposes, naturally used even more emphatic language, and especially made explicit the links between irreligion and political unrest. For instance, a Sheffield vicar, in 1840, after referring to the absence from church of most of his parishioners, went on to claim that:

> The moral condition of the people is precisely what might be anticipated. . . . Can it be surprising that the profane doctrines and licentious practices of the Socialists, so congenial to the animal appetites of the ignorant, find numerous abettors? It is quite natural that in such a population, the demagogue and political firebrand will find abundant materials for sedition, treason and rebellion.[19]

Not surprisingly this rhetoric caused some resentment on the part of those who were subjected to such sweeping judgements. The best-known response was perhaps that of Thomas Wright, 'The Journeyman Engineer', who wrote in 1868:

The classes who do habitually attend places of worship frequently do so for other than religious motives. . . . No person with the slightest knowledge of the world – and I take it that even clergymen should have some worldly wisdom – needs to be told that attendance at a place of worship is not necessarily a proof of religious feeling, and yet it is upon the grounds of non-attendance that the working classes are stigmatised as irreligious. If, however, we put aside this evidently unreliable criterion and judge them by the essentials of Christianity, it will be found that the working classes are not irreligious. Brotherly love abounds among them, and those who have the opportunity of seeing with what kindness they assist friends or neighbours in distress know that they have that charity that covers a multitude of sins. . . . To speak of a widespread infidelity among the working classes, or of their being actively opposed to religion or to religious institutions, is simply to talk nonsense.[20]

Such subtleties, however, were likely to be lost on most Victorian evangelicals, who were reluctant to meet outsiders on their own terms. The evident facts that the majority of working-class adults were not regular churchgoers and that many of them did not observe the sabbath was sufficient to establish in the minds of the more zealous evangelicals that they were not genuine Christians, and that any religious profession that they made was self-delusion.[21] (Of course, such zealots were well aware that much middle-class religiosity was superficial, but the fact that most middle-class people went to church services and so were subject to sermons and readings of the Bible, meant that the nature of the evangelist's task was different.)

The first of the city missions was established in Glasgow in 1826, and before long every British town of any size had an interdenominational organisation formed for the purpose of evangelism in working-class areas. Many congregations established their own mission in a poor neighbourhood near to the church, and though the initial purpose was to win recruits for the main congregation, the result tended to be the emergence of a second quite separate congregation, distinguished by shabbier clothes and the existence of a supporting apparatus of charitable provision.

Whatever the original intentions of those running such agencies, it would quickly become apparent that any attempt to evangelise the poor must take account of the conditions in which the poor lived – lack of food, clothing and fuel, inadequate housing, the frequency of illness and death, the compulsion to earn a living by means condemned by evangelicalism (e.g. Sunday labour) or by all forms of religion (e.g. prostitution or theft). Whether for reasons of compassion, or from a realisation that proving for the material needs of the poor might be a way of persuading them to listen to the spiritual message, or for both reasons, most evangelistic agencies found themselves sooner or later providing food or clothing, or other kinds of material help.[22] Even the Salvation Army, which began with a determination to preach the gospel and nothing else, was soon forced into a realisation that poverty left its victims with little surplus energy for anything that did not relate to the struggle for survival.[23] Others, like the south London-based Ranyard Mission, combined evangelism with humanitarian care from the start: founded in 1857, this mission employed Bible Nurses, who combined free medical care with the delivery of a religious message.[24]

The Wesleyan Central Missions, founded under the influence of Hugh Price Hughes in the 1880s, provide a good indication of the way many Nonconformists of the time envisaged the church of the future. These missions were the clearest expressions of a new current of thinking about evangelism, social work, political campaigning, and the connection between them. In the eyes of those such as Hughes, who espoused what Americans were calling the Social Gospel, all of these were inter-related, and each was a part of the church's mission. No distinction

143

should be made between what was 'sacred' and what was 'secular': all of human life was God's concern, and concern for human beings included a concern for their bodies, their minds and their souls – any work which limited itself to one part of the human personality was incomplete. Very similar ideas were being advanced by High Anglicans, who saw the Incarnation as lying at the heart of Christianity and who argued that if God had become man, human life was holy.[25] But in Hughes's thinking the new missions were also part of a power struggle. They were a means of 'winning back' the masses, and they were also a means of fighting the influence of the Church of England, with a view to 'capturing' the cities, and above all London, for the forces of Nonconformity. Military metaphors came readily to Hughes, as they did to many others of his generation.[26] Hughes's West London Mission provided the prototype.

The best description of this new kind of church appears in Alan Bartlett's study of the south London borough of Bermondsey, which housed not only the Wesleyan South London Mission, but also the Primitive Methodist St George's Hall and the Free Methodist Bermondsey Mission, which were run on very similar lines. Their buildings were all very big, and deliberately unecclesiastical. They looked more like a theatre or music-hall, 'and the style of worship bore similarities as well. There were platforms not pulpits. String and brass bands flanked the preacher. The singing was enthusiastic. Booth saw Flanagan leading the congregation, with his arms outstretched, in singing again and again the last and most moving verse of the hymn. Soloists, especially women, sang songs of appeal and lament. The services themselves were dramas which focused on the central figure of the preacher.'[27] The reputation of the preacher was a crucial factor in attracting people to the services, and the founding ministers of the Wesleyan and Primitive halls were both noted for their popular and highly emotional style. An array of social services proclaimed the church's compassion for those in need, and perhaps persuaded some of them to listen to the church's message and to join the Christian community. These services included teams of nurses, free legal advice, libraries, temperance cafes, and a seaside home for cripples. Ministers of these churches frequently got involved in social reforming campaigns, and in local Liberal or Labour politics. They also were frequently astute businessmen. In particular, Henry Meakin of the South London Wesleyan Mission had a very keen eye for publicity, which extended from the selection of a highly visible corner site, to the sale of 'South London Mission' handkerchiefs.[28]

In the first half of the nineteenth century the most important mission fields had been at home, but in the second half of the century overseas missions gradually came to take priority. Although the 1790s had seen the foundation of a series of societies for overseas mission, and pioneering missionary work in India, the number of British missionaries remained relatively small during the first half of the century, and the successes enjoyed by missionaries were relatively limited. During the second half of the century, enthusiasm for missions among the British Christian public seems to have run through a series of distinct peaks and troughs.

The first major peak, in the later 1850s, may have been influenced by the publication in 1857 of David Livingstone's immensely popular *Missionary Travels*; by the Indian Mutiny, in which a number of Indian Christians and British missionaries were murdered; and by the forcible 'opening up' of China to missionaries. There was another peak in the mid-70s, when the death of Livingstone in 1873 and the visit to Britain of Moody and Sankey in 1873–5 seem to have played a part in arousing interest in missions and in persuading significant numbers of young men that they might have a calling to engage in such work. And in the 1890s enthusiasm for overseas missions reached a higher point than at any other period before, with 1896 seeing record levels of recruitment.[29] The British conquest of huge areas of Africa during the 1880s and 1890s no doubt played a major part here, both in arousing interest in the people of that continent, and in making it possible for missionaries to gain access to many areas which they previously entered at their peril.

Most English denominations had at least one society for overseas missions – often dating back to the years around 1800, when the upsurge of missionary interest was linked with the millennial hopes aroused by the overthrow of the French monarchy and French Catholic church, and the apparently imminent downfall of the papacy.[30] In the course of the nineteenth century, a series of new Anglican missions were established representing various shades of high churchmanship, in rivalry to the evangelical Church Missionary Society, and various non-denominational missions were founded, usually of a strongly evangelical character, most notably the China Inland Mission (CIM), and other 'faith missions', which eschewed fund-raising and any attempt to get involved in education or medical care, as opposed to simply 'preaching the gospel'.

By the early twentieth century, Christian missionaries were active in nearly every part of the world, including India, China, Japan, the islands of the Pacific, and most parts of Africa. Only a very few countries, notably Nepal, Tibet and Afghanistan, remained closed to them.[31] The response to their efforts varied greatly. At one extreme were some Pacific islands, such as Fiji, where the great majority of the population was converted to Christianity in the middle years of the nineteenth century. At the other extreme were the Muslim countries of North Africa and the Middle East, where numbers of conversions were minimal. But the foundations were laid for a major shift in the centre of gravity within worldwide Christianity that has taken place within the twentieth century. It is estimated that between 1900 and 1985 the proportion of the world's Christians living in Africa or Asia rose from less than 5 per cent to 25 per cent.[32]

So far as Protestant missions were concerned the role

of missionaries from the British Isles and of English-based missions was crucial. British churches produced a regular supply of volunteers who were prepared to offer themselves for work in the mission fields and, equally important, they provided regular supplies of money to support missionary work. Statistics published in 1896 suggested that there were approximately 12,000 European and American Protestant missionaries working in the mission fields, of whom over 3000 were employed by the English societies: 903 were working for the evangelical Anglican Church Missionary Society and 612 for its High Anglican rival, the Society for the Propagation of the Gospel. The other giants were the China Inland Mission (604), the Wesleyan Missionary Society (388), the non-sectarian, but in practice mainly Congregationalist, London Missionary Society (261), and the Baptist Missionary Society (192). In terms of the total number of converts, the most successful was the London Missionary Society (LMS), which employed considerably more native pastors than European missionaries.[33] Numerous congregations raised funds for one of the missionary societies, and many of them had their 'own' missionary, whose portrait hung in a prominent place in the church building, whose letters were enthusiastically read out at church meetings, and whose work was supported by prayers and money.[34] Susan Thorne's research on the finances of Congregational churches in the period 1870–1913 suggests that overseas missions were the largest beneficiary of collections after the payment of the minister's salary and the upkeep of the buildings.[35]

In the later nineteenth century, as missionary enthusiasm reached its highest point, missionary exploits became staple fare in Sunday Schools.[36] Children thrilled to stories of voyages down uncharted rivers to the heart of Africa, of journeys across deserts or through impenetrable forests, of encounters with slave-traders and witch-doctors, and escapes from crocodiles and cannibals. Naturally, cruelty, duplicity and superstition featured prominently in accounts of life 'before' the missionary impact, though the emphasis

147

on the favourable results of missionary activity led to a
stress on the potential for good even within the most
apparently benighted human communities. Such teaching helped to shape more general attitudes towards Britain's Empire and its subject peoples. By highlighting the
less attractive aspects of life in the areas that had been
colonised, the benefits of imperialism were underscored.
A tract written by an LMS missionary in 1894, in which
he tried to justify the British South Africa Company's
invasion of Matabeleland, provides a compendium of
popular arguments for the social benefits of imperial rule
in combination with missionary work:

> One great obstacle of fear and dread in the way of our
> past progress – the club of Lobenguela – has been bro-
> ken. The people . . . will no longer be in fear and dread
> of the heathen monarch's tyrannical power to crush their
> ambition, enterprise, and desire for knowledge. . . . There
> will be no more slavery in the land, nor children brought
> to you for sale. The woman, too, will have some room
> to live, and have some reason to rejoice that she is free
> from the thraldom of her heathen master. . . . A new
> era will begin in the history of the country and the
> people will be free. The current of their thought will
> be directed into another channel – that of progress,
> education, civilisation and Christianity. Therefore, the
> future is full of hope and bright prospects.[37]

Here we have many of the key concepts of liberal missionary imperialism: heathenism meant fear, cruelty and
the oppression of women. British rule provided peace and
good government. Christian missions brought with them
a new era of freedom and development, in which every
area of life would be reshaped in accordance with the
new ideals. At the same time, the stress on the benefits
following christianisation undermined the influence of
those forms of imperial ideology which were based on
assumptions of the innate superiority of one race over

another. Missionaries frequently supported annexations both on religious and on humanitarian grounds – but the same considerations subsequently led to conflicts with the colonial authorities, whether because evangelistic work was being impeded, from political motives, or because the colonial authorities carried out or tolerated cruel or exploitative practices. The most famous example was Kenya in the 1920s, where missionaries led opposition to the conscription of African labour to work on European-owned farms. But many smaller clashes were taking place in the years before the First World War. Quite apart from humanitarian motives for such interventions, the credibility of the missionaries in the eyes of converts was at stake. In south-eastern Nigeria, for instance, missionaries were defending Africans against cruel or arbitrary punishments by the colonial authorities.[38]

In the later nineteenth century, emphasis on the social benefits of missionary work was tending to increased as the belief that all the unconverted would go to hell diminished. A comparison between statements made by would-be LMS missionaries in the years 1845–58 and in the years 1876–88 indicates the changes. The former group included many who referred to the 'perishing' heathen or stated their belief that those who had not heard the gospel would go to hell. In the latter group were fewer who stated such beliefs, and several who explicitly repudiated them.[39] This trend did not, however, affect some of the more strongly conservative of the evangelical missions, such as the China Inland Mission – in 1884 the CIM's founder, Hudson Taylor, went so far as to make belief in everlasting punishment part of the mission's statement of faith.[40]

Manliness

As the case of C. T. Studd indicates, missionaries (like soldiers and sportsmen) also played an important part in the attempt by many Christian propagandists in this period to give their faith a masculine image which, it was hoped, might appeal to young men – the section of the population thought to be most distant from the churches. Missionaries (at least in the early pioneering years) led exciting and dangerous lives. Some of them became martyrs, like James Hannington, the Anglican bishop murdered, together with a large group of African Christians, in Buganda in 1885. Others succumbed to tropical diseases, as did a very high proportion of the pioneering missionaries in West Africa in the middle decades of the century.[41] They lent themselves to heroic treatment, and the huge missionary literature exploited to the full the heroic dimensions of the subject. Biographies of missionaries emphasised their powerful physique, 'utter manliness', handiness with their fists, ability to bear pain and discomfort – and, of course, the passion for cricket, which proved that as well as being heroes and saints, they were reassuringly human, and thoroughly English.[42]

Interest in missions and missionaries thus interacted with two other characteristic concerns of the time. It had an obvious relationship with the sense of Britain as a nation blessed by God, with a crucial part to play in the spread of Christianity and the advance of civilisation. Less obviously it related to the contemporary obsession with physical fitness, sport, character-building and 'manliness'. Christian propagandists naturally presented the Christian faith, and organised their attempts to mobilise the Christian public, in terms which made sense to contemporaries, and which related to their concerns.

One example was the interaction between Christianity and the cult of sport and the sportsman, which was so characteristic of the later part of the nineteenth century. From about 1860, the public schools were devoting an increasingly large part of the curriculum to organised sport (principally, cricket, athletics, and the various forms of football); frequently headmasters used sermons in chapel to justify this innovation, which was seen above all as an exercise in character building, though a variety of other considerations also played a part. In spite of some degree of initial resistance, it seems that by the 1880s and 1890s a large proportion of the boys had internalised the games ethic, and had become as fanatic in their sporting enthusiasm as their teachers.[43] Meanwhile sport was becoming a matter of equally passionate interest to large numbers of working-class youths. (In their case, soccer ruled supreme, though boxing and cricket also had a significant place.) Once again, clergymen played a significant part, by forming teams in connection with their churches, or by setting up a gym. Many clergymen who had become avid sportmen at public school and university brought this enthusiasm with them to their working-class parishes. Boxing was particularly favoured by Anglicans, and the settlements founded in south and east London in the 1880s and 1890s often became major centres for amateur boxing, and training grounds for some future professionals. Both Anglicans and Nonconformists were enthusiastic players of football and cricket, and such famous football clubs as Aston Villa and Everton have chapel or church origins. Both in Birmingham in 1880 and in Liverpool in 1885, just under a quarter of the football teams in the city were affiliated to a church or chapel.[44]

The link between Christianity and sport had at least three dimensions. In the first place it was part of a broader conception of the Christian life. The ideal of the 'muscular Christian' was first preached in the 1850s by liberal Anglicans, such as Charles Kingsley and Thomas Hughes, who objected to what they deemed the excessive asceticism of many Tractarians and the fanaticism of Evangelicals, who saw their own enthusiasm for sport and the open air as part of a more life-affirming Christianity which enthusiastically enjoyed God's good gifts, and who accepted what was healthy in the life of upper-class males, instead of continually setting barriers between Christians and the world.[45] In a sermon of 1858, G. E. L. Cotton, the headmaster of Marlborough, who was an early champion of organised games, said that: 'God was the Creator of our bodies as well as our minds. His workmanship included physical as well as mental powers and faculties. In developing both we served Him who made us, no less surely than when we knelt in prayer.'[46]

Broad Church influences were strong in the public schools; but soon the same ideas were being pursued in High Church schools such as Lancing. Evangelicals tended to be more ambivalent about sport. C. T. Studd, for instance, regretted that he had made 'an idol' of cricket.[47] But they too recognised that sport, like music, could be an effective means of attracting newcomers to their churches, and thus placing them within hearing distance of the saving message. And they were equally aware that the sporting prowess of Christians like Studd was the most effective means of refuting the idea that Christianity was 'effeminate'. Also, Christians of every stamp shared the belief that sport, and especially team games, was an effective means of inculcating valuable qualities such as team spirit, the principles of fair play, determination, 'grit' and the will to win – an ideal balance, it was claimed, between individual ambition and loyalty to the community.[48]

A good example of these tendencies is the growing phenomenon of Christian militarism, which seems to have mainly developed in the period during and after the Crimean War, and was reflected in the vogue for hymns which used military language, and in the selection of military men (such as General Sir Henry Havelock, killed at Lucknow in 1857) as Christian heroes. The use of military language in hymns such as 'Fight the Good Fight' and 'Onward, Christian Soldiers' had a New Testament legitimation, since military metaphors were used in the epistle to the Ephesians (and, of course, battles play a prominent part in the Old Testament), but military language had played very little part in the hymns of the eighteenth and early nineteenth centuries. By the 1860s, however, pride in the achievements of the British armed forces, a more positive view of the moral credentials of the soldiery, and a growing acceptance of the armed forces as legitimate fields of Christian service, encouraged the tendency to provide a Christian legitimation for military activity, and to use military expressions in order to present Christianity in language that contemporaries would understand.[49]

The link between muscular Christianity and the spirit of patriotism was provided by the wave of uniformed organisations, founded from the 1880s onwards, which mixed Christianity, patriotism and sport. The most characteristic example was the Boys' Brigade, founded in 1883 in Glasgow, which remained strongest in Scotland but established many English branches, often attached to Nonconformist chapels. The imitators include the (Anglican) Church Lads' Brigade (1891), the Jewish Lads' Brigade (1895), the Catholic Lads' Brigade (1896), the non-military Boys' Life Brigade, started by a Congregational minister in 1899, and of course the Boy Scouts (1908), where the religious emphasis was weaker and the patriotic emphasis stronger than in the older bodies.[50] The main initial aim of the latter was probably to integrate working-class youth into the religious community. A subsidiary aim was simply to keep the youngsters off the streets. Equally important, in time, probably was the fact that both leaders and boys enjoyed brigade activities – especially the camps – and that became an end in itself. The most distinctive feature of the ideology which they inculcated was the mixture of character-building, religion, patriotism and the cult of discipline. The last of these was well portrayed in a fund-raising leaflet of the 1890s for the Church Lads' Brigade, juxtaposing a group of rough-looking and potentially criminal or riotous layabouts with a clean and tidy rifle-carrying uniformed lad, whose upright posture contrasted with their slouch, and whose impassive expression contrasted with their menacing looks.[51] The overall ethos of these bodies is best summed up in the objects of the Boys' Brigade, which include 'the advancement of Christ's Kingdom among Boys and the promotion of habits of Obedience, Reverence, Discipline, Self-Respect and all that tends towards a true Christian Manliness'.[52]

Similar ideas were propagated in the immensely popular *Boy's Own Paper,* which had been established by the Religious Tract Society in 1879. The original objective had been to provide an alternative to the widely read 'penny dreadfuls'. But soon the *B.O.P.* was outshining its rivals and setting new standards that others tried to imitate. Once again the prevailing ethos was that of muscular Christianity and patriotism. The favourite themes were sport, life at public schools, and adventure in far-flung parts of the Empire. The characters in the stories were noted for their 'loyalty, team spirit, patriotism, pluck and manliness' – virtues learnt at public school through the medium of team games, held together by an unostentatious Christian piety, and practised in extending, defending and ruling the Empire.[53]

While the religious message does not seem to have been too heavily emphasised, occasionally the adventure stories were mixed with articles with titles like 'The Manliness of Christ'. The ubiquitous 'Christian manliness' meant, above all, a combination of physical and moral strength – the physical strength being harnessed to noble ends. Very often this model Christian was seen as a teetotaller – someone whose self-discipline gave him a power that drinking men lacked. Part of the legend surrounding Sir Henry Havelock, the Indian Mutiny hero, was that his men derived additional strength and courage from the fact that they did not drink (though the brewers proved adept at co-opting such legends for their own quite different purposes, since this militant abstainer suffered the posthumous humiliation of having five London pubs named after him).[54] A similar story was associated with Hugh Price Hughes. On the day that he delivered his famous sermon denouncing Parnell, he rightly predicted that a large contingent of Irish Catholics would attend the service with the purpose of interrupting the sermon if anything derogatory of their leader were said. The evangelistic agent therefore arranged for a particularly tough contingent of reformed sinners attached to the Mission to be present, with the duty of ejecting any trouble-makers – '"Teetotallers all, sir, and only thirsty to show Irishmen the way to Piccadilly."'[55] The expected interruptions did take place, and the hecklers were thrown out. Hughes must have relished this episode a great deal in view of the considerable length at which the story is spun out in his daughter's biography. Evidently it was the combination of piety with physical strength, and willingness to use this strength in a fairly unceremonious way when occasion required, that appealed to Hughes.

The clergy of the 1880 and 1890s included many 'men's men', who combined a passionate interest in everything that was affirmable in the culture of their male parishioners with a determined rejection of the drunkenness, the swearing and the illicit sex which vitiated this culture. A characteristic figure was the Reverend A. Osborne Jay, vicar of the east London slum parish of Holy Trinity, Hoxton, who provided the model for the heroic Fr Sturt in Arthur Morrison's A Child of the Jago, the best-known novel to be written about the late Victorian East End. Jay was described by a researcher for Charles Booth's Life and Labour as 'a stout, plain, coarse-looking fellow with the appearance of a prize-fighter out of training'. He did indeed take a close interest in boxing, and at least one future professional was said to have learnt to box at Holy Trinity parish gym. He claimed to get on better with men and boys than with women, and his followers included a teenage gang called 'Father Jay's Boys'.[56]

Fr Jay was very much a 'man's man', and also emphatically an Anglo-Catholic. He was thus a living refutation of one of the most popular religious stereotypes of the time – that of the 'effeminate' Anglo-Catholic.[57] Charles Kingsley, the pioneer of muscular Christianity, was also a fervent critic of Anglo- and Roman Catholicism, and allegations of 'effeminacy' played a prominent part in his attacks on John Henry Newman. These soon became a standard feature of liberal or evangelical criticism of High Anglicanism. Prompted partly by the fact that many Anglo-Catholic priests practised celibacy, these criticisms had two dimensions. There was a general objection to what seemed an undue concern with ritual, the decoration of churches, and priestly vestments, none of which was seen as an appropriately 'masculine' concern – *Punch*, in 1865, published a humorous article entitled 'Parsons in Petticoats'. More specifically, Anglo-Catholic priests, especially those belonging to brotherhoods, were sometimes suspected of homosexuality.

While some prominent Anglo-Catholics may have been unconsciously homosexual, it seems that the homosexual sub-culture emerging in London in the 1880s and 1890s included a number of people, many of them writers and artists, who quite consciously combined homosexuality (or 'uranism', as it was often termed) with Roman Catholic or, more often, Anglo-Catholic religion. They tended to be attracted by the aesthetic dimensions (so much despised by the muscular Christians) of the Catholic forms of the faith, and they found among some High Church clergy a degree of sympathy and tolerance that was lacking on the Evangelical wing of the church. There was also in the Anglo-Catholicism of the time a dimension of rebellion – against puritanism, against respectability – that appealed to members of a persecuted minority. No doubt homosexuals were a relatively small minority among Anglo-Catholics, and Anglo-Catholics were a minority among homosexuals, but there was sufficient overlap between the two communities to provide the basis for a distinctive sub-sub-culture, with its principal base in various Anglican churches in London, Brighton and Oxford.

Female Piety

While accusations that Christianity was 'effeminate' were partly stimulated by dislike of allegedly 'unmanly' Anglo-

Catholic priests, a more important factor was the general observation that women seemed to be more active in the churches than men. Claims that women were the more religious sex went back at least to the early eighteenth century. In fact research by Clive Field on the membership records of Dissenting congregations shows that throughout the period from the 1660s to the present day women have tended to be disproportionately numerous.[58] Many writers have speculated on the reasons for these differences. Most emphasised the superior moral qualities of women, and/or the susceptibility to religious appeals arising out of their responsibility for the upbringing of children, the traumas following the loss of children and the dangers of sudden death in childbirth. Some stressed the tendency of men to become so caught up in the business of earning a living or so preoccupied with worldly affairs that they lost sight of more profound questions.[59]

Throughout the nineteenth century women attended church services in greater numbers than men. In Nonconformist congregations they were more likely than men to take the decisive step of applying for church membership. Within the Roman Catholic community nuns were more numerous than priests. There is also much evidence to suggest that in the majority of households women took the lead in religious matters. This was particularly the case in working-class families, where women would take responsibility for having the children christened, for teaching them their prayers, and later for ensuring that they went to Sunday School. Many fathers were so uninvolved in all this that they did not bother to turn up for the christening.[60] A London vicar commented in the 1890s that if, when he was visiting, the husband opened the door, he would say 'Ah, you're from the church: you want to see the missus.'[61] The notable point is that religiously indifferent husbands generally seem to have been content to let their more pious wives set the religious tone for the household. Only rarely do religious differences

157

seem to have been a cause of marital disharmony.

In Christian families the idea that the responsibility for household religion lay with women rather than men was a matter of social custom rather than religious tradition. In Judaism, on the other hand, there was a more clearly defined separation of male and female religious responsibilities: religious learning and public worship were the responsibility of men, while religious observances in the home were women's responsibility. But in the Jewish immigrant 'ghettos' of east London and north Manchester in the early twentieth century the religious role of men was declining, while that of women became increasingly crucial.[62] Jewish men were going to the synagogue less often – partly because of the pressure to work on Saturday, partly because of the counter-attractions of radical organisations, theatres or sport, partly because some relished the freedom that England offered. Women, however, continued to light candles and cook special meals on the Sabbath eve and on festivals, to keep a kosher kitchen, and to ensure that their sons (and, less often, their daughters) received a religious education. Thus women came to have a crucial role in the transmission of Judaism to the next generation – much as they did in the transmission of Christianity. Within both religions, mothers had become the most potent symbols of piety. Here, for instance, are the memories of one child of Russian-Jewish immigrants, of Friday evenings on Cheetham Hill in the early years of the twentieth century:

> Our mother looked beautiful and mysterious as she covered her head with a lace shawl, made ritual gestures over the candles in the shiny candlesticks, covered her face with her hands and murmured the prescribed blessing, praising God for his gift to mankind of a day of rest and spiritual refreshment. She appeared to me like a priestess, the guardian of the sacred fire, a ritual older than Judaism.[63]

In middle-class households, fathers were usually at least passively involved in religious activities, and quite often they took a much more active part, by for instance reading the Bible to the family. But still it was more frequently their wives who exercised the dominant religious influence. The prominent Birmingham Congregational minister John Angell James, in a volume of sermons published in 1852 entitled *Female Piety*, presented an idealised portrait of the religious role of women. After describing the work of Christians for the promotion of women's education and the suppression of polygamy, concubinage and various other forms of male oppression, he went on to say:

Well have women understood their privileges, for look into our congregations and churches, and see how largely they are composed of females, how many more of their sex than of the other avail themselves of the offer of gospel mercy and come under the influence of religion. It is in the female bosom, however we may account for the fact, that piety finds a home on earth. The door of woman's heart is often thrown wide open to receive the divine guest, when men refuse an entrance. And it is by this yielding to the power of godliness, and reflecting upon others the beauty of holiness, that she maintains her standing and influence in society. Under the sanctifying power of religion she ascends to the glory not only of an intelligent, but of a spiritual existence – not only gladdens by her presence the solitary hours of man's existence, and beguiles by her converse and sympathy the rough and tedious paths of life; but in some measure she modifies, purifies, and sanctifies him by making him feel how awful goodness is.[64]

As James indicated, devout women often had a strong influence on their husbands – and, or course, their children. Mary Ryan's research on the evangelical revivals in the United States in the first half of the nineteenth century demonstrated the strategic role of women, and especially of mothers. When several members of a family were converted, the first was in the great majority of cases a woman: typically, the conversion of a mother was later followed by the conversion of her husband or her children.[65] Although no equivalent research in English church records has been done, Clyde Binfield's examination of one eminent Congregationalist family reveals a similar process. In 1797 Charlotte Baines, wife of Edward Baines, later owner of the *Leeds Mercury* and MP for the town, had joined Salem Chapel. In 1820, one of her daughters became a church member, and in the next seventy years a further forty-seven members of the family became members of Salem or of one of its successor chapels in the Leeds suburbs. Yet Baines himself, one of England's most famous Dissenters, did not feel ready to become a member, as opposed to one who merely attended services, until 1839.[66]

Around the middle of the nineteenth century the crucial role of women in the religious life of the household, and the preponderance of women in most congregations, contrasted with the very restricted role of women in public religious life. The clergy, ministers and priests of the five largest denominations (the Anglicans, Wesleyan Methodists, Independents, Baptists and Roman Catholics) were all exclusively male. The Methodists had some tradition of preaching by women, which had been accepted, though only in exceptional cases by John Wesley. The Wesleyan Conference put a stop to it in 1803. The other large denominations had no such tradition, and so there was no need to stop it. In the eyes of most Protestants the decisive argument was Paul's prohibition, in the first epistle to the Corinthians, on women speaking in church. In Catholic eyes church tradition was the decisive factor. Many people on both sides argued that the modesty, the gentleness, and the grace, which were most becoming in women would all be lost if women entered the public sphere. Again, John Angell James's sermons provide a good summary of the mid-century orthodoxy. Arguing that the natures of men and women were largely different, and

that the interests of society were best served by allowing
the talents of each to blossom within their own special
sphere, he declared:

Neither reason nor Christianity invites women to the
professor's chair, nor conducts her to the bar, nor makes
her welcome to the pulpit, nor admits her to the place
of ordinary magistracy. Both exclude her – not indeed
by positive and specific commands, but by general principles and spirit, from the corruption of the camp, the
debates of the senate, and the pleading of the forum.
And they bid her beware how she overleaps the deli-
cacy of her sex, and listens to the doctrines of effeminate debaters, or becomes the dupe of modern reformers
or fashionable journalists. They forbid us to hear her
gentle voice in the popular assembly; and do not even
suffer her to speak in the Church of God. They claim
not for her the right of suffrage, nor any immunity by
which she may 'usurp authority over the man'. And yet
the Bible gives her her throne, for she is the queen of
the domestic circle. It is the heart of her husband. It is
the heart of her family. It is the female supremacy in
that interesting domain, where love, and tenderness, and
refinement, thought and feeling preside.[67]

As James implied, not everyone agreed with such limitations, even in 1852 – and in the following decades, the
sphere of women's public activity slowly but inexorably
grew. Women preachers and leaders were characteristic
of smaller, more plebeian or more heterodox denominations. These were of three main kinds. First, there were
various prophetic movements, whose impact tended to be
short-lived, but which were important in the turbulent years
of the French Revolutionary and Napoleonic wars, when
all familiar landmarks were being swept away, and many
people looked forward to an imminent millennium. Most
notably there were the Southcottians, led by a former
servant and former Methodist from Exeter, Joanna

Southcott, who claimed to be 'The woman clothed with the sun', mentioned in the book of Revelation, and who at one point said she was pregnant with Christ. Her position of leadership within a movement which for a time had a substantial nationwide following was legitimated by the direct revelations she claimed to have received. In any case, biblical references to prophetesses were sufficiently numerous to dispel any objections to female leadership that were based on the Bible. However, the Southcottian movement faded away after the death of its foundress in 1814.[68]

More important in the longer term were evangelical Protestant movements that were entirely orthodox in their theology, but whose plebeian character made them less susceptible to considerations of respectability, and whose heavily evangelistic orientation encouraged a pragmatic approach to questions of how the work of conversion might best be pursued. In the first half of the nineteenth century, the most important examples were the Primitive Methodists and Bible Christians. These two bodies both originated in the early years of the nineteenth century, the former in the industrial north midlands, and the latter in the rural south-west. In their early years, both were committed to preaching the gospel to as many people as possible in the shortest possible time. They needed all the preachers they could find. They found that there were many women who felt a call to preach, and that their preaching frequently resulted in conversions. This was taken as a sign that their work was 'owned' by God, and that objections by scriptural literalists were therefore irrelevant. They certainly recognised the Bible as their ultimate authority, and in most circumstances, their interpretation of the Bible was fairly literal. But in this instance they pointed to the many biblical passages, including some from the Pauline epistles, which seemed to suggest a more active religious role for women, and they concluded that Paul's prohibition only applied to the peculiar circumstances in Corinth.

In the 1820s, about 20 per cent of Primitive Methodist Travelling Preachers (those who would later be called 'ministers') were women. None the less, they did not enjoy full equality with their male colleagues. For instance, women preachers were paid less than men, and it seems that none ever became Superintendent of a Circuit. Moreover, as more men became available for ministerial positions, as more emphasis was placed on their formal training, and as the Primitive Methodist Connexion became more centralised and bureaucratised, women tended to slip back into a more restricted role (though one less circumscribed than, for instance, among the Anglicans or Wesleyans). While the smaller and more localised Bible Christians continued throughout the nineteenth century to have some women ministers, the last of the women travelling preachers in Primitive Methodism retired in 1860 – though there continued to be a relatively small number of women who acted as local preachers.[69]

A third category of church which allowed women a more extensive public role than in the mainstream denominations consisted of those which side-stepped the Pauline prohibitions by placing some other kind of authority on a higher level than Scripture. The most notable examples were the Quakers and Unitarians. The latter accepted the Bible as their principal authority but, as heirs to the eighteenth century Enlightenment, they insisted that it must be interpreted in the light of human reason. The former believed that the ultimate authority was 'the Christ within' or 'inner light', accessible to all human beings, and to women as much as men: the writers of the Bible were guided by the inner light, but the present-day reader, instead of following blindly whatever the Scripture said, had to interpret it in the light of 'that of God' within herself or himself. Around the middle of the nineteenth century, the Quakers stood out by the fact that women took an equal part with men in the meetings for worship, having the right and duty to give ministry when moved to do so. Indeed Elizabeth Fry was only the most famous of a number of women who had the status of 'recognised minister', and who travelled the country attending meetings for worship and addressing other meetings of Quakers. This is not to say, however, that a complete equality existed: while women and men were equal in the spiritual life of the Society of Friends, business matters remained a male preserve.[70] However, it is hardly surprising that the few women who were prominent public figures around the middle of the nineteenth century included a number of Quakers. Pre-eminent was Elizabeth Fry, who, among much else, was the first woman to give evidence to a Parliamentary committee.[71]

When the movements for the emancipation of women got under way from the 1860s onwards, led by women from the professional and business classes, Quakers and Unitarians, as well as agnostics, would all have a disproportionately large role, as the example of the campaign against the Contagious Diseases Acts reveals. Of twenty-two Ladies' National Association executive members whose religious affiliation is known, twelve were Quakers, four belonged to other branches of Nonconformity, four were atheists or agnostics, and only two were Anglicans. Indeed, Josephine Butler, though herself an Anglican, claimed to feel particularly at home among Quakers.[72]

The first religious body to abolish all formal distinctions between the roles of women and of men was, however, the Salvation Army, heir to the Primitive Methodist tradition of plebeian evangelicalism. William and Catherine Booth, who in 1865 founded the East London Mission, out of which the Salvation Army grew in the later 1870s, came from a Methodist background. The Booths branched out on their own when they found the Methodist New Connexion resistant to their style of no-holds-barred, revivalism. They too started with an overwhelming emphasis on evangelism, and a willingness to make use of anyone who was willing to work for them. Catherine Booth's influence on the movement's autocratic 'General' was doubtless an important factor in the development of the Army's policy of making all ranks open to members of either sex, and giving women a full part in their propaganda.[73]

The front-runners in any movement towards religious equality for women were always relatively small and idiosyncratic denominations, but changes in the larger denominations necessarily had a wider impact. In the second half of the nineteenth century nearly all the churches were seeing an expansion in women's public religious role, though the precise form that this took naturally varied. For instance, between 1820 and 1862 the proportion of Sunday School teachers who were women increased from less than 10 per cent to about 50 per cent.[74] There was also, between 1838 and 1860, a considerable increase in the relatively small number of women who were employed as evangelists by home missions – from about 50 to about 250. As in the days of the Primitive Methodist pioneers, evangelical zeal was one potential solvent of conventional gender divides. In the United States, which in this respect was a generation ahead of England, women had begun to win some degree of acceptance as preachers and as leaders of mixed prayer meetings during the revival associated with Charles Finney in the 1830s and 1840s. In England the revival of 1859 seems to have had a similar effect. The women preachers who came out of the revival included not only the Quakers and the working-class Methodists of former years, but middle-class women, some of them Anglicans, such as Geraldine Hooper, known as 'the female Spurgeon', who could attract audiences of up to 4000 to meetings. Another of the women preachers of the 1860s, Miss Robinson, acquired her own mission hall in Norwich. Baptist, Congregationalist and Primitive Methodist chapels were all open to women preachers, though preaching by women in Anglican churches would still be controversial in the 1920s.[75]

But the biggest growth in women's ministry came from about 1880 onwards in the mission fields. The decisive consideration was the recognition that in many parts of the world it was impossible for men to preach to women.

For instance, at the Mildmay Missionary Conference of 1878 it was argued that in countries such as China, where the progress of Christian missions was so far slow, women missionaries who could convert the mothers might be the key to the eventual conversion of the male population. One result was the Zenana mission, which employed women specifically to bring Christianity to women. But the exclusion of women from the pulpits at home meant that there were large numbers of women whose call to the Christian ministry could only be fulfilled overseas, and by the 1880s many of the principal English overseas missions were recruiting women missionaries. They soon made up a large proportion of the mission personnel. Women became particularly numerous in the China Inland Mission and other missions influenced by the Holiness movement, which played down lay/clergy distinctions and tended to disregard formal training, arguing that the direct inspiration of the Spirit was all important.[76] When, in 1887, the Church Missionary Society (CMS) decided to recruit single women as missionaries (before that the female input had very largely been limited to the wives of male missionaries), a flood of applications from women followed, and in the 1890s, 315 women were recruited, as against 356 men. By 1905 there were as many female as male CMS missionaries, and by 1915 the women were in a slight majority.[77]

The other expanding area for women who felt a vocation to full-time religious work was in the numerous sisterhoods formed in the nineteenth century. As Susan O'Brien points out. 'The nineteenth century was unique in the history of Christian religious life not only because of the number of new foundations that were made, but also because of the number made by and for women.'[78] The main growth was in the Roman Catholic orders, and by 1900 there were some 600 Roman Catholic convents in England and Wales, and betweeen 8000 and 10,000 nuns. But from 1845 there was a modest growth in Anglican sisterhoods, and by the end of the century, there were

about 60 communities of Anglican nuns.[79] By the 1880s
and 1890s there were also various Methodist sisterhoods
specialising in work in the urban slums. This practical
emphasis was characteristic of all the various kinds of sis-
terhood. Roman Catholic religious communities had historically been mainly contemplative, but women entering
the religious orders in the nineteenth century were usually
seeking a life of active service, in teaching or in care of
the sick. In England, as in the United States and in most
parts of western Europe, a large network of Catholic institutions was built up in the later nineteenth century,
with the aim of protecting Catholics from Protestant or
secular 'contamination'.[80] Most of these institutions were
eager for the services of nuns – both because they were
believed to be uniquely qualified for caring work, and
because their labour was cheap. Catholic schools, hospi-
tals, orphanages, and women's refuges all provided work
for nuns, and many Catholic parishes also used nuns to
visit the sick or those who had missed mass.

The movement to gain equality for women within the
churches progressed most rapidly within those Nonconformist denominations which were either relatively free
in their interpretation of the Bible, or placed an overrid-
ing stress on evangelism; it was somewhat slower in the
Anglican church (where liberals tended to be favourable,
but opposition came both from the more extreme evangelicals and from the more extreme Anglo-Catholics); it
was slower still in the Roman Catholic church; and it was
slowest of all in those Nonconformist churches which
combined a literalist approach to Scripture with a relatively low concern with evangelism. Generally speaking the
processes of change were faster in denominations with a
congregational polity, where local initiatives had considerable scope, than in more centralised denominations –
though a major exception to this rule is offered by the
highly-centralised Salvation Army.

The process of emancipation went through several stages.
First to be conceded was the right of women to vote in

church meetings or to vote for representatives in higher church bodies; then the right to preach; then the right to hold lay office; then the right to take pastoral charge of a congregation or parish; and finally the right to administer the sacraments. A first turning-point was the revival of 1859 and the various evangelistic campaigns during that year, and in the years immediately following. A second period of significant change was the 1890s, when the advances of secondary and higher education for girls and women were followed by increasingly vocal demands for women's rights in other spheres – most notably in politics, but also in the churches. In the Society of Friends women obtained formal equality; Unitarian, Congregationalist and Baptist congregations were beginning to admit women to lay offices; women took part in the Wesleyan Conference for the first time. The Unitarians (in 1904) were the first to give pastoral charge of a congregation to a woman, Gertrud von Petzold. The situation among the Congregationalists was suitably unclear – given the extreme decentralisation of that denomination. While some women were effectively acting as Congregational ministers before the First World War, the first formal ordination (of Constance Coltman) took place in 1917.[81] The Baptists followed shortly after the war.

In the Anglican church the movement to ordain women to the priesthood got under way on the eve of the First World War, as a spin-off from the Church League for Women's Suffrage, which enjoyed considerable support. However, at this stage Anglican opposition to women's ordination was so considerable that the more faint-hearted supporters of the cause soon abandoned it as hopeless. It was decisively rejected by the Lambeth conferences of 1920 and 1930.[82]

4

THE RELIGIOUS CRISIS

In 1900 A. L. Baxter, one of the researchers for Charles Booth's *Life and Labour of the People in London,* interviewed the Reverend Alfred Love, who had been vicar of St Paul's, Greenwich, in south-east London, for twenty-two years. He reported as follows:

As usual the general attitude of the people was described as 'indifferent' and the indifference and slackness is extending to those who are to some extent church-goers: they all take their religion much more lightly: there is much more tendency to believe that it will all come right in the end. In this regard Mr L. noticed:

1. That when he first came here night calls to give consolation to the sick or dying were common: they are now unknown. 2. A week used not to pass without letters of praise, inquiry or abuse with reference to sermons: they have completely ceased. 3. Those who used to come to church twice now only come once. 4. Those who had friends staying with them used as a matter of course to bring their friends to church: they now make it an excuse for staying away altogether. 5. The bicycle has captured many regular church-goers. 6. The attendance at prayer meetings is consistently declining, and it is increasingly difficult to get people to 'lead in prayer'. Altogether, as Mr L. said (with a cheerful smile), 'if

one's heart could be broken a dozen times mine would have been'.[1]

In the Edwardian years there were many prophets of gloom in the English religious world. In 1904, R. F. Horton, a prominent Congregational minister, with a church in the wealthy and cultured London suburb of Hampstead, declared that 'there was a great deal to be said for the view that the great majority of the English people were drifting towards a state of "non-religion"'.[2] J. H. Shakespeare, Secretary of the Baptist Union, addressing the Union's assembly in 1908 on 'The Arrested Progress of the Church', noted the chilling of the spiritual atmosphere during recent years, and concluded: 'It is as if our planet by some slight change on its axis, plunged these islands into a lower average temperature of twenty degrees.'[3] Signs of impending crisis had been building up for many years. But until recently they had often been mixed with other more hopeful signs. In the years immediately before the First World War, however, it seemed that all the religious indices were pointing in the same downward direction.

Symptoms of Crisis

Most obviously there was the decline in church-going. For much of the nineteenth century a very large proportion of the middle and upper-class population had attended one or more church services every Sunday. In the words of Horace Mann, in his famous commentary on the 1851 religious census, it had become 'one of the recognised proprieties of life'.[4] Church-going by the working class, whether in town or in country, was much less frequent, but there were none the less many areas of the country with large and flourishing working-class congregations. Between 1851 and 1881, when a series of local counts of church attendance took place, there was little change in

170

the level of church-going. The overall trend was slightly downwards, but the changes were hardly significant. In London, total attendances as a proportion of population fell from 30 per cent to 28.5 per cent between 1851 and 1886. Robin Gill has pieced together evidence from large numbers of censuses published in local newspapers, together with Anglican Visitation Returns, to build up a picture of the long-term patterns of church-going. Taking figures from twenty-eight large towns, he found a very slight drop in average attendance from 37 per cent to 35 per cent between 1851 and 1881.[6]

The average concealed considerable local differences. Many of these towns were experiencing spectacular growth in this period, usually associated with considerable changes in economy and social composition. Some, notably Nottingham, saw a severe drop in rates of attendance, while others, including Sheffield, Bradford and Bolton, saw an increase. There were also interesting variations between the fates of different denominations. The Church of England suffered a slight decline, while the major Nonconformist denominations and the Roman Catholics suffered a larger decline. However, the overall Nonconformist attendance rate remained more or less static because of the growth of some of the smaller denominations and the emergence of the Salvation Army.

But then, between 1886 and 1903, church attendance in the metropolis fell considerably further in seventeen years than it had in the previous thirty-five. In Inner London the drop was from 28.5 per cent to 22 per cent. Both Anglicans and Nonconformists were losing ground, but the biggest losses were suffered by the Anglicans. In Liverpool, the level of church-going was a little higher than in London, and the decline was slower, but the trend was the same. From 34 per cent in 1891, the rate had declined to 29 per cent in 1912. Again, both Anglicans and Nonconformists were declining, but the Anglicans were doing so at a slightly faster rate.[7]

In a further eight towns (mostly medium-sized, and all

in the north midlands or the north) it is possible to compare the results of the national religious census of 1851 with those of various local censuses conducted between 1902 and 1904. In 1851 these towns had a rather high average attendance of 44 per cent; by 1902–4 it had fallen dramaticallly to 27 per cent. While the Roman Catholic attendance rate remained unchanged, both the Anglicans and the Nonconformists had suffered major losses.[8] It seems likely, therefore, that a clear downward trend in urban church-going set in some time between 1881 and 1902. Two pieces of evidence point to the possibility that the crucial decade was the 1890s. One is the case of Liverpool, the only city where counts were held in both 1881 and 1891 and where attendance remained more or less static between these two dates; the second is the case of Birmingham, where comparison can be made between 1851 and 1892, showing only a small decline between those two dates.[9] Some contemporaries noted a sharp drop at the time. For instance, in 1894 a south London vicar claimed that 'Less come to church than did ten or even four years ago. The tendency seems to be in this direction increasingly.'[10] However, in view of the considerable differences between the patterns in different towns during this period, one cannot generalise from a small number of examples.

To sum up the denominational trends: Anglican attendance declined slightly between 1851 and 1881, and much more rapidly between the later 1880s and the First World War. The Nonconformist attendance rate remained about the same between 1851 and 1881, but decline set in during the later 1880s and 1890s, and continued up to the First World War. Initially, the decline was less rapid than that suffered by the Anglicans. The Nonconformist totals conceal, however, denominational variations: the larger and more middle-class branches of Dissent were already suffering falling attendances before 1881, while some of the more plebeian Nonconformist denominations were growing. The picture for Roman Catholicism is confusing. Most cities saw a fall in the rate of Roman Catholic attendance between 1851 and 1881, and in London this trend continued between 1886 and 1903; on the other hand Liverpool saw a slight increase between 1881 and 1912. While the proportion of Catholics in the total population seems to have changed little between the 1850s and the First World War, there were no doubt considerable local fluctuations. Moreover the Catholic figures are unusually tentative, as they so often depend on estimates because of the tendency of census-takers to undercount Catholic attendance by only including one out of the several masses usually held on a Sunday morning. As yet, unfortunately, Catholic statistics have not been subjected to the kind of detailed and expert scrutiny that Gill has devoted to the Anglican figures, and Currie and Gilbert to those of the Methodists.[11]

There is very little evidence concerning the trends in rural church-going. A study of rural life published in 1913 suggested an average attendance rate of between 25 per cent and 35 per cent in rural Oxfordshire.[12] If this is accurate, it would suggest an even sharpen decline in attendance than in urban areas, since the rural and small-town average for the county in 1851 had been around 45 per cent. A paper published in 1912 by the rector of Cavendish, in Suffolk, argued that attendance at both church and chapel was generally declining, though the quality of individual clergy could still make a difference. He did not provide any precise figures, although he made an estimate of 10–15 per cent attendance at Anglican services by male labourers, whom he identified as the least church-going section of the population.[13] Gill has carried out intensive research in a rapidly depopulating area of rural Northumberland which suggests that the rate of Anglican church attendance in this area reached a peak in 1866.[14] But until much more research has been done, it is impossible to judge whether this area is in any way typical.

The decline in church membership remained partly

concealed until the years 1907–14, when total membership of the largest Nonconformist denominations showed
a continuous (though not dramatic) drop.[15] *The British
Congregationalist* recognised the seriousness of the situation by publishing a special series of articles on 'The
Decline of Church Membership'.[16] There was no agreement as to the causes of the crisis, but everyone agreed
that major changes were taking place. In fact, more recent analysis of the statistics by historians suggests that
the peak of church membership in relation to population may have been reached in the 1880s. The best figures are those for the Methodists. The long-term decline
in Methodist membership as a percentage of the English
population appears to have set in between 1886 and 1891.[17]
The Particular Baptists peaked around 1880, and had fallen
back slightly by 1890. For the other major Nonconformist denomination, the Congregationalists, no adequate
figures are available for the later nineteenth century.
However, in the early twentieth century trends in Congregationalism were very similar to those among the Methodists and Baptists. In the period up to 1906 total numbers
had generally continued to grow, but in most years the
increase was smaller than the growth of population.

Some of the smaller denominations had different patterns of growth and decline. The 1880s and 1890s saw
the dramatic growth of a new denomination, the Salvation Army, which continued at a slower rate right up to
the First World War. Some older denominations such as
the Churches of Christ, the Quakers, and maybe the Brethren, showed a modest but steady increase in this period.
However, the gains made by these smaller churches were
insufficient to compensate for the decline suffered by the
larger Nonconformist denominations.[18]

Anglican membership trends are harder to assess, since
everyone who as an infant had been baptised at an Anglican font was regarded as a member of the church. Since
1919, when the National Assembly of the Church of England was established, and an electoral roll drawn up in

each parish of those Anglicans claiming the right to vote, numbers on the electoral roll have often been taken as the best indicator of the church's active membership. The other statistic commonly used is that of the numbers of Anglicans receiving Communion at Easter, as the church's canons formally require them to do. In spite of this requirement, there were large numbers of Anglicans in the nineteenth century who attended church regularly, but seldom or never received Communion. Sometimes this was because of a feeling of unworthiness. Sometimes the scruples were theological – doubts about particular Anglican doctrines, or more generalised lack of faith.[19] Numbers of Easter Communicants were rising in the late Victorian and Edwardian periods, and reached a peak in 1911 – but this probably reflects the growing importance attached to Communion at a time of rising Anglo-Catholic influence, rather than an increase in the number of zealous Anglicans. Robin Gill, who has examined communicant statistics both in the nineteenth century and at the present day, concludes (rightly, I think) that church attendance statistics are far more valuable as an indicator of the rise and fall of Anglican commitment.[20]

Customs were changing in other ways which contemporaries often saw as reflecting a decline of religion. To German or French eyes, the English Sunday still seemed a grim relic of puritanism. But to those who had lived through the early and mid-Victorian years, the English Sunday as it had become by the early twentieth century seemed a shadow of its former self. Admittedly the pace of change was faster in the vicinity of the great cities than in remoter country areas - especially those where Nonconformity was strong. There had always been a large section of the working class which had few or no sabbatarian scruples, whether because the struggle for survival forced them to work on Sunday, or because Sunday was the only time in the week when they had any relaxation, and they therefore meant to enjoy it.[21] But from about 1880 onwards, there had been some relaxation of sabbatarian rigour in the large section of society, stretching from the upper working class to the aristocracy, where some recognition of Sunday as a day set apart was regarded as normal.

In the eyes of many Evangelicals, all this Sunday activity was simply a desecration of the Lord's Day: Sunday was a day set apart for religious observances, and most forms of amusement were as unacceptable as work. But even those Christians who had somewhat more relaxed ideas about Sunday were likely to agree that religious activity should have first priority, and that the kind of Sunday that was becoming increasingly popular, which was simply a day of relaxation, was part of a worrying trend towards a frivolous and hedonistic way of life.[22]

While this might be open to debate, there was general agreement that England was moving from an age of religious 'certainties' to one of 'uncertainty' and 'Doubt'. 'Do we Believe?' was the title of a correspondence in the *Daily Telegraph,* published in 1904. Several thousand readers sent in their answers, and while most did admit to some kind of religious belief, it was clear that large numbers of middle-class people were very unclear about whether they believed or what they believed, and there was a general realisation that they lived in times when Christian orthodoxies were under widespread challenge, and that a wide range of alternatives were being presented. W. L. Courtney, in introducing a selection of the letters, summed up the situation as follows:

the letters which will be found in the body of this volume present a curiously interesting psychological study, and also an almost pathetic picture of moral and spiritual aspirations. Possibly no-one was aware how deeply average men and women were feeling their necessity for a faith that should be beyond the reach of sceptical doubt. It is a trite and commonplace remark that the age is a sceptical one – a prey to scepticism due to a variety of causes, most of all, perhaps, to the triumphant analysis of Science applied both to History and Biology.

When we learn the natural history of a thing we begin to wonder if it is of the same value as it seemed to be before this account of its origin and development was made known. . . . A man whose father was the ape, and whose remote ancestor was the worm, appears to have lost his position just because he is shown to be like the beasts that perish. In precisely similar fashion, when we study the history of Religion and discover how much that we thought peculiar to Christianity is not only to be found in more antique faiths, but is also due to certain antecedent conditions and influences of racial development, the unique sacredness of the faith once delivered to the saints seems to have disappeared. . . . [But] let a man dispassionately read some of the letters in the present correspondence, and he will find, it may be with some surprise, that people are not so sceptical as he supposed. . . . Dogmatic Christianity may indeed have decayed, but those instincts to which as a form of religion it appealed are as fresh and indomitable as ever.[23]

When contemporaries spoke of a 'crisis of faith', they might be referring to any one of several phenomena – for instance, a decline in the extent of religious belief, a change in the nature of religious belief, a decline in religious practice or church membership, or a decline in the influence of religious ideas on people's behaviour or their view of the world, or a decline in the social influence enjoyed by religious institutions. They might have been referring to all of these things at once – and indeed there is evidence that all of these things were happening in the late Victorian and Edwardian periods. It does not necessarily follow, however, that the phenomena were interconnected. It may be that there was a single 'crisis of faith' with common causes, but this should not be assumed in advance.

In the following section I shall look at changes in belief, changes in the level of involvement in the churches, and trends towards what might be termed (to use a highly controversial term) the 'secularisation' of society. By the latter, I mean a society in which religion has become to a considerable degree privatised. That is: it affects the thinking and behaviour of the individual believer, but no longer to any great degree shapes the taken-for-granted assumptions of the majority of the population, and religious institutions no longer exercise a dominant influence on areas of life that are not directly involved in 'religion'.[24]

There are at least four separate strands to the story of how this crisis had come about, and I shall examine each in turn. There are connections between them, but each strand is at least partly independent of the others.

I shall argue that the most important changes were those taking place within the upper middle class. This social group has played a crucial part in the religious revival of the early nineteenth century and in the 'religious boom' of the mid-Victorian years. The decline in the level of religious activity from about the 1880s onwards may well have begun with this hitherto very active section of society. And certainly the declining participation by this most powerful group had fateful consequences for the social role of religion more generally. Comparison of the religious censuses undertaken in London in 1886–7 and 1902–3 shows how serious a decline in church-going there had been in the wealthy suburbs – although these still had the highest levels of church attendance. Overall there had been a 23 per cent decline in church-going. However, if the districts of London are placed in four groups according to their social status, it is found that attendance had dropped in the top group from 36.3 per cent to 26.3 per cent in the second group from 33.3 per cent to 24.1 per cent, and in the third group from 25.6 per cent to 19.1 per cent. But in the bottom group, comprising the six poorest boroughs, the drop was only from 20.1 per cent to 18.5 per cent.[25] Working-class districts still had the lowest levels of church-going, but the gap had narrowed. In fact there may have been very little reduction in working-class church-going during this period. Two of the poorest boroughs, Bermondsey and Finsbury, recorded an increase in church attendance, and in a third, Bethnal Green, the decline was very slight. Admittedly the drop in some other working-class boroughs, such as Poplar, was more considerable; but a large part of this may be explained by the movement of middle-class residents further out into the suburbs.[26]

Very much the same pattern was found in Liverpool, where the results for 1902 can be compared with those for 1912. During this period the attendance rate for the Garston district, which included many of the wealthiest suburbs, dropped from 38.4 per cent to 30.5 per cent and that for the lower middle-class suburbs fell from 31.4 per cent to 24.4 per cent. However, in Protestant working-class districts there was a much smaller drop from 25.3 per cent to 22.4 per cent, and in Catholic working-class districts there was a slight increase, from 44.2 per cent to 46.4 per cent.[27]

Doubt

The first strand in the story of religious change in this period was the growth of religious unbelief, or at least 'doubt', to use a word that was very current in the later Victorian period. There was a slow growth of such unbelief in the 1850s and 1860s; it spread more widely in the 1870s; and in the 1880s and 1890s, agnosticism unmistakably became one of the generally available religious options, alongside the liberal, evangelical and Catholic versions of Christianity.

T. H. Huxley's coining of the word 'agnosticism' in 1869 may be seen as a symbolic turning-point, as doubters now had a socially acceptable and intellectually plausible means of defining their religious position. Older terms like 'infidel' and 'atheist' were both unsatisfactory. The latter term had a definiteness about it, and indeed a touch of arrogance – 'How do you *know* that there's no God?' – which the often hesitant doubter found unattractive. And the former term was one coined by believers in order to stigmatise the unbelievers – it had connotations both of extreme social radicalism and of doubtful morals, and so tended to be accepted only by the most imperturbable rebels. 'Agnosticism', however, struck just the right note to catch the mood of the time – it spoke a firm but courteous 'No' to the 'orthodox', as believers were often termed, and it neatly shifted the burden of arrogant assertion onto the orthodox side by declaring God to be not non-existent, but merely 'unknowable'. George Gissing, in a novel set in the early 1880s, caught well the mood of the times. Gissing's hero, Godwin Peak, declared that:

'Two kinds of book dealing with religion are now greatly popular and will be for a long time. On the one hand is that growing body of people who for whatever reason, tend to agnosticism, but desire to be convinced that agnosticism is respectable; they are eager for anti-dogmatic books written by men of mark. They couldn't endure to be classed with Bradlaugh, but they rank themselves confidently with Darwin and Huxley. Arguments matter little or nothing to them. They take their rationalism as they do a fashion in dress, anxious only that it shall be "good form". Then there's the other lot of people – a much larger class – who won't give up dogma, but have learnt that bishops, priests and deacons no longer hold it with the old rigour, and that one must be "broad", these are clamorous for treatises that pretend to reconcile revelation and science. It is pathetic to watch the enthusiasm with which they hail any man who distinguishes himself by this kind of apologetic skill, this pious jugglery.'[28]

Loss of faith during these years was very often a traumatic experience. The religious revival of the early nineteenth century had an overwhelming impact on large sections of the population – most notably on the upper middle class of business and professional families, but to a lesser extent on most other social groups. Families influenced by the evangelical movement brought up their children from a very early age with a strong awareness of the presence of God; of the absolute need of sinful human beings for an experience of conversion, in which they would accept Christ as their Saviour and experience God's forgiveness; and of the responsibility they had for the proper stewardship of all the gifts they had received from God. Religious unbelief was widely regarded as a result of sin – a need to rationalise one's desire to escape God's justice. Fear of hell acted very powerfully to keep temptations at bay, and to ensure that doubts were often suppressed.[29]

In the 1850s and 1860s the secular societies offered one possible home for such doubters. Secularists of this era mainly came from upper working-class or lower middle-class families, and many of them had been active members of a Nonconformist chapel. Only very slowly and painfully did such people shed their former faith and eventually find the comfort of a new faith shared with a community of fellow-believers.[30] But the political radicalism and strongly plebeian tone of these societies made them unattractive to members of the established middle class.

There were several factors contributing to this mood of religious uncertainty. None was in itself decisive, but all of them contributed to an atmosphere in which many people, whether they ended up on the Christian or the agnostic side of the fence – or indeed ended by sitting on the fence – felt that Christian faith rested on less secure foundations than it had thirty or fifty years earlier. (Of course, a hundred years earlier, in the golden age of eighteenth-century enlightened rationalism, Christianity had been widely challenged on other kinds of grounds, but eighteenth-century deism had been almost submerged by the tides of the evangelical revival in the first half of the nineteenth century.)

There were three main clusters of sources of such doubt. The first related to the reliability of the Bible, the foundation-stone of Protestantism, knowledge of and reverence for which was deep and widespread in nineteenth-century England.[31] Scientific discoveries called into question the literal accuracy of some biblical passages, notably the Creation accounts in Genesis. The first blow came in the 1830s and 1840s from geologists, who argued that the earth must be much older than the writers of Genesis had realised. More fundamental questions were raised by Darwin, whose theory of evolution through natural selection, set out in *On the Origin of Species* (1859) and *The Descent of Man* (1870), contradicted the biblical account of the separate creation of each species, culminating with the creation of humankind.

Many mid-Victorian Christians already argued, and others soon came to accept, that the Creation accounts, and indeed many other sections of the Old Testament, were to be understood allegorically rather than literally, so that these scientific developments did not necessarily undermine faith in the Bible. More important in some ways were developments in the critical study of the New Testament, which had been pioneered in England in the eighteenth century but had mainly been the achievement of German scholars, most notably the famous Tübingen School of the 1830s and 1840s. How accurate and how consistent one with another were the biblical accounts of the life and teaching of Jesus? How far were the various accounts distorted by the polemical purposes of their authors or by the need to square the events with Old Testament prophecies? How far did the mentality of the time lead to a presentation of the story in terms that no longer made sense to the 'modern mind'? Can we in fact ever know the truth?

A second cluster of problems related to science. Knowledge derived from science called into question knowledge derived from the Bible, as we have already seen. Moreover, the spread of scientific knowledge and of assumptions about the universal and inexorable operation of the laws of nature led to increasing uneasiness with the many accounts in the New Testament of miraculous events. The positivist teachings of the French philosopher Auguste Comte offered a plausible way of resolving the problem. Comte argued that knowledge passed through three phases, the first theological, the second metaphysical and the third scientific. In their day, religious accounts offered the best available means of understanding the phenomena of the world; but now, with scientific tools of understanding available, such interpretations had been superseded. Comte himself had gone on to devise a Religion of Humanity appropriate to the new scientific age. This had relatively few devotees in England, but in the 1860s and 1870s his philosophy of positivism had a considerable vogue among religiously sceptical members of the educated middle class, including George Eliot and John Stuart Mill. And the idea that science had superseded religion, or at least made it much harder to believe in any kind of religion, won considerably wider acceptance among many people who had never heard of Comte.[32]

The third cluster of doubts related to the morality of Christian doctrines. Most important here was the doctrine of hell – the everlasting punishment of the wicked. This doctrine had been widely questioned or at least pushed into the background in the seventeenth and eighteenth centuries. But it had been strongly re-emphasised by the preachers of the evangelical revival, who had readily appealed to the fear of hell in urging the need for repentance and conversion. It was certainly accepted, even if less loudly proclaimed by the Tractarians. In a *cause célèbre* of 1853 F. D. Maurice was dismissed from his chair of Theology at King's College, London, for questioning the eternity of punishment in hell, and in 1862 two contributors to the famous volume of liberal theology *Essays and Reviews* were convicted of heresy for the same reason – although they subsequently appealed successfully to the judicial committee of the Privy Council, where two of the three episcopal members rejected the appeal, but the four lay members all supported it.

The tide turned fairly soon after that. The key year was 1877, when a prominent Anglican, Canon F. W. Farrar of Westminster Abbey, and a well-known Baptist, Samuel Cox of Nottingham, preached and subsequently published a series of sermons questioning the existing teaching on hell.[33] In the latter years of the century, hell became one of the chief touchstones in the battle between conservatives and liberals in the various churches, and it was clear that opinion was moving fairly fast in the more liberal direction.

Also problematic was the doctrine of the Atonement. Over the centuries many people had asked the question 'Why did Christ die on the cross?' There had been many answers to the question, and often hot debates between theologians. But one of the most popular answers, and certainly one which held favour with the evangelicals of the early nineteenth century, ran like this: 'All human beings deserved to suffer in hell for their sins, and God's justice demanded that this should be so. But in his mercy God accepted the death of the one sinless man, Jesus Christ, as a substitute for fallen humanity.' But the whole idea of one person standing as a substitute to suffer for the wrong-doing of another seemed offensive to the moral sensibilities of many mid-Victorian English people. Nor did the idea that the whole human race had inherited a burden of sin from their first parents make sense to them. And the conception of God which was implicit in such doctrines repelled them.

Of course, many of those who remained Christian were unhappy with such ideas, and one consequence of this moral critique of existing orthodoxies was the liberalisation of Christian theology. But doubts over such doctrines could also be the first step in the dissolution of all faith – either because those concerned believed that such teachings were authentic Christianity and that Christianity stood or fell with them, or because doubts in such areas were a first step towards a wider critical appraisal of all areas of Christian doctrine. The prevailing belief that the whole of the Bible was inspired and that each part was consistent with every other part also caused problems, as some parts of the Old Testament, and particularly of the book of Genesis, recorded with approval behaviour which seemed cruel or immoral, and out of keeping with the ideals expressed elsewhere in the sacred book.

The 'Do We Believe?' correspondence published in the *Daily Telegraph* in 1904 suggests the kinds of religious objections which were being advanced by middle-class people at this time, and gives some indication of the relative frequency of various kinds of objection. Taking the 97 letters in the selection edited by W. L. Courtney which offered objections to Christianity or to religion in general, we find that the criticisms fall into four broad categories. (I have categorised each letter, which in most cases is unproblematic. However, there are a few cases in which the writer made several quite different points, and I have had to select one as being the principal theme.) Of the 97 letters, 29 focused on objections to the Bible, to specific Christian doctrines, or to 'dogma' in general; 23 expressed faith in science as the supreme source of knowledge, or argued that science had refuted religion; 18 focused on the relationship of Christianity to other religions or to humanism, often arguing that the essential points of all religions were much the same, or stressing the moral worth of those adhering to other religions or none; 12 argued either that the existence of evil in the world discredits God, or that atrocities and inconsistencies committed by Christians disprove Christianity. The remaining 17 letters fell into none of these categories. They included several written from a Social Darwinist perspective, arguing that Christian doctrines of compassion, care for the weak, etc., were contrary to the laws of nature.

Among those who cited objections to Christian doctrine, by far the most common objection was to the doctrine of everlasting punishment. But equally significant was the large group of correspondents who objected to 'dogma' as such. The word 'dogma', generally with negative connotations, occurred in numerous letters, the general argument being that in all fields knowledge was advancing, but that Christianity, through its rigid adherence to creeds, remained stuck in the past. A number of correspondents argued that religion needed to be progressive if it was going to meet humanity's needs in the modern age.

Objections to the Bible took many different forms, ranging from moral doubts about some Old Testament passages to doubts about the reliability of the account of the life of Jesus in the gospels. Arguments derived from science did not often refer to specific scientific discoveries or theories, though a few mentioned evolution. More often they focused either on the idea that the only reliable knowledge was scientific knowledge and that science had now superseded all other methods of intellectual enquiry, or on the claim that God is unknowable, and that Christianity should be rejected because it cannot be proved. One of the major bugbears here was 'anthropomorphism', which ranked second only to 'dogma' as a term of intellectual abuse.

A typical contribution referred to 'the secret presence that underlies it all' – 'to think of Him even is presumption, to pray to Him is impertinent, and to attempt to enter into His secret councils wicked'.[34] The first reaction of the present-day reader might be to ask how the correspondent knew God's gender while knowing nothing else. For someone reading this in 1904 the more obvious point would be the contrast with the extreme familiarity with God which characterised a great deal of Victorian evangelicalism. Believers, as well as doubters, were indeed becoming increasingly uneasy with the tendency to involve God in all the trivial decisions of everyday life, and the readiness with which pious language was used in contexts where it seemed superfluous. Many contributors to the correspondence posited a mysterious God, utterly remote from all human understanding.

Another common tendency was to relativise Christianity. Sometimes this was linked with the objection to rigid 'dogmas', and the belief that our understanding of God was 'evolving' and thereby developing and broadening. In the words of one characteristic contribution:

> Creeds began by asserting the revengeful savagery of a Supreme Being demanding holocausts of innocent victims and thence onwards through the idea of an outraged Father, unappeased without blood, towards the gentler teaching of the infinite compassion of a Mother–Father God. . . . We all believe something, but we need a wider conception of God as the basis of our creed – a belief in a God who loves and saves Hindoos and Buddhists and Mohammedans, as well as Christians of a hundred sects, and prepares each by the experience of one or more earthly lives for the next school of training in the great evolutionary march of embryonic souls from chaos towards that perfected state which can gaze upon the face of God Himself.[35]

Most often, however, Christianity was relativised by the application of moral criteria: belief systems should be evaluated on the basis of their moral fruits, and those of non-Christian religions, or of humanism, were as good as those of Christianity.

Another quite common line of argument (also used by many of the Christian contributors) was to judge a belief-system by the quality of its most eminent representatives. Christians were accustomed to arguing that there could not be much wrong with a religion that had produced Lord Shaftesbury, Mr Gladstone and Clerk Maxwell,[36] and unbelievers hit back by claiming as their comrades in unbelief Socrates, Lucretius, Darwin, and even Descartes.[37] The number of correspondents using the 'argument from evil' or referring to examples of Christian hypocrisy or cruelty was relatively small. This probably reflects the mainly middle-class character of those taking part in this correspondence. It is highly likely that in any group of working-class doubters and unbelievers, arguments of this kind would have predominated.[38]

Questioning of religious orthodoxy in early and mid-Victorian England was often an intensely private matter. The shocked reactions of those in positions of authority when such doubts were publicly voiced encouraged a considerable degree of caution. The secularist leader Charles Bradlaugh, told the vicar of his Anglican parish of his religious doubts, and the clergyman's hostile reaction started the process which eventually led to Bradlaugh becoming an uncompromising atheist. Parents and spouse might be equally alarmed to know that unbelief (often visualised as something akin to a deadly form of contagion) was at work within the family.

In working-class districts, secularist orators held forth in parks on Sunday afternoons – alongside evangelical and temperance preachers of every kind – and secularist papers were available in small newsagents' shops.[39] It was in fact one such park orator who first attracted the attention and aroused doubts within the mind of the young Bradlaugh. But these forms of anti-religious propaganda were regarded as crude and vulgar by most middle and upper-class people. For them, however, there was an extensive periodical press, which represented many shades of religious opinion and acted as an important medium for the spread of new ideas. In the 1850s and 1860s the most 'advanced' currents of opinion were available in the *Westminster Review*. In the 1860s and 1870s it was joined by the *Fortnightly Review*, which combined agnosticism in religion with advanced Liberal politics. In 1899 a mid-point between the mandarin style of the Reviews and the tub-thumping of the secularists was found when the Rationalist Press Association was formed with the objective of publishing cheap editions of anti-religious classics or of works by scientists deemed damaging to religion. These were printed in editions running into tens of thousands, and became a major channel for the diffusion of religious criticism.[40]

England, like most other European countries in the later nineteenth century, had its secular gurus, who wrote popular works of anti-religious criticism, or who acted as patrons to the secular movement and symbols of the fact that agnosticism had gained respectability and was perhaps beginning to gain an ascendancy. In the latter category, the leading figure was T. H. Huxley, the most outspokenly agnostic of eminent scientists.[41] (Darwin, who was both an agnostic and a pre-eminent scientist, had no desire to get involved in religious polemic.) In the former category, England never produced a writer to rival the popularity of Büchner or Haeckel in Germany,[42] of Renan in France, or Multatuli in the Netherlands. The most widely read work of popular freethought in England was probably Robert Blatchford's *God and my Neighbour* (1904), which combined socialism with Darwinism. But the fact that Blatchford was a well-known socialist journalist, which ensured a large working-class readership for his book, was likely to deter many possible middle-class readers.

The full impact of these changes in religious thinking was felt after about 1880. E. E. Kellett, brought up in the mid-Victorian years, the son of a Wesleyan minister, later claimed that he had 'seen no such rapid or complete change as that which took place in the eighties and nineties':

> it was like one of those 'catastrophes' which the old geologists used to postulate in order to explain the alterations in the earth: sudden, immense, and I think irrevocable. There is far more difference between the mind of 1900 and that of 1880 than between 1880 and 1640.

Referring to the combined impact of Darwinism and the Higher Criticism of the Bible, he argued that this was experienced most strongly by the younger generation, 'untramelled by their fathers' doubts and fears'.[43]

189

The first generally noticeable change was a move in the Anglican church and in most Nonconformist churches towards a wider definition of the acceptable limits of orthodoxy.[44] The Anglican church had, in the mid-nineteenth century, its Broad Churchmen, who disliked theological controversy, who had a very positive view of science and of the beneficial effects of education, and rejected literalistic interpretation of the Bible. But their position was precarious, as was indicated by the prosecution for heresy of two of the contributors to *Essays and Reviews*.[45] However, their eventual acquittal in 1864 marked a turning-point in the church's evolution towards a broader definition of the limits of orthodoxy. Bishops occasionally refused to ordain or to license a clergyman whose orthodoxy was suspect, but heresy trials were very rare, and a clergyman, once appointed as incumbent of a parish, would have to be very outspoken to attract disciplinary action of this kind.

The most important development was the emergence of the 'liberal catholic' form of modernised High Anglicanism, which would come to dominate the Church of England in the first half of the twentieth century. *Lux Mundi* (1889), which offered a middle way between the radical modernisers and the conservatism of the Tractarians and most evangelicals, was the key text for this form of modern yet orthodox Anglicanism, which accepted the theory of evolution and a critical approach to the Bible, and was enthusiastic about the new vogue for social Christianity, but also emphatically believed in the Incarnation (which became the focal point of liberal catholic theology) and more generally in miracles.[46]

Even more decentralised were the Baptist and Congregational denominations, where each congregation was supreme and considerable diversity resulted. The Congregationalists in particular were marked by increasing liberalism from the 1870s onwards, and particularly in the 1880s there were fierce battles within particular congregations between conservative deacons and young ministers, often trained at Spring Hill College, Birmingham, a stronghold of liberal Congregationalism. 'Many in the 1870s and 1880s', comments Binfield, 'must have found the experience of their first pastorate strangely like the hell in whose disbelief lay their undoing.'[47] Apart from doctrinal disputes over such issues as biblical authority, hell, and the existence of a personal devil, there were also clashes on matters of life-style and aesthetics. D. W. Simon, the principal of Spring Hill, had been thrown out of his Royston pulpit in the later 1850s following rumours that he went to the theatre and condoned dancing. H. R. Reynolds, the principal of Cheshunt College, was said to have defined delight as 'Mendelssohn, Ullswater and a glass of Champagne'[48] – the general spirit of this observation would have been approved by other liberalisers, though most would probably have preferred ginger beer to champagne. In late Victorian Nonconformity, liberalising theology often went hand in hand with enthusiasm for music and the arts, which was reflected in a great concern for the beauty of church buildings and a more positive view of the value of ritual.[49]

The liberals and the aesthetes were weaker among the Baptists, but the prevailing mood was sufficiently liberal, especially in terms of the rejection of hell, to cause the resignation from the Baptist Union in 1887 of their most famous preacher, C. H. Spurgeon.[50] The Methodist churches were more centralised, and an all-powerful Conference was able to impose official doctrinal standards. The years around the end of the century therefore brought some fierce battles, and attempts to exclude liberals from positions in denominational colleges, or even from the ministry. But here too, the years 1880–1914 brought a considerable extension of the limits of acceptable orthodoxy.[51]

As a generalisation, one can say that a moderate liberalism in matters of theology, combined with a strong emphasis on the social implications of Christianity, and a continuing interest in the church's missionary task both at home and abroad, were the predominant Christian

191

responses to the challenges of the time. The fundamentalist option, which was important in the United States, remained very much a marginal phenomenon in England.[52] Even rarer in England was the emphatic political conservatism with which many Lutherans in Germany and Catholics in France and Spain reacted to the modernising trends in these years.

Liberalisation meant a change in attitudes to the Bible, which had been at the heart of the evangelical movements of the earlier part of the nineteenth century. Crucial to the spread of such movements as Methodism had been the belief that the Bible was the inspired word of God, that it contained within it all the knowledge that was necessary for salvation, and that its meaning was readily accessible to anyone who could read. Protestants believed that the Bible should be in every home, and that it should be read every day – preferably with the head of the household reading, while everyone else listened. The corollary of this was the assumption that interpretation of the Bible was not the preserve of priests or of those who had taken a university degree, but that everyone had the right and the duty to study the book themselves, and to check the teaching of their clergy against the printed page. The underlying premiss of this assumption was that the Bible was not a difficult book: it could indeed be understood literally, and provided it had been accurately translated, the meaning would be clear. The Bible not only described the creation and early history of the human race, explained God's plan for humanity, described man's fall and set out the way to salvation: it also provided practical guidance in all the trials of daily life. According to one widely held belief, the perplexed could open the Bible at random, and find a passage which answered their questions. Many other people would search the Scriptures in a more systematic way to provide guidance in times of trouble.

The critical approach to the Bible, which stressed the difficulties inherent in deciding what the Bible did say, placed all this in jeopardy. In particular, it erected a new kind of priesthood, since the educated minister in the pulpit who had made an academic study of the Bible was once again able to claim privileged knowledge that was not available to members of his congregation. Similarly, the idea that there could be tensions, and even inconsistencies, between different parts of the sacred book made a nonsense of the idea that you could simply open it at random to discover 'what the Bible says'. The liberals kept their reverence for the Bible, but made it such a difficult book that the average reader was frightened off. Meanwhile the secularists were trying to destroy all reverence for the book, and the agnostics were tending simply to ignore it. The overall effect was primarily to confuse the average church or chapel-goer, but secondly to make it a lot harder to preach the kind of uncomplicated evangelical message which had worked so well for the Methodists in the early part of the century, and which was still being preached by the Salvation Army, and later by the Pentecostalists, but with rather less effect.[53]

In the longer term, the liberalisation of theology contributed to the growth of a more tolerant view of other faiths, which weakened the missionary impulse. Admittedly, more liberal beliefs did not at first weaken the missionary impulse, but changed its motives. Would-be missionaries perceived the African and Asian societies which they hoped to convert as racked by slavery, by polygamy and other forms of injustice towards women, and by fear-inducing superstitions of all kinds. Only in the 1920s would a more respectful attitude towards many non-Christian religions combine with a greater scepticism about the virtues of European 'civilisation' to produce a major loss of faith in the value of missions. But a crucial pillar of the missionary edifice was removed when Christians began to doubt that all those who did not know Christ were lost.

Meanwhile, the churches were finding it harder to recruit clergy to work at home. In the Church of England, there had been a spectacular increase in the numbers of clergy in the 1840s, as a result of which the ratio of clergy to population in 1851 was 1:1035. Up until 1891 the growth in the numbers of clergy almost kept pace with the rise of the population. In that year the ratio was 1:1196. After reaching a peak of 814 in 1886, the number of ordinations had dropped to 650 in 1900 and 569 in 1901. Between 1901 and 1911 there was a slight drop in the total number of clergy and by the latter date the ratio of clergy to population was 1:1451.[54] The reasons for this were no doubt complex. Partly it reflected the expansion of secular professions, and the growing autonomy of those such as teaching and social work which had been in the shadow of the church. But intellectual factors also played a part. Some men who considered ordination were being held back by an inability to subscribe to certain orthodox doctrines. We know, for instance, that the later Liberal politician C. F. G. Masterman was strongly attracted by the Anglican ministry in the 1890s, but was held back by doubts about New Testament miracles.[55] Several years later, the future Archbishop of Canterbury, William Temple, was initially refused ordination by the High Church Bishop of Oxford, because his views on the Virgin Birth were held to be unorthodox, although he was later ordained by the Archbishop of Canterbury, a Broad Churchman.[56]

No doubt the growth of agnosticism in the middle and upper classes reduced the pool of potential ordinands, as the Church of England was reluctant to recruit clergy from lower down the social scale. Haig has also argued that the declining rate of ordination among the intellectual elite predated the more general decline, and played a part in undermining the prestige, and thus the attractiveness, of the ministry. He shows that in the period 1841–3, 65 per cent of those obtaining Firsts at Cambridge went on to be ordained. In 1861–3 it was 50 per cent, and by 1881–3 the proportion was down to 18 per cent.[57]

The decline in the numbers of Nonconformist ministers set in slightly later, with the more middle-class branches of Dissent following closest on the heels of Anglicanism, while the more plebeian branches were a little further behind. The numbers of Congregational ministers peaked in 1908, United Methodists in 1910, Wesleyans and Unitarians in 1911, Baptists in 1912, and Primitive Methodists in 1918. The number of Salvation Army officers peaked in 1939.[58]

By the early twentieth century, this failure of recruitment was feeding through to the parishes, where clergy were in shorter supply, and the type of well-staffed parish, with a vast network of organisations, that had been characteristic of the later nineteenth century, was becoming harder to maintain. Bartlett's study of Bermondsey shows that a peak in the numbers of Anglican church workers was reached in 1894, and that by 1907 there had been a 17 per cent decline. The drop in the number of clergy was as yet small, though the number of parishes where a solitary vicar worked without a curate had increased from two to five between 1899 and 1915.[59] But there had been a much bigger drop in the number of lay workers, paid or voluntary, who played a crucial part in enabling the church to remain in contact with a major part of the population. Most of these had been single women, and, in Bartlett's view most were middle-class, though the evidence on this is inconclusive. He comments that 'a non-churchgoing family would have had more contact with a lay worker, probably a woman, than with a clergyman, let alone the vicar', and that 'the lady workers did the brunt of the everyday visiting, ran the clubs and societies for girls and women, helped in the Sunday schools and above all supervised relief'.[60] In Croydon serious shortages of district visitors and Sunday School teachers were being reported by many Anglican parishes from the later 1890s onwards. As one vicar commented in 1906, the shortage of visitors made it 'almost impossible for the clergy to begin to get in touch with a very large number of those to whom they should minister'.[61]

Thus, from about the 1890s onwards, men and women of the middle and upper middle class were becoming less willing to seek ordination or to work voluntarily for one of the churches, and they were also becoming less willing to give money. As Stephen Yeo points out, in the case of Reading, large donations had made an important contribution to the expansion of religious work in the town between about 1850 and 1890. 'Elaborate churches and chapels in Reading were, in significant numbers of cases, the expression of the impulse and donations of local wealthy men, and could not have been built without them.'[62] Many of these wealthy men were themselves very active in the churches which they patronised. A representative figure of this era was the seed merchant Alfred Sutton, one of the town's largest employers, and an evangelical Anglican. He lived in the town, sat on the School Board, was a Sunday School Superintendent, and in later years a churchwarden and Bible Class leader, and built a coffee house, a reading room, and three churches or missions. Between 1890 and 1914, figures like Sutton were becoming rarer. Business leaders were increasingly unlikely to be prominent in church or chapel, or even to live in the town, and they were becoming less willing to give money to local religious organisations.

The Leisure Revolution

The second strand in the story of religious change in these years is the rising importance of leisure in English life. While changes in belief obviously affected, and sometimes challenged, existing religious ideas and practices in a direct way, the relationship between changes in leisure and changes in religion was much less obvious. Yet the effects may have been equally profound. The period between about 1870 and 1914 saw a leisure revolution, in terms of the range and forms of leisure available, how it was provided, when it was practised, and what kind of ethos informed it.

For much of the nineteenth century, the most important recreational centres had been pubs, and the chief recreational activity had been drinking – though admittedly, other leisure pursuits, ranging from card-playing and listening to music to watching cock-fights, often accompanied the drinking. However, three-quarters of the population were largely excluded from such forms of amusement, since the majority of pubs catered mainly or entirely for adult males. The chief alternative centres for recreation were churches and chapels, where tea took the place of beer, and where the inclusion of women and children acted as a discouragement to many men.

The big growth from about 1870 was in forms of amusement that were independent of the pub and could be (though were not always) independent of the church. Major developments included the emergence of sport as a national obsession, the growth of various forms of popular theatre, the rise of popular holiday resorts, and the emergence of a mass daily newspaper press. The 1870s were an important decade, bringing the introduction of bank holidays, and, in many firms, of Saturday half-holidays, as well as the first cycling craze, and many sporting developments.

A considerable proportion of the world sports of today were formalised in Britain during the latter part of the nineteenth century.[63] The most widely popular, and most extensively professionalised at the time, were cricket (county championship established and first international matches played in the 1870s), and soccer (professional league started in the 1880s and first international matches played in the 1870s). But rugby, tennis and golf all grew fast in this period – and golf quickly became a central part of the culture of business and professional men. At the same time, two older sports retained their popularity and developed in new directions. Boxing, which, in the form of prize-fighting, had been illegal, with all that this implied in terms of underworld associations and illicit thrills for those taking part, was reformed, civilised and legalised, and as an amateur sport became widely popular with working-class youth (as well as Anglican clergymen). At the same time, horse-racing came to play an equally big part in the lives of the older generation of working-class people (women as much as men) – most working-class people never saw a horse race, but they placed bets with a bookie, who communicated by electric telegraph with the race-course. In some ways the most important leisure innovation of all was the bicycle – the ownership of which had become by the 1890s every young person's dream, and which, with its connotations of freedom and mobility (for women as much as for men), became a part of the spirit of the age.[64]

The later nineteenth century was also the golden age of the music-hall, which became the characteristic form of urban popular entertainment in this period and which was succeeded in the early twentieth century by the cinema. Music-hall artistes, such as Marie Lloyd and Dan Leno, were to the late Victorian and Edwardian eras what film-stars were to the 1920s and 1930s.[65]

What is the relevance of all this to the decline of the churches? Contemporary Christian observers quite often claimed to see a connection – though, of course, it does not necessarily follow that they were right. Most directly threatening was the fact that quite a lot of this increasing leisure activity was taking place on Sundays. Already in the 1840s many railway companies were running Sunday excursion trains, and such resorts as Brighton, Southend and Blackpool came to thrive on the patronage of excursionists. In 1856 Sunday bands were briefly provided in London parks, but then withdrawn as a result of pressure by sabbatarians, and for long after that the majority of museums, galleries and public sporting facilities remained closed on Sundays – as well as all theatres.

For a long time, most Sunday leisure was of an unorganised kind. Up until about the 1880s the main distinction was between working-class areas and middle or upper-class areas. In the former, we know that many people did observe sabbatarian restrictions of one kind or another, but Sunday was also a popular day for fishing, pigeon-flying, whippet-racing and informal games of football (as well as for more surreptitious forms of sport, such as cock-fights), and those who took part in such amusements were far more visible than those who stayed at home. In the latter areas, on the other hand, Sundays tended to be very quiet, and at least an external observance of Sunday was regarded as being a normal requirement of respectability.

By the 1880s this was beginning to change. Gradually the taboos on Sunday recreation were lifted. In London Society, Sunday dinner parties were becoming fashionable, and wealthy families with their own tennis courts and croquet lawns were beginning to lift the ban on Sunday play. In the 1890s, Sunday became the great day for cycling – and indeed the bicycle became the supreme symbol of a new kind of Sunday, unpuritan without necessarily being irreligious, best described by a contributor to a newspaper correspondence on Sunday observance in 1905, who praised the man who 'takes his bicycle, entailing no Sunday labour on others, and goes forth to worship God in His bright sunshine, amid His wonderful lakes and fells'.[66] During the 1890s many private golf clubs began to open on Sundays, though public courses tended to remain closed.[67]

Two other aspects of these developments, although less clearly defined, were of broader significance. First, sport was becoming the emotional centre of many people's lives, offering them their deepest experience of fulfilment, sustaining them through the workaday grind, and sometimes (through passionate involvement with a particular club) providing their most strongly felt form of social identity. In this sense, sport did for some people many of the same things that religion did for others. Sport and religion were not of course mutually exclusive alternatives. But the constant parading by the religious press of Christian sporting stars like C. T. Studd was eloquent testimony both to the high status which sportsmen enjoyed, and to the fact that many people saw a tension between sport and religion.

The dominant place which sport had come to occupy in many people's lives was most clearly demonstrated in the case of the public schools, where, by about 1900, organised games were being played on every day but Sunday. Elaborate rituals surrounded the games, complex systems of rewards had been devised to bestow status on those who excelled at sport, and intense rivalries surrounded house matches and, to a lesser extent, inter-school matches. As Mangan shows, a circular system had evolved whereby public schools inculcated a passion for games; Oxford and Cambridge colleges vied with one another for the custom of talented athletes; and the latter then returned to the public schools as masters, determined to pass on their sporting passion to the next generation.[68]

Lowerson notes the irony that churchmen had been among the most enthusiastic proponents of the benefits of sport, but by the end of the century sport was often being presented as an alternative to religion: enthusiasts for tennis and soccer were claiming that playing these games provided a moral training superior to that obtained by attending church, and in parts of the sporting press 'the Churches were portrayed repeatedly as boring, with dim clergy and dull sermons'.[69] In the later nineteenth century the tendency was still to justify an obsession with sport by reference to its 'envigorating' qualities, or the release it offered from stress.[70] By the 1920s all such pretexts tended to be dropped, and people were much readier to make candid confessions of sporting fanaticism. The great England fast bowler Harold Larwood, recalling his years as a Nottinghamshire miner in the early 1920s, claimed 'Cricket was my reason for living', and in 1926 P. G. Wodehouse felt constrained to point out that 'Golf is only a game.' Meanwhile, in the troubled years immediately after the end of the war, the head of the Home Office's Intelligence Branch saw the obsession of most working men with football as offering the best hope of diverting them from the path of revolution.[71]

Secondly, the growing preoccupation with leisure during this period, especially on the part of the upper and middle classes, but also among the more prosperous sections of the working class, was part of a widespread reaction against the cult of work, the emphasis on saving, the restraint and the puritanism, which had played such a central role in many areas of English life in the early and middle years of the nineteenth century. 'We are living in the midst', said the letter from the Wesleyan Conference to the Methodist societies in 1890, 'of a great reaction from Puritanism. Sympathy is turning from the spiritual to the natural side of things. Town life has produced a passion for rural nature. Civilisation is creating artificial wants. Art is clothing objects in sensuous garments which are most attractive. Ingenuity is manufacturing new forms of enjoyment. Travel is contributing to the knowledge of the world.'[72] Many Christian preachers were anxious to show that the new mood of freedom was (within limits) good, and Anglo-Catholics, in particular, danced, sang and drank with missionary zeal in the years around 1900. But there were limits to the willingness of even the most unpuritan Christians to accept the new gospel of enjoyment. And many of the devotees of the cult of leisure saw the rejection of all churches and formal creeds as an integral part of their search for individual self-fulfilment.

At the upper end of the social hierarchy, the cult of leisure was reflected in a greater determination to enjoy the possibilities which wealth offered. Country-house weekends and holidays in Biarritz and Monte Carlo were taking the place of the Sunday School teaching and the attendance at borough council meetings that had filled the free hours of many of the older generation of industrialists. Meanwhile a generation of writers dedicated themselves to pouring scorn on the Victorian regime of 'cant and rant', and to pulling the rug from under the feet of anyone who insisted on taking life with undue solemnity. In a less self-conscious way, many middle-class households were dropping all the restrictions and taboos that stood in the way of a relaxed enjoyment of life.[73]

The Decline of Paternalism

A third strand of religious change arises out of the decline of paternalism and the rebellion of oppressed social groups.

In the English countryside the 1870s were a decade of dramatic change. The early 1870s were the final phase of a period of considerable prosperity, in which landowners and tenant farmers benefited from the high prices of English corn, and farm labourers' wages improved somewhat because of the migration to the growing cities and a consequent dwindling of the labour supply. Labourers' wages were still, however, very low by industrial standards. The 1860s had seen a growth of trade union organisation among farm workers, and this culminated in 1872 and 1873 in the 'Revolt of the Field', marked by the formation of two nationwide organisations of agricultural workers and a series of strikes.

The attitude of the Anglican clergy varied. Some were sympathisers or indeed active supporters – though the most prominent clerical champion of the labourers, Bishop Fraser of Manchester, was hardly in the midst of the countryside.[74] The majority of the Anglican clergy, however, seem to have taken a more critical line. They saw themselves charged with maintaining harmonious relations between the various sections of the rural community, and in their eyes the labourers' movement, with its denunciations of gentry and farmers, was a disruptive force, spreading enmity. Some clergy also taught that social superiors had been placed in a position of God-given responsibility, and that rebellion was a sin.

In many rural parishes relations between the clergy and the labouring population deteriorated in these years. In the strongholds of Primitive Methodism, notably large parts of Norfolk, relations were often already bad, and the Revolt of the Field served to emphasise the cleavage between church and chapel. In areas where most labourers were Anglican, the effect was to alienate many of the rural poor from their own parish church. In the diocese of Oxford, for instance, the episcopal visitation of 1875 found many rural incumbents complaining to the bishop of the 'slanders' of the Union, or of the decline in church-going since the onset of the labourers' movement. In one parish the vicar claimed that 'three years ago the church was full, but now there are many empty benches'.[75] By the late 1870s some of these clergy were reporting that attendances had risen again with the decline of the Union. However, it seems that there were many rural parishes where tradition continued to hold that the clergy had stood against the people in the time of crisis, and had condoned the victimisation of activists that followed the decline of the Union.[76]

From about 1875, the whole rural community was facing a common challenge of catastrophic proportions. That year saw the beginnings of the agricultural depression which hit farmers all over Europe, as a result of the importation of cheap American grain. As farm prices plummeted, the labourers were hit by falling wages, and the gentry by falling rents – and the clergy suffered too as income from tithes or glebe dropped. The labourers responded in huge numbers by getting out – whether to London and Birmingham, or to Australia and New Zealand, and the last quarter of the century saw a flood of emigration from the countryside. The gentry were also leaving, though this was a more gradual process. Some were selling freeholds to the farmers, some were selling their estates to industrialists and bankers, and some were diversifying their sources of income by buying shares or seeking directorships. (There were also others who tried to leave, but could not find any buyers for their land, and were forced to make stringent economies.)

The farmers stayed, and survived mainly by switching from arable farming to pasture, or from cereals to fruit and vegetables. And the clergy stayed, but more modest life-styles were increasingly required of them. According to Haig,[77] the middle decades of the nineteenth century had been 'without doubt the most prosperous in the Church's history, for its rural clergy'. But from the late 1870s onwards there was a severe drop in income. A report of the early 1900s noted that large country vicarages had an air of neglect, and that their occupants mixed less easily with the gentry, and no longer had carriages or belonged to London clubs.[78]

There were still in 1914 many 'close' parishes, where squire and parson worked hand in hand to keep the inhabitants God-fearing and law-abiding, and in return recognised a responsibility for their material well-being, but this situation was becoming increasingly untypical. A volume of 1912 contrasted the 'Old Squire' with the 'New Squire'. The 'New Squire' saw the countryside as a pleasant place to live, but recognised no special personal tie with the people living in his village. He recognised no obligations towards them, nor was it any business of his whether the children went to school or their parents went to church. He would live his own life and leave the villagers to live their's.[79] Increasingly, therefore, the village parson was on his own, without the assistance that many of them had been used to. Declining clerical incomes also meant that they were less able to continue with the extensive charitable help which had been an important means of retaining the loyalty of the poor. They had to find ways of winning hearts and minds, without relying on external pressures.

Meanwhile, the cultural independence of the countryside was being gradually eroded through the growing dominance of influences originating from the cities. One of the biggest steps in this direction had been the spread of Methodism to most rural areas in the first half of the nineteenth century. The process continued in the second half of the century with the completion of the national railway network and the national network of elementary schools, the organisation of rural trade unions, the enfranchisement of the rural labourer in 1884, and the growing penetration of newspapers into the newly literate countryside. Unfortunately, historians have not yet gone very far in exploring the religious implications of these changes. Obelkevich's classic study of rural religion stops in 1875. But the decisive stage in the decline of specifically rural cultures probably took place in the period between 1875 and the First World War.

Industrial paternalism had also had a very important influence on life in many towns and industrial villages in the third quarter of the nineteenth century, though it was seldom that industrialists obtained the degree of control over urban life that landowners often enjoyed in rural areas. One difference was that all towns and even most industrial villages contained a variety of significant employers. And even where one individual or company was overwhelmingly the largest employer, he or it seldom owned all or most of the land, as squires often did. Moreover, the close monitoring of individual behaviour that was carried out by squire and parson in some agricultural villages was not practicable in a larger community. Direct coercion certainly played a part in maintaining the industrial paternalist's authority – mainly in dealing with direct attacks through trade union militancy or unwelcome forms of political action. Involvement by paternalist industrialists in local religious life took the form more of patronising approved forms of religion, and encouraging its practice by employees, rather than forcing the latter to attend an approved place of worship, as often happened in the countryside.

In the 1880s and 1890s, and more especially in the early years of the twentieth century, culminating in the 'Great Labour Unrest' of 1911–14, industrial paternalism was in decline and working-class militancy was growing. To some extent the same factors were involved. Foreign competition, especially in this case from Germany, led to mergers between companies, and the introduction of styles of management that were more impersonal and also to some extent more aggressive, as firms struggled to maintain profit margins in the face of falling prices for their products.

At the same time there was a tendency for the younger generation of industrialists to adopt more luxurious lifestyles, and to shun the intimate relations between owners and workers which had frequently characterised the mid-Victorian period. Owners of factories were showing less interest in supporting local churches and chapels, or encouraging their managers, foremen and workers to do the same.

Trade unions, Co-operative Societies and back-street chapels had been the principal institutions which symbolised the spiritual autonomy of the working class – especially the skilled working class. But these institutions could maintain an uneasy co-existence with the power of industrial paternalism. In particular, Liberal politics and Nonconformist religion provided a bond between many employers and many of their workers, and much of the trade unionism of the later nineteenth century rested on principles of give and take, which assumed that owners and union leaders, if they approached the task in the right spirit, could reach agreements that were acceptable to both sides.

All this was under threat from the 1880s onwards. Owners were less willing to play their side of the game. On the side of the workers, there was a growing mood of rebellion. The severe depression of the later 1870s, followed by another period of high unemployment in the mid-1880s, led many to conclude that the capitalist system was at fault, and that a new economic system was needed. Socialist ideas were spreading slowly in the 1880s and 1890s, and then much more rapidly in the years immediately before the First World War. The London Dock Strike of 1889 touched off a brief but intense movement of unionisation among previously unorganised unskilled workers. Other strikes had a powerful, but more localised influence – for instance, the Manningham Mills strike of 1891 in Bradford, or the Hull dockers' strike of 1893. Above all, the 'Great Labour Unrest' was marked by the greatest wave of strikes that England had ever seen.

The religious implications of these developments were complex. There was no simple equation between rejection of the authority of employers and rejection of the church, as happened in a number of European countries.[80] The relationship between religion and the power-structure was also a lot more complicated than in the English countryside. Both employers and workers were likely to belong to a multiplicity of different religious denominations, and there was seldom much agreement among the clergy of any one denomination on the ways in which to handle situations of social conflict.

Most Anglican clergy were Conservative by choice, but no attempt was made by the Anglican authorities to impose a common political line on the clergy. Congregational and Baptist ministers might risk the loss of their pulpits if they took a line which the majority of church members opposed, but they were subject to no central discipline. The Methodists were far more centralised and, in the first half of the nineteenth century, connexional discipline had been used in various branches of Methodism, most notably the Wesleyans, to restrict freedom of political expression. By the later nineteenth century there was no question of expelling a member for political reasons, as had happened in the aftermath of the Peterloo Massacre in 1819; but local preachers might face disciplinary action if they preached 'politics from the pulpit' – which in practice seems to have meant preaching socialist politics, since Liberal politics could be accepted as unexceptionable platitudes.[81] Since most Anglican clergy were Conservatives and most Nonconformist ministers were Liberals, a church member who became actively involved in the Social Democratic Federation or Independent Labour Party was unlikely to meet with positive encouragement from clergy or lay leaders and might meet with positive opposition. Moreover, the trade unionist or socialist might take the view that his church or chapel was part of the local authority structure, and hand in glove with employers, especially if employers held important church offices.[82] And indeed socialism became for many people, in these years, a new revelation, indeed a religion superseding all previous revelations.[83] So it is not surprising that some socialists and trade unionists moved out of the churches.

The most striking development was the formation, beginning in Manchester in 1891, of new Labour Churches – providing what was called in the terminology of the time 'a Sunday home' for those socialists who could not attend the existing churches and chapels because of their links with the older political parties.[84] About a hundred Labour Churches sprang up in the next twenty years – most of them in a first burst of enthusiasm. These, however, fairly soon went into decline, partly because many socialists were so deeply involved in political work that they no longer felt the need for such a 'Sunday home', and partly because of disagreement as to what the nature of the religion taught in the Labour Churches should be.

Autobiographical notes by A. J. Waldegrave, who at one point was Secretary to the Labour Church Union, suggest some of the complexities of the relationship between religion and socialism in this period, and also some of the reasons why the Labour Church movement proved short-lived. Waldegrave was born in 1872. He became a pupil-teacher, and then came to London in 1891 to work in the civil service. At this stage he was a fervent Wesleyan, active in the South London Mission, which preached 'the evangelical doctrine of individual salvation in an atmosphere of brotherliness'. In 1892 he became a Fabian and in 1894 he left the church, influenced partly by scientific criticisms of Christianity, and partly by dissatisfaction with the church's apparent lack of interest in 'abolishing the slums'. He wanted a 'great new church', which would take account of modern knowledge, and would give priority to transforming society. His answer was the Labour Church, and he joined the small Tottenham branch, mainly supported by discontented Nonconformists, who were in continuous tension with those who were dogmatic Marxists.

Waldegrave summarised the membership of the Labour Churches as consisting of five disparate and incompatible elements: (1) 'those who had been active members of a church, usually a nonconformist one, & had found their efforts to interpret the teaching of Jesus in the socialistic way (which seemed to them the natural and obvious way) obstructed by the brethren who found nothing in that teaching inconsistent with individualistic commercialism'. Apart from that 'they were as much Christian as they had always been – Christians of a simple and uncritical sort, having no quarrel so far as they knew with orthodox theology'. (2) Former church members who had become 'Rationalistic Humanists'. (3) The largest section were 'working men (& often their wives) who were class-conscious members of trade unions', who had 'an idealism often tinged by the religious conception of a kingdom of Heaven on earth', but whose primary concerns were political. (4) Socialists influenced by John Ruskin and William Morris. (5) 'Hard-shell Marxists'.[85]

Autobiographical accounts show that conversion to socialism was often part of a more general process of questioning, in which orthodox religion was placed in doubt. Sometimes religious doubts led to the discovery of a new socialist faith; sometimes involvement in the socialist movement led to a more critical attitude either towards the church or towards official doctrine; sometimes they came to see socialist activism as the main practical expression of their Christianity, and gradually to regard the church as relatively unimportant.

Some examples recorded by oral historians indicate ways in which this could happen. A Bristol woman recalls that her father, who was a boot checker and later a co-op manager, was a keen reader, especially of the Bible and of history. He began with the Strict Baptists. Finding them too dogmatic, he joined another Baptist church, and then became a Unitarian. Then he got interested in socialism, 'which he felt was a practical form of Christianity, with people, if they are really true Socialists wanting the good of everybody and, well, as people have said, working towards what Christ was trying to teach'.[86] A Preston factory worker, born in 1884, and brought up as a Methodist, gave up religion as a young man as a result of reading Blatchford, Huxley, Darwin and Wallace. His discovery of the Independent Labour Party seems to have come later (though the chronology is not clear), and followed a holiday in the Lake District with a group of other young men, the leader of whom was an 'ILPer'. He was not so much converted by arguments – 'it was more a matter of company', though he became so vocal in voicing socialist opinions that his Liberal father threatened to throw him out of the home. He also became active in the Clarion Cyclists, which for many of his generation of socialists played as big a part in their conception of socialism as the strictly political work.[87]

As an example of the difficulties sometimes faced by those who mixed Christian and socialist activism, the Labour Church at Wilsden in Yorkshire was formed in 1906 after a Wesleyan local preacher was prevented from finishing a sermon in which he expressed socialist views. Also involved was another socialist preacher who had faced opposition from the leaders of his church. Admittedly, the attraction of the Labour Churches was so strong in the 1890s that they were pulling people away from the chapels even where there was no corresponding push. For instance, at the Northgate End Unitarian Church in Halifax, where the members of the Mutual Improvement Society underwent a mass conversion to socialism in 1893, a large section of them left to join the Labour Church in 1894 – much to the chagrin of the minister, who was himself sympathetic to socialism.[88]

Of course there was a large section of the working class which had little involvement in organised religion and little interest in politics. However, the growing mood of working-class militancy had important repercussions for the churches and chapels, because the religiously committed minority of the working class – those who were active in churches, chapels or secular societies – were strongly over-represented among those who became involved in working-class political organisations. However, the links between political radicalism and rejection of organised religion must not be exaggerated. In the first place it should be noted that many clergy were sympathetic towards, or even actively supported, the various working-class movements of this period. Even more important was the fact that many working-class activists saw a direct connection between their Christianity and their socialism. The most important development in this period was probably a switch of focus. Some of the politically-active working class were simply rejecting Christianity. More widespread, however, was a tendency to give religious questions a lower priority and to take a more sceptical view of what churches and chapels might achieve, while pushing political and social changes to the top of the agenda. So far as the decline of church attendance and membership were concerned, the losses to the churches were more qualitative than quantitative. The number of those who left their churches or chapels because of their conversion to socialism or their preoccupation with political activism was relatively small. But many of those who did leave for such reasons had been exceptionally committed and able.

The Marginalisation of the Churches

There was also a fourth and more elusive strand in the 'decline of religion' in the later Victorian period. In subtle ways the churches' sphere of operation was being narrowed down and the influence of religious categories on people's ways of thinking was being reduced.

To some extent this followed on naturally from the spread of agnosticism in the later nineteenth century. While fewer men of the upper and upper middle classes were entering the ministry, there was an increasing number who sought purely secular solutions to the nation's problems, and assumed that religion and the churches had little to contribute. Secular Utilitarianism had indeed been a significant influence of the Whig reforms of the 1830s. But the dominant position of the churches in education and in many areas of charitable provision continued to be accepted for most of the Victorian period.

In the latter years of the century there were various signs of change. One was the system of non-sectarian Board Schools created in the wake of the 1870 Education Act. After initial hesitations, these were warmly supported by Nonconformists, but they also came to assume a messianic significance for some secular Liberals, who enthused about the fact that they were under public control, that they reached almost the whole working-class population and so were much more effective than the churches as agencies of civilisation, and that they provided pure knowledge, uncontaminated by dogma or sectarian prejudice.[89] In Joseph Chamberlain's Birmingham, it was noted that Board Schools actually looked like churches. Indeed the same could be said about public libraries and baths, which were also part of the same drive by urban authorities to bring the benefits of civilisation to the whole population, regardless of creed. Not that there was any avowedly secularist motivation behind this movement. As Jeffrey Cox has shown, many of its strongest supporters were Nonconformists.[90] But the effect was to make the churches seem less necessary to social progress.

A more self-consciously secular trend in contemporary elite thinking is represented by Toynbee Hall, the settlement in the East End of London established in 1884 by Canon Samuel Barnett, a Broad Church Anglican, and his wife Henrietta Barnett. In the next years, Toynbee Hall became a formidably influential institution, where a succession of future leaders in politics, the civil service and the universities spent time engaged in social work and the study of social problems, between 'coming down' from Oxford or Cambridge and entering on a career. They included Clement Attlee, William Beveridge and R. H. Tawney. Politically the tone of Toynbee Hall was mainly Liberal, religiously it tended towards agnosticism – the tolerant, undogmatic Anglicanism of the founders created a haven in which those without any religious faith could feel safe to pursue what really interested them. In the case of such influential Toynbee figures as William Beveridge, sub-warden from 1903 to 1905, and Ernest Aves, who held the post in the 1890s, their principal aim was the reorganisation of society on rational and efficient lines, with the help of unlimited facts and figures, and without being diverted by emotive language or the unrealistic hopes of religious or political idealists.[91]

Meanwhile, more ambitious schemes by local authorities to further the welfare of the population were encroaching on territory hitherto dominated by the churches. This process has been fully documented by Jeffrey Cox in his study of the south London borough of Lambeth.[92] Nonconformist chapels in Lambeth had been providing evening classes since the 1850s, but by the 1890s these were in decline because of the classes provided by the London School Board. Generations of poor children had enjoyed free or very cheap breakfasts provided by churches; but the Education (Provision of Meals) Act of 1906 led to this responsibility being largely taken over by the London County Council. In 1912 Lambeth Borough Council began to enter the field of infant welfare, where, as so often, much of the pioneering provision had been by churches and chapels. The tendency for churches to pioneer social provision in previously neglected areas continued in the inter-war period when, as Cox shows, most of the youth clubs in Lambeth had a religious basis. The churches' involvement in welfare work did not die out, but shifted to new areas. None the less the expanding sphere of responsibility of central and local government meant that the overall presence of the churches in these areas was declining.

The social role of the churches and clergy was also

threatened by the appearance of ever greater numbers of 'experts', with claims to exclusive jurisdiction over particular areas of knowledge or particular fields of social action, and a vested interest in keeping the clergy out.[93] The most obvious example was the rising influence of scientists, and especially the effective campaigning of such champions of the profession as T. H. Huxley to obtain a complete separation of spheres of influence between scientists and theologians. In the first half of the nineteenth century, a number of the most prominent British scientists were clergymen, and up to about 1865 numerous clergymen held prominent positions in the Royal Society and the British Association for the Advancement of Science. The clerical scientists, and many of the most eminent lay scientists of the era, were powerfully influenced by the assumption that in studying nature they were studying the works of God, and by the 'argument from design', according to which the existence of God could be demonstrated by referring to the evidence of design in nature.

From the 1850s the role of the clergy in the scientific community was under fierce attack by a younger generation of professionals, led by Huxley, who argued that the prestige of science suffered from the prevalence of amateurism. Huxley suspected scientists who were clergymen (and even those laymen who were strongly committed believers) of having a dangerously divided loyalty. Theological preconceptions could divert scientific explanation into predetermined channels. Huxley and his colleagues, including the even more polemical Francis Galton, launched violent attacks on churches and clergy, in which the latter were presented as fanatical obscurantists who would do everything in their power to block the free pursuit of scientific enquiry. 'Extinguished theologians', declared Huxley, 'lie about the cradle of every infant science as the strangled snakes beside that of Hercules.'[94]

By the 1870s members of Huxley's circle occupied many of the most influential positions in the scientific establishment, and the role of clergymen within such institutions as the British Association had been drastically reduced. The longer-term process whereby the theologian's sphere of influence was marginalised and the scientist moved to the centre of the stage took place much more gradually. But the 'Do we Believe?' correspondence of 1904 indicated that this trend had already gone a considerable distance. Many correspondents juxtaposed 'dogmatic assertions' and 'scientific truth', referred to scientific heroes such as Copernicus, Galileo, Darwin, or Huxley himself, or insisted that since religion by its nature did not lend itself to proof, it was best left on one side.

Another example of the emergence of the 'expert', claiming exclusive jurisdiction within particular areas, was the development of the medical profession. Doctors were, for instance, among the strongest supporters of the Contagious Diseases Acts, and they bitterly resented the intrusion of moralists like Josephine Butler into their domain.[95] The influence of the medical profession also favoured the growth of a strictly secular understanding of disease. The first major cholera epidemic of the century, in 1831–2, was widely seen as a divine visitation. An official Day of Fasting and Humiliation was decreed by Parliament, and the ending of the epidemic soon after this was seen by many as an answer to prayer. But already at the time of the next major epidemic in 1848–9 opinion was changing. The epidemic was indeed accompanied by a temporary religious revival, as sinners flocked into churches to pray for escape, or maybe to put themselves right with God before it was too late. But this time there was no national day of prayer, and the Bishop of London, in speaking about the epidemic in the House of Lords, put the main stress on the need for more effective public health measures. In 1854, at the time of yet another cholera epidemic, Lord Palmerston rejected calls for a national day of prayer, arguing that prayers were only appropriate after all necessary medical and sanitary precautions had been taken. (It should be noted, however, that when in

the same year the Crimean War broke out, the government did order a national day of prayer, which illustrates
the fact that, rather than there being a uniform decline
in the use of religious language, such language continued
to flourish in some areas of life while seeming increasingly
out of place in others.)[96]

Not that Victorian medical men were often irreligious,
or saw themselves in direct rivalry with the clergy – as
quite often happened in France. For most doctors, being
a church-going Anglican was simply a part of the expected
behaviour of a person in their social position. Christianity
also acted as an important motivation for a medical career
– the healer being someone who followed in the footsteps
of Christ. But they wanted it to be quite clear that it was
they, and not any priest or theologian, who pronounced
why a person was sick and how they might be cured.

By the early twentieth century, social work was beginning to emerged as a profession in its own right and similar
processes were taking place. As in other 'caring professions', religious motivation remained very important in
recruitment. But as social work moved from being a branch
of the church to being a profession in its own right, it
became increasingly difficult to work according to rules
and in pursuit of objectives determined by religious goals,
such as the conversion of sinners or the establishment of
the Kingdom of God. Social work too was influenced by
the ideal of a religiously-neutral 'scientific' approach. This
was pioneered by the Charity Organisation Society (COS),
which eventually came to be discredited by its dogmatism
and its evident unpopularity with the poor. But the ideal
remained, and had special attractions in a pluralistic society where religious denomination was always a potential source of division.

Finally, the religious dimension of politics, after reaching a peak in Gladstone's first ministry of 1868–74, was
declining in importance. The reasons for this were complicated, and it did not necessarily reflect any decline in
the proportion of Members of Parliament who were strongly

influenced by religion. Indeed, the Liberal-dominated 1906 Parliament may have included an abnormally high proportion of strongly religious individuals. About half the Liberals and over half the Labour MPs were Nonconformists. Though there certainly were some whose free-church credentials, amounting to little more than family tradition or attendance at a Nonconformist Sunday School, were paraded for the purposes of attracting Nonconformist voters,[97] there were plenty of others, such as Keir Hardie or Arthur Henderson, whose religion was a much more fundamental influence. But overtly religious issues were playing less part in politics, and religion was diminishing in importance as a line of division between the parties. The most obvious point was that the questions of religious equality which had been so important for most of the century had lost some of their force, since most of the demands of the various religious minorities had been met.

There was one major exception: the Church of England continued to be the established church of England and Wales. In Wales, the Liberals were able to turn this into a major election issue, and a Bill to disestablish the church in Wales was approved by the House of Commons in 1894, only to be rejected by the House of Lords. Welsh disestablishment was finally enacted in 1914, and put into effect in 1920. In England, however, the disestablishment loudly preached by militant Dissenters since the 1840s, and seized upon by Joseph Chamberlain in his Radical phase in the 1870 and 1880s, never quite took off.[98] The fact that Gladstone was a fervent High Anglican meant that there was no chance of the Liberals taking up the cause while Gladstone was leader; the fact that many Anglicans voted Liberal meant that any Liberal government was likely to hesitate before possibly alienating a large section of its supporters; and the Church of England (whatever might have been true in the 1830s) was no longer quite reactionary enough to provoke a full-blooded anti-clerical movement of the French or Spanish kind.

Apart from religious equality, the other great sectarian

issue was elementary education and, indeed, the years between 1902 and 1908 saw a last great upsurge of sectarian passion. But in fact the 1870 Education Act had provided the basis for what proved to be a workable compromise. This Act established the 'dual system', whereby publicly-controlled Board Schools supplemented, rather than replaced, the system of partly publicly-funded church schools. The Board Schools were Christian in the sense that teaching of the Bible could be (and usually was) provided, though it had to be strictly non-denominational. Most Nonconformists regarded these schools as acceptable, and most of their schools were handed over for control by the School Board. While many Anglican, as well as Catholic, schools retained their independence, the Board Schools soon established an ascendancy in most urban areas outside Lancashire, and won acceptance from many Anglican, as well as Nonconformist, parents and clergy. Although the Conservative Education Act of 1902 provoked the fury of militant Nonconformists, and the Liberal Bill of 1906 had a similar effect on militant Anglicans, the issue failed to achieve a comparable degree of resonance with the wider public. When the Liberal government chose to fight the House of Lords, it was not on the issue of education, but on Lloyd George's 'People's Budget' of 1909.

This reflected the growing importance of class issues in politics, and the significance of class as a basis for political alignment. The Second Reform Act in 1867 enfranchised a large part of the urban working class, and except in Lancashire the main beneficiaries were the Liberals. The Conservatives were gaining ground in the towns from 1874, as a result of their growing appeal to middle-class voters. The enfranchisement of rural labourers in 1884 further emphasised the importance of class, and weakened the significance of the urban/rural divide, since most rural workers voted Liberal. Religion remained a vitally important influence on voting. But by the 1880s and 1890s loyalty to the Liberal Party was wearing thin among Nonconformists at both ends of the social hierarchy.

The Nonconformist elite were disturbed by symptoms of what they saw as the party's growing radicalism. The year 1886 marked a first turning-point. In that year Gladstone was converted to the cause of Irish Home Rule. The Liberal Party split, and many wealthy Nonconformists joined the motley band of Whig aristocrats, militant Protestants and Birmingham radical Chamberlainites in seceding to form the Liberal Unionists. Some prominent preachers joined the exodus, notably Spurgeon, though generally ministers remained faithful to the Liberal Party for longer than the lay elite. The second turning-point was Lloyd George's 'People's Budget', of 1909, which caused even more heart-searching among wealthy Nonconformists, leading many to desert not only the Liberal Party, but Nonconformity itself.[99] There had been a long-standing tendency for the sons and daughters of prosperous Nonconformist families to move over to the Church of England. In the early twentieth century, when the chapels seemed to be deeply implicated in the radical policies of the Liberal government, such defections were exceptionally numerous. Ironically there was equal restiveness among many working-class Nonconformists, who felt that radical Liberalism did not go far enough, and who were converts to the new gospel of socialism. Often the split ran along generational lines, with the older generation remaining faithful to Liberalism, while the younger generation were attracted to the ILP.[100]

Labour was religiously pluralistic, and this was a vital factor in the growing disengagement between religion and politics. Both Nonconformists and secularists were over-represented among Labour activists. But in parts of Lancashire there were many Catholics in the various Labour and Socialist organisations. In the East End of London, Jews were important – initially mainly secular Jews, but later religious Jews too. And there was even a number of Anglicans who were prominent in the Labour movement, most notable George Lansbury.

This religious pluralism had several important consequences. First, Labour was much less closely identified than either Liberals or Conservatives with a specific religious standpoint – so that religious and political loyalties were much less likely to be mutually reinforcing than in the older parties. Secondly, as Labour attracted working-class voters, regardless of denomination, and the Conservatives increasingly attracted middle-class people, regardless of denomination, both Labour and Conservatives had a motive for playing down religious issues, which might divide their own supporters.[101] Thirdly, and particularly important, was the fact that the Labour Party never acquired the anti-religious or anti-clerical character of many of its continental counterparts. This meant that Labour Party leaders were reluctant to bring church issues to the fore, and that the older parties seldom tried to win votes by posing as champions of Christianity. In most continental European countries, religion continued for much of the twentieth century to mark a major political dividing line because the Socialists and Communists were vehemently anti-clerical, while right-wing parties claimed to be 'Christian'; in England religion lost a good deal of its political force, as religious and non-religious people, and members of various denominations, were scattered across the political spectrum.

CONCLUSION

This book began with three questions, none of which can be satisfactorily answered in a simple Yes/No fashion. My first conclusion, therefore, must be that much more nuanced answers are needed than those that are provided in a large part of the existing literature.

The first question is the one that can be answered with the greatest degree of confidence. It should be clear that the 'religious boom' was not an exclusively middle-class phenomenon, but that it influenced in some degree all sections of the population, including the urban as well as the rural elites, and both the rural and the urban working class. As was shown in Chapter 2, the influence of Christianity and the churches penetrated most areas of life; and, as was shown in Chapter 1, even the least church-going section of the population, the urban working class, included a substantial minority of those who were actively involved in church or chapel. It remains true, however, that the upper middle class was *more* strongly affected by the 'religious boom' than any other section of the population, and this had important implications for the nature of the religion of the time. It meant that plenty of funds were available for religious purposes of all kinds, ranging from church-building to overseas missions to a variety of charitable schemes.

It also meant that religion played an important part in most of the systems of authority operating in English society, and that most areas of religious life thus had an important class dimension. Deference could be expressed in a religious idiom, and so could defiance and rebellion.

221

Wickham, Inglis, and the many historians who followed their lead, were quite right to emphasise the class dimension of Victorian religion, but they analysed it in too one-sided a way, and made exaggerated claims for the extent of working-class alienation from the churches or from religion in general. More recently the 'revisionist' historians of the later 1980s and early 1990s have more than redressed the balance, and the tendency in their work is to understate the role of class divisions and antagonisms.

The question of whether religion acted primarily as an instrument of authority or a force for reform cannot be answered in any general way. As was suggested in Chapter 2, the pervasive influence of Christianity in Victorian society was such that it played a major part both in most systems of authority, and in most emancipatory movements. The more interesting accounts of the social role of Victorian religion are not those which one-sidedly emphasise one aspect or the other, but those which explore the tensions between more conservative and more liberal or radical understanding of Christianity or of Judaism, or the tensions between more religious and more secular versions of conservative, liberal or radical ideology. The most interesting studies have not been those which assume a neat fit between religion and social roles, but those which have explored the unintended consequences of people's beliefs, and the contradictions between different deeply held convictions. This is one area in which ambiguity is all-important, and clear-cut answers are generally wrong.

I shall conclude by briefly summing up the view of the Victorian religious crisis that has been presented here. First, I am suggesting that most accounts have been vitiated by an insistence on identifying some master-factor, which provides the key to the crisis: my argument is that no such key exists, and indeed that there was not one crisis, but a series of crises, that were only loosely related to one another. Secondly, as regards chronology, I would agree with those historians who have identified the period 1890–1914 as the one in which there was a general *con-*

sciousness of religious crisis, but I would also agree with those who have argued that the roots of the crisis lie in an earlier period, and that in looking at the various causes of the crisis it is not possible to concentrate on this period alone. This crisis had at least three partly independent dimensions: the growth of unbelief or doubt, mainly after about 1860; the decline in church membership and attendance, mainly after about 1890; and a weakening of the social role of religion, which was a much more gradual and long-drawn-out process, affecting different areas of life at different times.

Throughout the nineteenth century, working-class church membership and attendance had been relatively low (though there may have been some increase in the second half of the century). The new development in the last quarter of the century was the declining participation of the upper middle class. Three quite separate types of factor were involved: the growth of religious doubt, partly because of new scientific developments, but more especially because of changes in moral sensibilities, which made many aspects of existing Christian orthodoxy harder to accept; the growing preoccupation with leisure, and the associated reaction against 'puritan' taboos and restrictions; and the decline of the social paternalism, of which religious institutions and ideology had often been an integral part.

The declining religious involvement of both urban and rural elites had various repercussions for the rest of the population: less money was available for religious purposes, and from about 1890 many churches were facing serious financial problems; fewer men were entering the ministry and fewer women were doing voluntary religious work, so that, by the turn of the century, parishes were finding it increasingly hard to maintain the huge parish organisation that had characterised the mid-Victorian years. Meanwhile, for a variety of very different reasons, the role of religion and the churches in education and social welfare was diminishing – in some areas, very rapidly. All of this had effects on working-class and lower middle-class religious participation: for instance, the declining role of the churches in charity weakened their links with the poor; the decline of paternalism and the trend towards more impersonal social relations meant that those at the lower end of the social hierarchy were less often under pressure to go to church; and declining resources made it harder for the churches to maintain contacts with non-church-goers through visiting or the provision of leisure facilities. Meanwhile, the new agnosticism and the rebellion against 'puritanism' also had an effect on the lower middle class and upper working class (though the impact was not as great as it was further up the social scale). Sometimes linked with this, and sometimes quite separate, was the growth in class-consciousness and political militancy in the working class and among some white-collar workers, especially in the years immediately before the First World War.

The religious implications of this were complex, but to some extent this militancy led to a rejection of religion or of the churches, either because they were too closely linked with employers and the older political parties, or because politics now seemed to offer the way to salvation, and religion therefore seemed to be a secondary issue. Meanwhile, and to some degree independently of all the other factors mentioned, there were long-term trends towards the privatisation of religion. The most important development during this period was the decline in the religious dimensions of politics, but, as was explained in Chapter 4, this had relatively little to do with the decline in religious belief and participation that was also taking place at this time.

NOTES

(Unless stated otherwise, all works cited were published in London.)

Notes to the Introduction

1. E. R. Wickham, *Church and People in an Industrial City* (1957), ch. 4.
2. Robert Currie, *Methodism Divided* (1968); Alan Gilbert, *Religion and Society in Industrial England: Church, Chapel and Social Change, 1740–1914* (1976); Robert Curie, Alan Gilbert and Lee Horsley, *Churches and Churchgoers: Patterns of Church Growth in the British Isles since 1700* (Oxford, 1977); John Kent, *Holding the Fort* (1978).
3. Jeffrey Cox, *English Churches in a Secular Society: Lambeth, 1870–1930* (Oxford, 1982); Callum G. Brown, 'Did Urbanization Secularize Britain?', *Urban History Yearbook* (1988), pp. 1–14. See also Stephen Yeo, *Religion and Voluntary Organisations in Crisis* (1976).
4. See, for instance, Bernard Lightman, '*Robert Elsmere* and the Agnostic Crises of Faith', in Richard J. Helmstadter and Bernard Lightman (eds), *Victorian Faith in Crisis* (Basingstoke, 1992), pp. 283–311. Lightman shows how Mary Ward understood her loss of faith in purely intellectual terms, and attempted to reproduce her own experiences in her best-selling novel of agnosticism, *Robert Elsmere*. It is noteworthy, however, that none of the contributors to this collection regards an explanation of the crisis in such terms as adequate.
5. For Christian responses to new intellectual developments, see Owen Chadwick, *The Victorian Church*, 2 vols (1966–70)

225

vol. 2, pp. 1–150; James R. Moore, *The Post-Darwinian Controversies* (Cambridge, 1979).

6. G. Kitson Clark, *The Making of Victorian England* (1962), p. 147.

7. Frank M. Turner, 'The Victorian Conflict between Science and Religion: A Professional Dimension', in Gerald Parson (ed.), *Religion in Victorian England*, 4 vols (Manchester 1988), vol. 4, pp. 170–97.

8. Josef L. Altholz, 'The Warfare of Conscience with Theology', in ibid., pp. 150–69; H. R. Murphy, 'The Ethical Revolt against Christian Orthodoxy in Early Victorian England', *American Historical Review*, 40 (1955), pp. 800–17; Susan Budd, *Varieties of Unbelief* (1977).

9. Wickham, op. cit.; K. S. Inglis, *Churches and the Working Classes in Victorian England* (1963).

10. Cox, op. cit., pp. 90–105.

11. Sarah Williams, 'Religious Belief and Popular Culture: A Study of the South London Borough of Southwark, c. 1880–1939' (University of Oxford D. Phil. thesis, 1993); Mark Smith, *Religion in Industrial Society: Oldham and Saddleworth, 1780–1865* (Oxford, 1994); Callum G. Brown, 'The Mechanism of Religious Growth in Urban Societies', in Hugh McLeod (ed.), *European Religion in the Age of Great Cities* (1995), pp. 239–62.

12. Patrick Joyce, *Work, Society and Politics* (Brighton, 1980).

13. Robert Moore, *Pit-men, Politics and Preachers* (1974).

14. Tapes and transcripts of these interviews are to be found respectively in the Department of Sociology, University of Essex; the Centre for North-West Regional Studies, University of Lancaster; and Avon County Reference Library, Bristol. For fuller information about the two former projects, see Paul Thompson, *The Edwardians* (1975); and Elizabeth Roberts, *A Woman's Place* (1984).

Notes to Chapter 1: Patterns of Religious Belonging

1. Michael R. Watts (ed.), *Religion in Victorian Nottinghamshire: The Religious Census of 1851*, 2 vols (Nottingham, 1988), vol. I, p. xiv.

2. Alan Haig, *The Victorian Clergy* (1984).

3. Interviews on Family Life and Work Experience before 1918, University of Essex Oral History Archive [hereafter cited as Essex Oral History], interview no. 83 (informant born 1900, Tonbridge).

4. Charles Booth, *Life and Labour of the People in London*, 17 vols (1902–3); B. S. Rowntree, *Poverty, A Study of Town Life* (1901); Ellen Ross, 'Hungry Children: Housewives and London Charity', in Peter Mandler (ed.), *The Uses of Charity: The Poor on Relief in the Nineteenth-Century Metropolis* (Philadelphia, 1990), pp. 161–96; Alun Howkins, *Poor Labouring Men: Rural Radicalism in Norfolk, 1870–1923* (1985), p. 35.

5. Essex Oral History, interviews no. 359, p. 59 (informant born 1898, Charles, north Devon); no. 368, p. 42 (informant born 1897, east London); no. 311, pp. 56–7 (informant born 1902, East Bergholt, Suffolk).

6. Ibid., interview no. 417, p. 22 (informant born 1899, east London).

7. Howkins, op. cit., p. 31.

8. Thomas Wright, *The Great Unwashed* (1868), as quoted in Gerald Parsons (ed.), *Religion in Victorian Britain*, 4 vols (Manchester, 1988), vol. 3, p. 324.

9. E. N. Bennett, *Problems of Village Life* (1913), pp. 134, 139.

10. Elizabeth Roberts, interview with Mr C1P, p. 72 (informant born 1884, Preston).

11. F. Bettany, *Stewart Headlam* (1926), p. 125. See also E. R. Norman, *The Victorian Christian Socialists* (1988); and Kenneth Leech's chapter on Headlam in M. Reckitt (ed.), *For Christ and the People* (1968).

12. Clyde Binfield, '"A Crucible of modest though concentrated Experiment": Religion in Sheffield, c.1840–1950', in Hugh McLeod (ed.), *European Religion in the Age of Great Cities* (1995), p. 197.

13. Essex Oral History, interview no. 38, pp. 17–18 (informant born 1895, Swerford, Oxfordshire).

14. See B. I. Coleman, *The Church of England in the Mid-Nineteenth Century: A Social Geography* (1980); Paul Ell and T. R. Slater, 'The Religious Census of 1851: A Computer-mapped Survey of the Church of England', *Journal of Historical Geography*, 20 (1994), pp. 44–61.

15. B. I. Coleman, 'The Church Extension Movement in London, c.1800–1860' (University of Cambridge PhD thesis, 1968).

16. Hugh McLeod, *Class and Religion in the Late Victorian City* (1974), p. 306.
17. Ibid., ch. 8.
18. Essex Oral History, interview no. 398, p. 26 (informant born 1892, west London).
19. Walter Arnstein, 'Queen Victoria and Religion', in Gail Malmgreen (ed.), *Religion in the Lives of English Women, 1750–1930* (1986), pp. 101, 103, 111–21.
20. [T. H. S. Escott], *Society in London* (1885), pp. 162–3.
21. Hugh McLeod, 'Class Community and Region: The Religious Geography of Nineteenth-Century England', in Michael Hill (ed.), *A Sociological Yearbook of Religion in Britain*, 6 (1973), p. 52.
22. Frank Prochaska, *Women and Philanthropy in 19th Century England* (Oxford, 1980), pp. 5–7.
23. David Jeremy, 'Important Questions about Business and Religion in Nineteenth-century Britain', in David Jeremy (ed.), *Business and Religion in Britain* (Aldershot, 1988), pp. 16–17; Jane Garnett and A. C. Howe, 'Churchmen and Cotton Masters in Victorian Lancashire', in ibid., pp. 72–94.
24. W. Hale White, *The Autobiography of Mark Rutherford* (1988), p. 29 [first published 1881].
25. Sec, for instance, Alan Bartlett, 'Churches in Bermondsey, 1880–1939' (University of Birmingham PhD thesis, 1987), pp. 286–94, which stresses the role of the Ryall and Bustin families in the history of the borough's mission halls.
26. Hugh McLeod, 'White Collar Values and the Role of Religion', in Geoffrey Crossick (ed.), *The Lower Middle Class in Britain, 1870–1914* (1977), pp. 61–88.
27. Coleman, 'Church Extension', pp. 120–4.
28. Geoffrey Crossick, 'The Labour Aristocracy and its Values', *Victorian Studies*, 19 (1976), pp. 301–26.
29. Essex Oral History, interview no. 54, pp. 12, 31 (informant born 1895, Bolton).
30. Ibid., interview no. 38, p. 14 ((informant born 1895, Swerford, Oxfordshire).
31. Bartlett, op. cit., pp. 130–4; Frank Prochaska, 'Body and Soul: Bible Nurses and the Poor in Victorian London', *Historical Research*, 60 (1987), pp. 336–48.
32. Watts, op. cit., pp. xxx–xxxi. See also James Obelkevich, *Religion in Rural Society: South Lindsey 1825–1875* (Oxford, 1976), p. 155.

33. Essex Oral History, interview no. 110 (informant born 1881, Bures, Essex).
34. For an overview of Nonconformity in this period, see James Munson, *The Nonconformists* (1991). Also relevant in D. W. Bebbington, *Evangelicalism in Modern Britain* (1989).
35. Robin Gill, *The Myth of the Empty Church* (1993), p. 305. See also McLeod, 'Class, Community and Region', pp. 46–7.
36. See Peter Ackers, 'West End Chapel, Back Street Bethel', forthcoming in *Journal of Ecclesiastical History*.
37. Munson, op. cit., pp. 4, 114–20.
38. Robert Currie, 'A Micro-theory of Methodist Growth', *Proceedings of the Wesley Historical Society*, 36 (1967), pp. 67–73.
39. K. D. M. Snell, *Church and Chapel in the North Midlands* (Leicester, 1991).
40. Theodore Koditschek, *Class Formation and Urban-Industrial Society: Bradford, 1750–1850* (Cambridge, 1990), p. 257.
41. See Jeremy (ed.), op. cit.; Clyde Binfield, *So Down to Prayers: Studies in English Nonconformity, 1780–1920* (1977).
42. Essex Oral History, interview no. 190, pp. 5, 41–2, 44 (informant born 1894, Eastwood).
43. Robert Moore, *Pit-men, Politics and Preachers* (1974). See also A. Ainsworth, 'Religion in the Working Class Community and the Evolution of Socialism in Later Nineteenth Century Lancashire', *Histoire Sociale*, 10 (1977), pp. 354–80.
44. Booth Collection, B183, pp. 97, 123–7 (London School of Economics Library).
45. Judith Champ, 'The Demographic Impact of Irish Immigration on Birmingham Catholicism, 1800–1850', in W. J. Sheils and Diana Wood (eds), *The Churches, Ireland and the Irish*, Studies in Church History, 25 (Oxford, 1989), pp. 235, 241. See also John Bossy, *The English Catholic Community, 1570–1850* (1975).
46. See, for instance, Gerard Connolly, 'The Transsubstantiation of Myth: Towards a New Popular History of Nineteenth-century Catholicism in England', *Journal of Ecclesiastical History*, 35 (1984), pp. 78–104.
47. Champ, op. cit., pp. 239–40.
48. Steven Fielding, *Class and Ethnicity: Irish Catholics in England, 1880–1939* (Buckingham, 1993), p. 40.
49. Susan O'Brien, 'Terra Incognita: The Nun in Nineteenth-Century England', *Past and Present*, 121 (1988), pp. 123–4; Jennifer Supple-Green, *The Catholic Revival in Yorkshire,*

1850–1900 (Leeds, 1990), pp. 27–30.

50. Fielding, op. cit., ch. 2.

51. McLeod, *Class and Religion*, pp. 140–1.

52. Sheridan Gilley, 'Papists, Protestants and the Irish in London', in G. J. Cuming and D. Baker (eds), *Popular Belief and Practice*. Studies in Church History, 8 (Cambridge, 1972), p. 263; G. Connolly, 'Irish and Catholic: Myth or Reality?' in Roger Swift and Sheridan Gilley (eds), *The Irish in the Victorian City* (1985), p. 229.

53. Lynn Lees, *Exiles of Erin: Irish Migrants in Victorian London* (Manchester, 1979).

54. For discussion of the relationship between poverty and religious alienation (including some London Irish examples), see Hugh McLeod, *Piety and Poverty: Working Class Religion in Berlin, London and New York, 1870–1914* (New York, 1995), ch. 6.

55. Fielding, op. cit., chs 3–4.

56. Hugh McLeod, 'Building the "Catholic Ghetto": Catholic Organisations, 1870–1914', in W. J. Sheils and Diana Wood (eds), *Voluntary Religion*, Studies in Church History, 23 (Oxford, 1986), pp. 411–44.

57. McLeod, *Class and Religion*, p. 74.

58. J. D. Holmes, *More Roman than Rome* (Tunbridge Wells, 1978).

59. The most recent of the many studies of Victorian anti-Catholicism is J. R. Wolffe, *The Protestant Crusade in Great Britain, 1829–1860* (Oxford, 1991). A good overview is G. F. A. Best, 'Popular Protestantism in Victorian Britain', in R. Robson (ed.), *Ideas and Institutions of the Victorians* (1967), pp. 115–42.

60. Booth, op. cit., 3rd series, vol. 7, p. 401.

61. See examples in Bartlett, op. cit.; and Hugh McLeod, 'New Perspectives on Victorian Working Class Religion: The Oral Evidence', *Oral History*, 14 (1986), p. 33.

62. Jennifer Supple, 'Ultramontanism in Yorkshire, 1850–1900', in Parsons (ed.), op. cit., vol. 4, pp. 141–2; Fielding, op. cit., p. 54.

63. Population figures taken from Geoffrey Alderman, *Modern British Jewry* (Oxford, 1992), pp. 2, 102–3, 119.

64. Aubrey Newman, *The United Synagogue, 1870–1970* (1976).

65. Alderman, op. cit., p. 101.

66. Geoffrey Alderman, *The Federation of Synagogues, 1887–1987* (London, 1987).

67. David Feldman, 'Immigrants and Workers, Englishmen and Jews: Jewish Immigrants to the East End of London, 1880–1906' (University of Cambridge PhD thesis, 1985), p. 325.

68. David Feldman, 'Popery, Rabbinism and Reform: Evangelicals and Jews in Early Victorian England', in Diana Wood (ed.), *Christianity and Judaism*, Studies in Church History, 29 (Oxford, 1992), pp. 379–86.

69. Todd Endelman, 'Communal Solidarity among the Jewish Elite of Victorian London', *Victorian Studies*, 28 (1985), pp. 491–526.

70. Todd Endelman, 'The Social and Political Context of Conversion in Germany and England, 1870–1914', in T. Endelman (ed.), *Jewish Apostasy in the Modern World* (New York, 1987), pp. 94–100.

71. Feldman, 'Immigrants and Workers', pp. 318–24. See also W. J. Fishman, *East End Jewish Radicals* (1975).

72. Elaine R. Smith, 'Jews and Politics in the East End of London, 1918–39', in David Cesarani (ed.), *The Making of Modern Anglo-Jewry* (Oxford, 1990), p. 144.

73. See Susan Budd, *Varieties of Unbelief* (1977).

74. George Levine, 'Scientific Discourse as an Alternative to Faith', in Richard J. Helmstadter and Bernard Lightman (eds), *Victorian Faith in Crisis* (Basingstoke, 1990), pp. 225–61; Noel Annan, *Leslie Stephen, The Godless Victorian* (Chicago, 1984), pp. 232–66.

75. C. S. Davies, *North Country Bred* (1963), p. 116.

76. Basil Willey, *More Nineteenth Century Studies: Some Honest Doubters* (1956), pp. 98–105.

77. See Walter Arnstein, *The Bradlaugh Case* (Oxford, 1965).

78. Edward Royle, *Radicals, Secularists and Republicans: Popular Freethought in Britain, 1866–1915* (Manchester, 1980), pp. 128, 335–42.

79. Ibid., pp. 154–5.

80. Davies, op. cit., chs 8–11.

81. James R. Moore, 'Theodicy and Society: The Crisis of the Intelligentsia', in Helmstadter and Lightman (eds), op. cit., pp. 153–86; Pietro Corsi, *Science and Religion: Baden Powell and the Anglican Debate, 1800–1860* (Cambridge, 1988), pp. 205–12.

82. A. R. Cunningham, 'The "New Woman Fiction" of the 1890s', *Victorian Studies*, 17 (1973–4), pp. 177–86.

83. P. A. M. Taylor, *Expectations Westward* (Edinburgh, 1965).

84. W. S. Smith, *The London Heretics, 1870–1914* (1967), ch. 5; Robert Currie, Alan Gilbert and Lee Horsley, *Churches and Churchgoers: Patterns of Church Growth in the British Isles since 1700* (Oxford, 1977), p. 193.

85. J. M. Winter, 'Spiritualism and the First World War', in R. W. Davis and R. J. Helmstadter (eds), *Religion and Irreligion in Victorian Society* (1992), pp. 185–200.

86. Logie Borrow, *Independent Spirits: Spiritualism and English Plebeians, 1850–1910* (1986), pp. 4–29.

87. Geoffrey Nelson, *Spiritualism and Society* (1969), p. 141.

88. Barrow, op. cit., pp. 225–6.

89. Cf. Holbrook Jackson, *The Eighteen Nineties* (1913).

90. George Bourne, *Change in the Village* (1912), p. 295.

91. Patrick Joyce, *Work, Society and Politics* (Brighton, 1980), p. 242.

92. This point has been forcefully argued by Jeffrey Cox, *English Churches in a Secular Society: Lambeth 1870–1930* (Oxford, 1982), pp. 103–5, and more fully developed by Sarah Williams, 'Religious Belief and Popular Culture: A Study of the South London Borough of Southwark, c.1880–1939' (University of Oxford D. Phil. thesis, 1993).

93. Obelkevich, op. cit., pp. 213–17.

94. Ibid., p. 157.

95. D. W. Bebbington, *The Nonconformist Conscience* (1982), p. 46. The standard work is Brian Harrison, *Drink and the Victorians* (1971).

96. Douglas A. Reid, 'Religion, Recreation and the Working Class: Birmingham 1844–1885', *Bulletin of the Society for the Study of Labour History*, 51 (1986), p. 9. For fuller discussion, see D. A. Reid, 'Labour, Leisure and Politics in Birmingham ca.1800–1875' (University of Birmingham PhD thesis, 1985).

97. See, for instance, Robert Moore, op. cit., pp. 142, 147.

98. Roberts, interview with Mrs P1P, p. 30 (informant born 1898, Preston).

99. Royle, op. cit., p. 129.

100. See Timothy Hands, *Thomas Hardy: Distracted Preacher? Hardy's Religious Biography and its Influence on his Novels* (1989).

101. Geoffrey Robson, 'Between Town and Countryside: Contrasting Patterns of Church-going in the Early Victorian Black Country', in D. Baker (ed.), *The Church in Town and*

Countryside, Studies in Church History, 16 (Oxford, 1979), pp. 402–3.

102. See McLeod, 'Class, Community and Region'.

103. Ibid., pp. 49–52; McLeod, 'White Collar Values', pp. 87–8.

104. Rosemary Chadwick, 'Church and People in Bradford and District, 1880–1914' (University of Oxford D.Phil. thesis, 1986), pp. 160–1.

105. Clive Field, 'The Social Structure of English Methodism, Eighteenth–Twentieth Centuries', *British Journal of Sociology*, 28 (1977), pp. 199–225.

106. Snell, op. cit., pp. 39–45.

107. Mark Smith, *Religion and Society in Oldham and Saddleworth, 1780–1865* (Oxford, 1994), chs 4–5; cf. Alan Gilbert, *Re-ligion and Society in Industrial England* (1976), pp. 112–14.

108. 'Religious Worship (England and Wales', *Parliamentary Papers*, 1852–3, vol. 89, pp. clviii–clxii.

109. Joyce, op. cit., p. 244.

110. For the debate on this issue, see Callum Brown, 'Did Urbanization Secularize Britain?', *Urban History Yearbook* (1988), pp. 1–14.

111. Clive Field, 'Adam and Eve: Gender in the English Free Church Constituency, 1650–1980', *Journal of Ecclesiastical History*, 44 (1993), pp. 63–79.

112. Chadwick, op. cit., p. 163.

113. Ibid., pp. 171–3.

114. See Richard Mudie-Smith, *The Religious Life of London* (1904).

115. Field, op. cit., p. 75.

116. Alderman, *Modern British Jewry*, p. 198.

117. The best discussion of Anglican and Nonconformist views is Leonore Davidoff and Catherine Hall, *Family Fortunes: Men and Women of the English Middle Class, 1780–1850* (1987), pp. 107–48. For briefer discussion of Catholic views, see Fielding, op. cit., pp. 59–61.

118. See, for instance, Sheila Wright, 'Quakerism and its Implications for Quaker Women: The Women Itinerant Ministers of York Meeting, 1780–1840', in W. J. Sheils and Diana Wood (eds), *Women in the Church*, Studies in Church History, 27 (Oxford, 1990), pp. 413–14.

119. Elizabeth Roberts, *A Woman's Place* (1984), pp. 118–19.

120. For the distinctive cultural features of this region, see D. J. Rowe, 'The North-east', in F. M. L. Thompson (ed.),

The Cambridge Social History of Britain, 1750–1950, 3 vols (Cambridge, 1990), vol. 1, pp. 443, 467–9.

121. Gareth Stedman Jones, *Outcast London* (Oxford, 1971), pp. 84–7, 125; Ellen Ross, ' "Fierce Questions and Taunts": Married Life in Working-Class London, 1870–1914', in Gareth Stedman Jones and David Feldman (eds), *Metropolis, London* (1989), p. 220.

122. Frank Prochaska, 'A Mother's Country: Mother's Meetings and Family Welfare in Britain, 1850–1950', *History*, 74 (1989), pp. 379–99.

Notes to Chapter 2: A Christian Country?

1. Simon Green, 'Religion in the Industrial Town, with special reference to the West Riding of Yorkshire, c.1870–1920' (University of Oxford D.Phil. thesis, 1989), p. 92.
2. This is a central theme of Robin Gill, *The Myth of the Empty Church* (1993).
3. *Facts and Figures about the Church of England*, 3 (1965), p. 54.
4. James Obelkevich, *Religion in Rural Society: South Lindsey 1825–1875* (Oxford, 1976), p. 127.
5. Essex Oral History, interview no. 5, p. 15 (informant born 1883, Edmonton).
6. Alan Bartlett, 'Churches in Bermondsey, 1880–1939' (University of Birmingham PhD thesis, 1987), pp. 182–8.
7. Ibid., p. 184; Sarah Williams, 'Religious Belief and Popular Culture: A Study of the South London Borough of Southwark c.1880–1939' (University of Oxford D.Phil. thesis, 1993), p. 190.
8. Ibid., pp. 190–1.
9. Bartlett, op. cit., pp. 184–7.
10. These estimates are based on responses to a question in the Essex Oral History survey.
11. Essex Oral History, interview no. 313, pp. 21–2 (informant born 1897, Shalford, Essex).
12. Raphael Samuel, East End MS (in his possession).
13. Bristol Oral History Project interview no. 11, p. 11 (informant born 1897, Bristol).
14. Ibid., interview no. 34, p. 12 (informant born 1895, Bristol).
15. Ibid., interview no. 2, p. 11 (informant born 1899, Bristol).

16. Ibid., interview no. 9, p. 6 (informant born 1886, Bristol); interview no. 15, p. 39 (informant born 1901, Bristol); interview no. 2, p. 5 (informant born 1899, Bristol).

17. Elizabeth Roberts, interview with Mrs P1P, pp. 1–3 (informant born 1898, Preston).

18. Raphael Samuel, *East End Underworld: Chapters in the Life of Arthur Harding* (1981), p. 27.

19. Gillian Rose, interviews (informant born 1910, east London) (tape in possession of Gillian Rose).

20. Thomas W. Laqueur, *Religion and Respectability: Sunday Schools and Working Class Culture, 1780–1850* (New Haven, 1976), pp. 179–86.

21. Booth Collection, B287, pp. 49–51; Richard Mudie-Smith (ed.), *The Religious Life of London* (1904), p. 190.

22. Essex Oral History, interview no. 368. p. 26 (informant born 1897, east London).

23. Laqueur, op. cit., pp. 246–7; Gill, op. cit., p. 301.

24. Robert Tressell, *The Ragged Trousered Philanthropists* (1965), p. 153 [first published 1914]; Samuel, *East End Underworld*, p. 24.

25. Elizabeth Roberts, *Working Class Barrow and Lancaster* (Lancaster, 1976), pp. 63, 68; Laqueur, op. cit., pp. 235–6.

26. Samuel, *East End Underworld*, pp. 26–7.

27. Laqueur, op. cit., p. 226.

28. An Old Potter, *When I was a Child* (1903), pp. 218–29, 236. See also S. J. D. Green, 'Religion and the Rise of the Common Man: Mutual Improvement Societies, Religious Associations and Popular Education in Three Industrial Towns in the West Riding of Yorkshire', in Derek Fraser (ed.), *Cities, Class and Communication* (Hemel Hempstead, 1990), pp. 25–44.

29. Steven Fielding, *Class and Ethnicity: Irish Catholics in England* (Buckingham, 1993), p. 64.

30. J. R. de S. Honey, *Tom Brown's Universe: The Victorian Public School* (1977).

31. Roberts, interview with Mrs D1B, p. 4 (informant born 1899, Barrow); and Mr S4P, p. 35 (informant born 1915, Preston).

32. Standish Meacham, *A World Apart* (1977), p. 53; P. J. Waller, *Democracy and Sectarianism: A Political and Social History of Liverpool, 1868–1939* (Liverpool, 1981), p. 238.

33. Roberts, interview with Mr C1P, pp. 88–9 (informant born 1884, Preston).

34. Bristol Oral History, interview no. 11, p. 12 (informant born 1897, Bristol).
35. Essex Oral History, interview no. 143, pp. 13–14, 48–9, 52 (informant born 1886, Dewsbury).
36. E. R. Dodds, *Missing Persons* (1977), p. 84.
37. Hugh McLeod, 'Building the "Catholic Ghetto": Catholic Organisations 1870–1914', in W. J. Sheils and Diana Wood (eds), *Voluntary Religion*, Studies in Church History, 23 (Oxford, 1986), pp. 441–3.
38. Obelkevich, op. cit., p. 201.
39. Bristol Oral History, interview no. 2, p. 13 (informant born 1899, Bristol); Roberts, interview with Mr T2P, p. 42 (informant born 1903, Preston); Essex Oral History, interview no. 368, p. 28 (informant born 1897, east London); Robert Moore, *Pit-men, Politics and Preachers* (1974), p. 70.
40. Frank Neal, *Sectarian Violence: The Liverpool Experience* (Manchester, 1988), p. 64; Bartlett, op. cit., p. 357; Gillian Rose, 'Locality, Politics and Culture: Poplar in the 1920s' (University of London PhD thesis, 1989), pp. 319–26; Bristol Oral History, interview no. 14, p. 3 (informant born 1895, Bristol).
41. Hugh McLeod, 'White Collar Values and the Role of Religion', in Geoffrey Crossick (ed.), *The Lower Middle Class in Britain, 1870–1914* (1977), p. 74; Peter Marsh, *Joseph Chamberlain: Entrepreneur in Politics* (New Haven, 1994), pp. 14–17, 25.
42. Essex Oral History, interview no. 348, p. 30 (informant born 1894, Mousehole).
43. Roberts, interview with Mr C1B, p. 18 (informant born 1900, Barrow).
44. Stan Shipley, 'The Boxer as Hero: A Study of Social Class, Community and the Professionalisation of the Sport in London, 1890–1905' (University of London PhD thesis, 1986), pp. 290–3; Edward Royle, *Radicals, Secularists and Republicans: Popular Freethought in Britain, 1866–1915* (Manchester, 1980), pp. 141–4; Geoffrey Alderman, *Modern British Jewry* (Oxford, 1992), p. 307.
45. Roberts, *Barrow and Lancaster*, pp. 63–4.
46. Douglas A. Reid, 'Religion, Recreation and the Working Class: Birmingham, 1844–1885', *Bulletin of the Society for the Study of Labour History*, 51 (1986), pp. 9–10.
47. Shipley, op. cit., p. 356; Roberts, *Barrow and Lancaster*, p. 64.

48. Roberts, interview with Mr G1P, pp. 82–3 (informant born 1903, Preston); Charles Booth, *Life and Labour of the People in London*, 17 vols (1902–3), 3rd series, vol. 1, pp. 96–8.

49. Roberts, interview with Mr M1B, p. 12 (informant born 1892, Barrow).

50. John Vincent, *Pollbooks: How Victorians Voted* (Cambridge, 1967).

51. Clyde Binfield, *So Down to Prayers: Studies in English Nonconformity, 1780–1920* (1977), p. 61; G. Kitson Clark, *The Making of Victorian England* (1962), p. 161.

52. Kenneth D. Wald, *Crosses on the Ballot* (Princeton, 1983), p. 197.

53. Jewish voting habits seem to have fluctuated more frequently than those of any other religious community. See Geoffrey Alderman, *The Jewish Community in British Politics* (Oxford, 1983); and *London Jewry and London Politics, 1889–1986* (1989).

54. Wald, op. cit., chs 7–8.

55. See D. W. Bebbington, *The Nonconformist Conscience* (1982); G. I. T. Machin, *Politics and the Churches in Great Britain, 1869 to 1921* (Oxford, 1987).

56. Fielding, op. cit., ch. 5.

57. Wald, op. cit., p. 197.

58. See Neal, op. cit.

59. Patrick Joyce, *Work, Society and Politics* (Brighton, 1980), pp. 250–62.

60. James Bentley, *Ritualism and Politics in Victorian Britain* (Oxford, 1978).

61. Theodore Koditschek, *Class Formation and Urban-Industrial Society: Bradford 1750–1850* (Cambridge, 1990), pp. 182–95.

62. Diane K. Drummond, *Crewe: Railway Town, Company and People, 1840–1914* (1994).

63. Jeffrey Cox, *English Churches in a Secular Society: Lambeth 1870–1930* (Oxford, 1982), p. 175.

64. Flora Thompson, *Lark Rise to Candleford* (1954), pp. 229–30 [first published 1939].

65. Roberts, *Barrow and Lancaster*, p. 69.

66. Joyce, op. cit., p. 254; Cox, op. cit., p. 159; Marsh, op. cit., p. 71.

67. Joyce, op. cit., pp. 254–61.

68. S. C. Carpenter, *Winnington-Ingram* (1949), pp. 155–7, 279–91; Alan Wilkinson, *The Church of England and the First World War* (1978), pp. 251–4. David Cannadine, *The Decline and*

Fall of the British Aristocracy (1992), p. 263, includes Winnington-Ingram in a group of Edwardian prelates whom he ridicules for their attempts to combine aristocratic or gentry origins with leftish political learnings. Winnington-Ingram seems to me out of place here: the fact that as Bishop of London he criticised slum housing hardly makes him a 'Christian Socialist', and the claim that he was anti-imperialist is clearly wrong.

69. Charles Dickens, *Little Dorrit* (1857), ch. 3.
70. George Gissing, *Born in Exile* (1970), pp. 288–9 [first published 1892].
71. An Old Potter, op. cit., pp. 1–9.
72. Essex Oral History, interview no. 339, pp. 33–4, 45 (informant born 1900, Keighley).
73. Edward Derrington, Journal, 27 November 1837; 13 March 1838 (Carr's Lane Collection, Birmingham Reference Library).
74. Hugh McLeod, *Piety and Poverty: Working Class Religion in Berlin, London and New York, 1870–1914* (New York, 1995), p. 158.
75. J. Wigley, *The Rise and Fall of the Victorian Sunday* (Manchester, 1980), p. 83.
76. Essex Oral History, interviews no. 348, p. 30 (informant born 1894, Mousehole); no. 188, pp. 5–6 (informant born 1882, Hastings); no. 359, p. 34 (informant born 1898, Charles, north Devon); Bristol Oral History, interview no. 30, pp. 3–4 (informant born 1898, Bristol).
77. D. H. Lawrence, *Selected Poems* (Harmondsworth, 1972), p. 21. See also the discussion in Jim Obelkevich, 'Music and Religion in the Nineteenth Century', in Jim Obelkevich, Lyndal Roper and Raphael Samuel (eds), *Disciplines of Faith* (1987), pp. 550–65.
78. J. Lawson, *Letters to the Young on Progress in Pudsey during the last Sixty Years* (Stanningley, 1887), pp. 33–4; Roberts, interview with Mrs S2B, p. 16 (informant born 1895, Barrow).
79. E. P. Thompson, *The Making of the English Working Class* (2nd edn., Harmondsworth, 1968), pp. 639–40; Alun Howkins, *Poor Labouring Men* (1985), p. 39. See also Nigel Scotland, *Methodism and the Revolt of the Field: A Study of the Methodist Contribution to Agricultural Trade Unionism in East Anglia, 1872–96* (Gloucester, 1981).

80. Essex Oral History, interview no. 235, p. 12 (informant born 1899, south London).
81. Howkins, op. cit. pp. 140–1.
82. Helen Corke, *D. H. Lawrence: The Croydon Years* (Austin, 1965), p. 61.
83. Edward Derrington, Journal, 21 February 1838 (Birmingham Reference Library, Local History Collection), W. Cooke-Taylor, *Notes of a Tour of the Manufacturing Districts of Lancashire* (1842), pp. 301–2.
84. Essex Oral History, interviews no. 354, pp. 37–8 (informant born 1897, Trumpatory, south Devon); no. 359, p. 31 (informant born 1898, Charles north Devon); no. 339, p. 34 (informant born 1900, Keighley); Bristol Oral History, interview no. 34, p. 7 (informant born 1895, Bristol).
85. F. Linden, *Sozialismus und Religion* (Leipzig, 1932), pp. 139, 163.
86. Susan Budd, *Varieties of Unbelief* (1977), p. 107.
87. Warren Sylvester Smith, *The London Heretics, 1870–1914* (1967), pp. 61–7. See also the discussion in Joss Lutz Marsh, '"Bibliolatry" and "Bible-Smashing": G. W. Foote, George Meredith and the Heretic Trope of the Book', *Victorian Studies*, 34 (1990–1), pp. 315–36.
88. Essex Oral History, interview no. 149, p. 45 (informant born 1900, Keighley).
89. Ibid., interview no. 206 (informant born 1903, Oakworth). See also discussion in Joyce, op. cit., pp. 175–7.
90. Honey, op. cit., p. 313.
91. R. Dahl, *Boy* (Harmondsworth, 1986), pp. 144–6. See also J. A. Mangan, 'Social Darwinism and Upper-class Education in Late Victorian and Edwardian England', in J. A. Mangan and James Walvin (eds), *Manliness and Morality: Middle Class Masculinity in Britain and America, 1800–1940* (Manchester, 1987).
92. Olive Anderson, 'The Growth of Christian Militarism in Mid-Victorian Britain', *English Historical Review*, 86 (1971), pp. 56–68.
93. Essex Oral History, interview no. 313, pp. 19, 75 (informant born 1897, Shalford, Essex).
94. Peter d'A. Jones, *The Christian Socialist Revival, 1877–1914* (Princeton, 1968), p. 24; Bartlett, op. cit., p. 365; Hugh McLeod, *Class and Religion in the Late Victorian City* (1974), p. 119.

95. Bruce Coleman, 'The Church Extension Movement in London, c.1800–1860' (University of Cambridge PhD thesis, 1968), p. 182; Simon Green, 'The Death of Pew-Rents, the Rise of Bazaars, and the End of the Traditional Political Economy of Voluntary Religious Organisations: The Case of the West Riding of Yorkshire, c.1870–1914', *Northern History*, 27 (1991), p. 211.

96. Ibid., pp. 210–11; Alderman, *British Jewry*, pp. 103–6.

97. Essex Oral History, interviews no. 143, p. 48 (informant born 1886, Dewsbury); no. 91, p. 31 (informant born 1894, Guildford).

98. William Haslam Mills, *Grey Pastures* (1924), pp. 9–10, 35–40.

99. Moore, *Pit-men*, pp. 161–8.

100. Hugh McLeod, *Religion and the Working Class in Nineteenth-Century Britain* (Basingstoke, 1984), pp. 46–7; Logie Barrow, *Independent Spirits: Spiritualism and English Plebeians, 1850–1910* (1986), pp. 112–24; Peter Ackers, 'West End Chapel, Back Street Bethel', forthcoming in *Journal of Ecclesiastical History*.

101. Eileen Yeo, 'Christianity in Chartist Struggle, 1838–42', *Past and Present*, 91 (1981), pp. 109–39; Scotland, op. cit.; McLeod, *Class and Religion*, p. 63.

102. The prominent First World War Conscientious Objector Stephen Hobhouse was so successful in persuading his fervently pro-War mother that war was inconsistent with the New Testament that she abandoned Christianity.

103. David Hilliard, 'UnEnglish and Unmanly: Anglo-Catholicism and Homosexuality', *Victorian Studies*, 25 (1981–2), pp. 198–200. See also E. R. Norman, *The Victorian Christian Socialists* (Cambridge, 1987).

104. Scotland, op. cit., pp. 57–74. For a local study, see R. W. Ambler, *Ranters, Revivalists and Reformers: Primitive Methodism and Rural Society in South Lincolnshire, 1817–1875* (Hull, 1989), pp. 81–5.

105. Scotland, op. cit., p. 89.

106. Norman, op. cit., p. 70.

107. Scotland, op. cit., p. 63.

108. Howkins, op. cit., ch. 3.

109. E. P. Thompson, 'Homage to Tom Maguire', in Asa Briggs and John Saville (eds), *Essays in Labour History* (1960), p. 289.

110. Jill Liddington, *The Life and Times of a Respectable Radical*

(1984), pp. 37–8; Moore, *Pit-men*, p. 170.

111. Thompson, 'Tom Maguire', pp. 289–90; D. F. Summers, 'The Labour Church and Allied Movements of the Late 19th and Early 20th Centuries' (University of Edinburgh PhD thesis, 1958), pp. 236–42; Henry Pelling, *The Origins of the Labour Party, 1880–1900* (2nd edn. Oxford, 1965), p. 140.

112. See Linden, op. cit. Eric Hobsbawm argues in 'Religion and the Rise of Socialism', in his collection of essays, *Worlds of Labour* (1984), p. 33 that 'there was no important working-class Christian socialism, merely the standard socialism, elaborated by secular thinkers and translated into the familiar biblical terminology'. However, I am more convinced by those who have argued that the large Christian influence on the British labour movement had an important influence on the way in which it developed. See (for a mainly positive assessment) A. Ainsworth, 'Religion in the Working Class Community and the Evolution of Socialism in Late Nineteenth Century Lancashire', *Histoire Sociale*, 10 (1977), pp. 354–80; and (mainly negative) William Knox, 'Religion and the Scottish Labour Movement', *Journal of Contemporary History*, 23 (1988), pp. 609–30.

113. Bristol Oral History, interview no. 1, pp. 2, 9–10, 14. See also interviews no. 9 (informant born 1899, Bristol), and no. 10 (informant born 1895, Bristol).

114. See the collection in Birmingham Reference Library. Also, Geoffrey Robson, 'The Failures of Success: Working Class Evangelists in Early Victorian Birmingham', in D. Baker (ed.), *Religious Motivation*, Studies in Church History, 15 (Cambridge, 1978); J. A. Burdett, 'A Study of the Relationship between Evangelical Urban Missionaries and the Working Class Poor in Birmingham, Norwich and Edinburgh, c.1830–1860' (University of Birmingham M. Phil. thesis, 1994).

115. K. S. Inglis, *Churches and the Working Classes in Victorian England* (1963), pp. 194–9.

116. Essex Oral History, interview no. 245, pp. 10, 24–8.

117. Howkins, op. cit., p. 33.

118. Essex Oral History, interview no. 222, p. 40 (informant born 1904, Nottingham).

119. Ibid,, interview no. 304, p. 37 (informant born 1902, Darlington); John Fletcher, interview with Louise Cook

(A. J. Cook's sister), 29 September 1977 (tape in his possession).

120. Essex Oral History, interviews no. 354, p. 42 (informant born 1897, Trumpatery); no. 250, p. 50 (informant born 1905, Newcastle upon Tyne).

121. James Obelkevich, *Religion in Rural Society: South Lindsey 1825–1875*, ch. 6; H. C. Keiner, 'Clergy and Community: The Church of England in Buckinghamshire, 1830–1914' (University of Connecticut PhD thesis, 1981); Michael Snape, '"Our Happy Reformation", The Church of England in the Parish of Whalley, 1688–1791' (University of Birmingham PhD thesis, 1994).

122. See Keith Thomas, 'The Double Standard', *Journal of the History of Ideas*, 20 (1959), pp. 195–216.

123. Judith R. Walkowitz, *Prostitution and Victorian Society* (Cambridge, 1980), pp. 21–5; John R. Gillis, 'Servants, Sexual Relations and the Risks of Illegitimacy in London, 1801–1900', in Judith L. Newton, Mary P. Ryan and Judith R. Walkowitz (eds), *Sex and Class in Women's History* (1983), p. 132.

124. [T. H. S. Escott] *Society in London* (1885), pp. 108–9.

125. See Walkowitz, op. cit.; Paul McHugh, *Prostitution and Victorian Social Reform* (1980).

126. Ibid., p. 17.

127. John Vincent, *The Formation of the Liberal Party, 1857–1868* (1966), pp. 3–5.

128. Tressell, op. cit., pp. 170–1

129. Malcolm Kirby, 'The Failure of a Quaker Business Dynasty', in David Jeremy (ed.), *Business and Religion in Britain* (Aldershot, 1988), pp. 157–8.

130. E. N. Bennett, *Problems of Village Life* (1913), p. 136.

Notes to Chapter 3: Signs of the Times

1. Article on Butler in *Dictionary of National Biography*.

2. Paul McHugh, *Prostitution and Victorian Social Reform* (1980), pp. 175–6.

3. Ibid., p. 187.

4. Lilian Lewis Shiman, *Women and Leadership in Nineteenth Century England* (Basingstoke, 1992), p. 184.

5. Ibid., p. 147.
6. D. W. Bebbington, *The Nonconformist Conscience* (1982), pp. 38–42.
7. K. S. Inglis, *Churches and the Working Classes in Victorian England* (1963), p. 288.
8. Dorothea Price Hughes, *The Life of Hugh Price Hughes* (1907), pp. 75–6.
9. John Kent, 'Hugh Price Hughes and the Nonconformist Conscience', in G. V. Bennett and J. D. Walsh (eds), *Essays in Modern English Church History* (1966), pp. 181–205.
10. Hughes, op. cit., p. 349; see also Bebbington, op. cit. p. 12.
11. Hughes, op. cit., p. 557.
12. Norman Grubb, *C. T. Studd, Cricketer and Pioneer* (1933), p. 45.
13. Ibid., chs 10, 13 and 16.
14. Ibid., pp. 52–4, 125.
15. See Deryck Lovegrove, *Established Church, Sectarian People* (Cambridge, 1988).
16. Essex Oral History, interview no. 143, p. 24 (informant born 1886, Dewsbury).
17. Donald M. Lewis, *Lighten their Darkness: The Evangelical Mission to Working-Class London, 1828–1860* (Westport, Conn., 1986), pp. 49–50.
18. Hugh McLeod, *Class and Religion in the Late Victorian City* (1974), p. 104.
19. E. R. Wickham, *Church and People in an Industrial City* (1957), p. 87.
20. Thomas Wright, *The Great Unwashed* (1868), as quoted in Gerald Parsons (ed.), *Religion in Victorian Britain*, 4 vols (Manchester, 1988), vol. 3, pp. 321–2.
21. See, for instance, the excerpts from the diary of the London missionary J. Oppenheimer, in Lewis, op. cit., pp. 131–49.
22. See J. A. Burdett, 'A Study of the Relationship between Evangelical Urban Missionaries and the Working Class Poor in Birmingham, Norwich and Edinburgh, c.1830–1860' (University of Birmingham M. Phil. thesis, 1994).
23. Inglis, op. cit., pp. 194–9.
24. See Frank Prochaska, 'Body and Soul: Bible Nurses and the Poor in Victorian London', *Historical Research*, 60 (1987), pp. 336–48.
25. David M. Thompson, 'The Emergence of the Nonconformist Social Gospel in England', in Keith Robbins (ed.), *Protes-*

tant Evangelicalism (Oxford, 1990), pp. 255–80; D. Bowen, *The Idea of the Victorian Church* (Montreal, 1968).

26. Alan Bartlett, 'The Churches in Bermondsey, 1880–1939' (University of Birmingham PhD thesis, 1987), p. 261.
27. Ibid., p. 264.
28. Ibid., pp. 261–85.
29. Brian Stanley, *The Bible and the Flag* (Leicester, 1990), pp. 78–84.
30. Ibid., pp. 60–1.
31. Stephen Neill, *Christian Missions* (Harmondsworth, 1964), p. 253.
32. John Taylor, 'The Future of Christianity', in John McManners (ed.), *The Oxford Illustrated History of Christianity* (Oxford, 1990), p. 636.
33. *The Church Missionary Atlas* (1896), pp. vii–xi.
34. Susan Thorne, 'Protestant Ethics and the Spirit of Imperialism: British Congregationalists and the London Missionary Society' (University of Michigan PhD thesis, 1990), pp. 95–6.
35. Ibid., pp. 98–9.
36. Ibid., p. 90.
37. Ibid., p. 165.
38. R. Oliver, *The Missionary Factor in East African History* (1952); Holger Hansen, 'Mission and Colonialism in Uganda: A Case Study in Forced Labour', in T. Christensen and William R. Hutchinson (eds), *Missionary Ideologies in the Imperialist Era: 1880–1920* (Aarhus, 1982), pp. 104–17; A. E. Afigbo, 'Christian Mission and Secular Authorities in South-eastern Nigeria from Colonial Times', in O. U. Kalu (ed.), *The History of Christianity in West Africa* (1980), pp. 187–8.
39. C. A. Oddie, 'India and Missionary Motives 1850–1900', *Journal of Ecclesiastical History*, 25 (1974), p. 69.
40. Stanley, op. cit., p. 67.
41. Goeffrey Moorhouse, *The Missionaries* (1973), pp. 229–30; *Church Missionary Atlas*, p. 32. See also David Hilliard, 'The Making of an Anglican Martyr: Bishop John Coleridge Patteson of Melanesia', in Diana Wood (ed.), *Martyrs and Martyrologies*, Studies in Church History, 30 (Oxford, 1993), pp. 333–45.
42. J. A. Mangan, *The Games Ethic and Imperialism* (Harmondsworth, 1986), pp. 172–7.

43. J. A. Mangan, *Athleticism and the Victorian and Edwardian Public School* (Cambridge, 1981), ch. 4.

44. James Walvin, *Leisure and Society, 1830–1950* (1978), p. 87; Stan Shipley, 'The Boxer as Hero: A study of Social Class, Community and the Professionalisation of Sport in London, 1890–1905' (University of London PhD thesis, 1986), pp. 251–3, 290–300, 334–56.

45. Norman Vance, *The Sinews of the Spirit* (Cambridge, 1985).

46. Mangan, *Athleticism*, p. 27.

47. Grubb, op. cit., p. 57.

48. Mangan, *Games Ethic*, pp. 168–92 (discussing the role of missionaries in propagating the games ethic).

49. Olive Anderson, 'The Growth of Christian Militarism in Mid-Victorian Britain', *English Historical Review*, 86 (1971), pp. 46–72.

50. John Springhall, *Youth, Empire and Society* (1977), p. 37.

51. Ibid., illustration 7.

52. John Springhall, 'Building Character in the British Boy: The Attempt to Extend Christian Manliness to Working-class Adolescents, 1880–1914', in J. A. Mangan and James Walvin (eds), *Manliness and Morality: Middle-Class Masculinity in Britain and America, 1800–1940* (Manchester, 1987), p. 53.

53. Ibid., p. 66.

54. Anderson, op. cit., pp. 50–2.

55. Hughes, op. cit., p. 349.

56. Hugh McLeod, *Piety and Poverty: Working Class Religion in Berlin, London and New York, 1870–1914* (New York, 1995), p. 155.

57. This paragraph is based on David Hilliard, 'Un-English and Unmanly: Anglo-Catholicism and Homosexuality', *Victorian Studies*, 25 (1981–2), pp. 181–210.

58. Clive Field, 'Adam and Eve: Gender in the English Free Church Constituency, 1650–1980', *Journal of Ecclesiastical History*, 44 (1993), pp. 63–79.

59. Jane Rendall, *The Origins of Modern Feminism: Women in Britain, France and the United States, 1780–1860* (Basingstoke, 1985), pp. 74–7.

60. Bartlett, op. cit., pp. 185–6, 194–5.

61. Booth Collection, B185, p. 173.

62. Rickie Burman, '"She Looketh well to the Ways of her Household": The Changing Role of Jewish Women in

Religious Life, c.1880–1930', in Gail Malmgreen (ed.), *Religion in the Lives of English Women, 1760–1930* (1986), pp. 231–59.

63. Ibid., p. 250.
64. John Angell James, *Female Piety* (1852), pp. 16–17.
65. Mary Ryan, *Cradle of the Middle Class* (Cambridge, 1981), pp. 78–98.
66. Clyde Binfield, *So Down to Prayers: Studies in English Non-conformity, 1780–1920* (1977), pp. 71–3.
67. James, op. cit., p. 62.
68. See J. K. Hopkins, *A Woman to Deliver her People* (Austin, 1982).
69. Deborah Valenze, *Prophetic Sons and Daughters: Female Preaching and Popular Religion in Industrial England* (Princeton, 1985); Dorothy Graham, 'Chosen by God: The Female Itinerants of Early Primitive Methodism' (University of Birmingham PhD thesis, 1987).
70. Elizabeth Isichei, *Victorian Quakers* (Oxford, 1970), pp. 94–5, 107–9.
71. Olive Banks, *Faces of Feminism* (Oxford, 1981), pp. 23–6.
72. Judith R. Walkowitz, *Prostitution and Victorian Society* (Cambridge, 1980), p. 122; McHugh, op. cit., p. 191.
73. Glenn K. Horridge, *The Salvation Army: Origins and Early Days, 1865–1900* (Godalming, 1993), pp. 23, 116; Pamela J. Walker, 'Proclaiming Women's Right to Preach', *Harvard Divinity Bulletin*, 23:3/4 (1994), pp. 20–3, 35.
74. Olive Anderson, 'Women Preachers in Mid-Victorian Britain', *Historical Journal*, 12 (1969), pp. 467–8.
75. Donald M. Lewis, '"Lights in Dark Places": Women Evangelists in Early Victorian Britain, 1838–57', in W. J. Sheils and Diana Wood (eds), *Women in the Church*, Studies in Church History, 27 (Oxford, 1990), p. 415; Anderson, 'Women Preachers', pp. 470–3; Brian Heeney, *The Women's Movement in the Church of England, 1850–1930* (Oxford, 1988), pp. 120–5.
76. Peter Williams, '"The Missing Link": The Recruitment of Women Missionaries in some English Evangelical Missionary Societies in the Nineteenth Century', in Fiona Bowie, Deborah Kirkwood and Shirley Ardener (eds), *Women and Missions, Past and Present* (Providence, 1993), pp. 45–55.
77. Stanley, op. cit., p. 80; Heeney, op. cit., pp. 60–2.
78. Susan O'Brien, 'Terra Incognita: The Nun in Nineteenth-

Century England', *Past and Present*, 121 (1988), p. 111. See also H. C. B. Stone, 'Constraints on Mother Superiors: Anglican and Roman Catholic Sisterhoods, c.1850–1900' (University of Leeds PhD thesis, 1993).

79. Ibid., pp. 110–12.
80. Hugh McLeod, 'Building the "Catholic Ghetto": Catholic Organisations 1870–1914', in W. J. Sheils and D. Wood (eds), *Voluntary Religion*, Studies in Church History, 23 (Oxford, 1986), pp. 411–44.
81. Elaine Kaye, 'A Turning-point in the Ministry of Women', in Sheils and Wood (eds), *Women in the Church*, pp. 505–12.
82. Heeney, op. cit., pp. 128–9.

Notes to Chapter 4: The Religious Crisis

1. Booth Collection, B287, pp. 5–7.
2. Hugh McLeod, *Class and Religion in the Late Victorian City* (1974), p. 233.
3. Jeffrey Cox, *English Churches in a Secular Society: Lambeth 1870–1930* (Oxford, 1982), p. 224.
4. Religious Worship (England and Wales), *Parliamentary Papers*, 1852–3, vol. 89, p. clviii.
5. Robin Gill, *The Myth of the Empty Church* (1993), p. 313.
6. Ibid., p. 303.
7. Hugh McLeod, 'White Collar Values and the Role of Religion', in Geoffrey Crossick (ed.), *The Lower Middle Class in Britain, 1870–1914* (1977), pp. 87–8.
8. Gill, op. cit., p. 322.
9. Ibid., p. 161.
10. McLeod, *Class and Religion*, p. 232.
11. Gill, op. cit; Robert Currie, *Methodism Divided* (1968); A. D. Gilbert, *Religion and Society in Industrial England* (1976).
12. E. N. Bennett, *Problems of Village Life* (1913), p. 122.
13. W. K. Lowther-Clarke, *Facing the Facts, or An Englishman's Religion* (1912), pp. 154, 161.
14. Gill, op. cit., p. 37.
15. See Robert Currie, Alan Gilbert and Lee Horsley, *Churches and Churchgoers: Patterns of Church Growth in the British Isles since 1700* (Oxford, 1977).
16. McLeod, *Class and Religion*, p. 258.

17. Gilbert, *Religion and Society*, p. 32.
18. Ibid., pp. 42–4; Currie, Gilbert and Horsley, op. cit., p. 157.
19. James Obelkevich, *Religion in Rural Society: South Lindsey 1825–1875* (Oxford, 1976), p. 139; Roy Jenkins, *Sir Charles Dilke* (1958), p. 24.
20. Gill, op. cit., pp. 16–18.
21. J. Wigley, *The Rise and Fall of the Victorian Sunday* (Manchester, 1980) pp. 83–4.
22. John Lowerson, 'Sport and the Victorian Sunday: The Beginnings of Middle Class Apostasy', *British Journal of Sports History*, 1 (1984), pp. 202–20.
23. W. L. Courtney (ed.), *Do we Believe?* (1905), pp. 1–4.
24. A useful guide to current thinking in this much disputed area is Steve Bruce (ed.), *Religion and Modernization: Historians and Sociologists debate the Secularization Thesis* (Oxford, 1992).
25. McLeod, 'White Collar Values', pp. 86–8.
26. McLeod, *Class and Religion*, p. 314.
27. McLeod, 'White Collar Values', pp. 87–8.
28. George Gissing, *Born in Exile* (1970), p. 119 [first published 1892].
29. Frank M. Turner, 'The Victorian Crisis of Faith and the Faith that was Lost', in Richard J. Helmstadter and Bernard Lightman (eds), *Victorian Faith in Crisis* (Basingstoke, 1990), pp. 9–39.
30. Susan Budd, *Varieties of Unbelief* (1977), ch. 5.
31. A useful brief summary of the impact of new developments in biblical interpretation is Gerald Parsons, 'Biblical Criticism in Victorian Britain: From Controversy to Acceptance', in Parsons (ed.), *Religion in Victorian Britain*, 4 vols (Manchester, 1988), vol. 2, pp. 237–57. However, very little study seems to have been made of changes in popular understanding of the Bible, as opposed to changes in the views of scholars.
32. For an overview, see John Hedley Brooke, *Science and Religion* (Cambridge, 1991). For the impact of Comte, see T. R. Wright, *The Religion of Humanity* (Cambridge, 1986).
33. Geoffrey Rowell, *Hell and the Victorians* (1974).
34. Courtney (ed.), op. cit., pp. 189–90.
35. Ibid., pp. 136–7.
36. Ibid., pp. 149–50, 159, 161.
37. Ibid., pp. 211–13.

38. See Hugh McLeod, *Piety and Poverty: Working Class Religion in Berlin, London and New York, 1870–1914* (New York, 1995), ch. 6.
39. Edward Royle, *Radicals, Secularists and Republicans: Popular Freethought in Britain, 1866–1915* (Manchester, 1980), ch. 9.
40. Budd, op. cit., p. 133.
41. Ibid., pp. 146–9.
42. Owen Chadwick, *The Secularization of the European Mind in the Nineteenth Century* (Cambridge, 1975), ch. 7.
43. E. E. Kellett, *As I Remember* (1936), pp. 105–6.
44. Parsons, 'Biblical Criticism'.
45. I. Ellis, *Seven against Christ* (Leiden, 1980).
46. J. Carpenter, *Charles Gore: A Study in Liberal Catholicism* (1960).
47. Clyde Binfield, 'Chapels in Crisis', *Transactions of the Congregational Historical Society*, 20 (1968), p. 246.
48. Ibid., p. 254.
49. Clyde Binfield, '"We claim our part in the great inheritance": The Message of Four Congregational Buildings', in Keith Robbins (ed.), *Protestant Evangelicalism: Britain, Ireland, Germany and America c.1750–c.1950* (Oxford, 1990), pp. 201–24.
50. Patricia Stallings Kruppa, *Charles Haddon Spurgeon: A Preacher's Progress* (New York, 1982), pp. 429–44.
51. D. W. Bebbington, 'The Persecution of George Jackson: A British Fundamentalist Controversy', in W. J. Sheils (ed.), *Persecution and Tolerance*, Studies in Church History, 21 (Oxford, 1984), pp. 421–33.
52. D. W. Bebbington, 'Baptists and Fundamentalism in Inter-War Britain', in Robbins (ed.), op. cit., p. 326.
53. Peter Ackers, 'West End Chapel, Back Street Bethel', forthcoming in *Journal of Ecclesiastical History*.
54. Alan Haig, *The Victorian Clergy* (1984), p. 3; Owen Chadwick, *The Victorian Church*, 2 vols (1966–70), vol. 2, p. 249.
55. Philip Hesketh, 'C. F. G. Masterman' (University of London PhD thesis, 1994).
56. John Kent, *William Temple* (Cambridge, 1992), p. 13.
57. Alan Haig, 'The Church, the Universities and Learning in Later Victorian England', *Historical Journal*, 29 (1986), pp. 187–201.
58. Currie, Gilbert and Horsley, op. cit., pp. 203–12. See also Kenneth D. Brown, *A Social History of the Nonconformist*

Ministry in England and Wales 1800–1930 (Oxford, 1988), pp. 222–4.

59. Bartlett, 'The Churches in Bermondsey, 1880–1939' (University of Birmingham PhD thesis, 1987), p. 120.

60. Ibid., pp. 133–178.

61. J. N. Morris, *Religion and Urban Change: Croydon 1840–1914* (Woodbridge, 1992), p. 183.

62. Stephen Yeo, *Religion and Voluntary Organisations in Crisis* (1976), p. 149.

63. Among the main works relating the development of sport and of mass gambling to its social context during this period are Tony Mason, *Association Football and English Society, 1863–1915* (Brighton, 1980); Stan Shipley, 'The Boxer as Hero: A Study of Social Class, Community and the Professionalisation of the Sport in London, 1890–1905' (University of London PhD thesis, 1986); Carl Chinn, *Better Betting with a Decent Feller* (Brighton, 1991); John Lowerson, *Sport and the English Middle Classes* (Manchester, 1993). For longer perspectives, see Tony Mason (ed.), *Sport in Britain: A Social History* (Cambridge, 1989); Richard Holt, *Sport and the British* (Oxford, 1989).

64. David Rubinstein, 'Cycling in the 1890s', *Victorian Studies*, 21 (1977–8), pp. 47–71.

65. James Walvin, *Leisure and Society, 1830–1950* (1978), pp. 109–11.

66. *Daily Telegraph*, 6 October 1905.

67. Lowerson, *Sport and the Middle Classes*, pp. 224–5.

68. J. A. Mangan, *Athleticism and the Victorian and Edwardian Public School* (Cambridge, 1981).

69. Lowerson, *Sport and the Middle Classes*, pp. 271–2.

70. Ibid., pp. 17–19.

71. Harold Larwood, *The Larwood Story* (Harmondsworth, 1985), p. 25; John Lowerson, 'Golf', in Mason (ed.), *Sport in Britain*, p. 187; Christopher Nottingham, 'More Important than Life or Death: Football, The British Working Class and the Social Order', in Lex Heerma van Voss and Fritz Holthoon (eds), *Working Class and Popular Culture* (Amsterdam, 1988), pp. 147–8.

72. *Minutes of the Wesleyan Conference* (1890), pp. 353–4.

73. On changes in the life-style of industrialists, see Yeo, op. cit., pp. 102–7. For the rather jaudiced views of a contemporary clergyman, see William Gascoyne-Cecil, 'The Upper

Classes: The Old Squire and the New', in Lowther-Clarke (ed.), pp. 48–50.

74. See G. Kitson Clark, *Churchmen and the Condition of England, 1832–85* (1973).
75. Pamela Horn, 'The Labourers' Union in Oxfordshire', in J. P. Dunbabin, *Rural Discontent in Nineteenth-Century Britain* (1974), p. 97.
76. Bennett, op. cit., pp. 129–31.
77. Haig, *Victorian Clergy*, p. 297.
78. Chadwick, *Victorian Church*, vol. 2, p. 170.
79. Gascoyne-Cecil, 'The Old Squire and the New', in Lowther-Clarke (ed.), op. cit., pp. 29–54.
80. For overviews of the connections between rising class-consciousness and alienation from the church in various parts of Europe, see Eric Hobsbawm, 'Religion and the Rise of Socialism', in his *Worlds of Labour* (1984), pp. 33–48; Hugh McLeod, 'The Dechristianisation of the Working Class in Western Europe, c.1850–1900', *Social Compass*, 27 (1980), pp. 191–214.
81. Robert Moore, *Pit-men, Politics and Preachers* (1974), pp. 155–68.
82. See, for instance, the comments on links between Nonconformist ministers and employers in Bradford in E. P. Thompson, 'Homage to Tom Maguire', in Asa Briggs and John Saville (eds), *Essays in Labour History* (1960), pp. 289–90.
83. Stephen Yeo, 'The Religion of Socialism in Britain 1883–96', *History Workshop Journal*, 4 (1977), pp. 5–56.
84. E. J. Hobsbawm, *Primitive Rebels* (2nd edn, Manchester, 1970), pp. 142–5.
85. D. F. Summers, 'The Labour Church and Allied Movements of the Late Nineteenth and Early Twentieth Centuries' (University of Edinburgh PhD thesis, 1958), pp. 687–90.
86. Bristol Oral History, interview no. 34, pp. 47–8 (informant born 1895, Bristol).
87. Roberts, interview with Mr C1P, pp. 20, 71 (informant born 1884, Preston).
88. Summers, op. cit., p. 468; S. J. D. Green, 'Religion and the Rise of the Common Man', in Derek Fraser (ed.), *Cities, Class and Communication* (Hemel Hempstead, 1990), pp. 38–9.
89. Peter T. Marsh, *Joseph Chamberlain, Entrepreneur in Politics*

(New Haven, 1994), p. 87; Cox, op. cit., pp. 188–90.

90. Ibid., pp. 162–75.
91. For Beveridge, see Standish Meacham, *Toynbee Hall* (1987), pp. 130–54; for Aves, see McLeod, *Class and Religion*, pp. 250–3.
92. Cox, op. cit., ch. 6.
93. Frank M. Turner, 'The Victorian Conflict between Religion and Science: A Professional Dimension', in Parsons (ed.), op. cit., vol. 4, pp. 170–97.
94. Ibid., pp. 172–3.
95. Judith R. Walkowitz, *Prostitution and Victorian Society* (Cambridge, 1980) p. 85.
96. R. J. Morris, *Cholera 1832* (1976); John Wolffe, *God and Greater Britain: Religion and National Life in Britain and Ireland, 1843–1945* (1994), p. 120.
97. Cf. Kenneth D. Brown, 'Nonconformity and the British Labour Movement', *Journal of Social History*, 8 (1975), pp. 116–18.
98. G. I. T. Machin, *Politics and the Churches in Great Britain, 1869 to 1921* (Oxford, 1987), pp. 2–3.
99. Cox, op. cit., pp. 238–42; N. Blewett, *The Peers, the Parties and the People* (1972), pp. 346–9.
100. See, for instance, the account of the divisions in early twentieth-century Durham Methodism in Moore, *Pit-men, Politics and Preachers.*
101. Stephen Koss, *Nonconformity in Modern British Politics* (1975), p. 184 and passim.

APPENDIX

1851 RELIGIOUS CENSUS

TABLE 1 *Total reported attendances at services in England*

	Attendances	As % of churchgoers	As % of population
Church of England	5,102,845	51.5	30.5
Wesleyans	1,440,962	14.4	8.6
Independents	997,830	10.1	6.0
Baptists	759,508	7.7	4.5
Primitive Methodists	497,112	5.0	3.0
Roman Catholics	375,257	3.8	2.1
Other Methodists	355,748	3.6	2.1
Presbyterians	80,510	0.8	0.5
Unitarians	46,249	0.5	0.3
Countess of Huntingdon	43,592	0.4	0.3
Mormons	28,874	0.3	0.2
Quakers	28,333	0.3	0.2
Brethren	17,276	0.2	0.1
Moravians	10,594	0.1	0.1
Swedenborgians	10,352	0.1	0.1
Jews	5,952	0.1	0.1
Others	112,798	1.1	0.7
Total	9,913,792	100	59.4

Appendix

TABLE 2 *Registration Districts with the highest and lowest Indices of Attendance: Attendances as percentage of population*

Highest

All denominations
St Ives (Hunts) 116.4, Luton (Beds) 115.2, Warminster (Wilts) 110.2, Dursley (Glos) 109.4, Bedford (Beds) 109.2, Royston (Herts) 108.9, Fordingbridge (Hants) 108.4, Westbury (Wilts) 107.9, St Neots (Hunts) 107.0, Scilly Isles (Cornwall) 106.6.

Church of England
Catherington (Hants) 69.0, Wilton (Wilts) 68.9, Brackley (Northants) 66.9, Warminster (Wilts) 66.2, Blandford (Dorset) 64.9, Marlborough (Wilts) 64.4, Amesbury (Wilts) 63.6, Droxford (Hants) 63.5, St. Faiths (Norfolk) 63.2, Alresford (Hants) 62.7.

Nonconformists
Luton (Beds) 85.9, Leighton Buzzard (Beds) 78.3, Westbury (Wilts) 75.3, Melksham (Wilts) 72.8, St Ives (Hunts) 71.3, North Witchford (Cambs) 69.2, Dursley (Glos) 66.2, Bedford (Beds) 63.4, Braintree (Essex) 62.7, Amersham (Bucks) 62.1.

Roman Catholics
Garstang (Lancs) 19.1, Chorley (Lancs) 16.4, Liverpool (Lancs) 15.6, Clitheroe (Lancs) 13.5, Cheadle (Staffs) 12.3, West Derby (Lancs) 11.8, Preston (Lancs) 11.2, Prescot (Lancs) 10.8, Wigan (Lancs) 10.2, Manchester (Lancs) 9.5.
(If districts of London are included, St George's, Southwark 12.5, and St Olave 10.2, would also be counted in this list. To do this would, however, be misleading, since most other cities are largely, or entirely, contained within a single Registration District, with rich and poor areas, areas of different ethnic composition, etc., mixed together; only in London does each area of the city form a separate Registration District.)

Lowest

All denominations
Longtown (Cumbs) 15.9, Haltwhistle (Northumbs) 24.2, Wigton (Cumbs) 24.4, Brampton (Cumbs) 24.5, Radford (Notts) 25.8, Chester le Street (Durham) 27.9, Stafford (Staffs) 28.1, Meriden (Warwicks) 30.8, Kings Norton (Worcs) 30.9, Rothbury (Northumbs) 31.4.
(If districts of London are included, the following would also be counted in this list: Shoreditch 18.5, St George's in the East 23.6, Bethnal Green 26.0, Strand 27.7 Clerkenwell 27.7.)

BIBLIOGRAPHY

One way of tracing the evolving historiography of religion and society in Victorian and Edwardian England is to look at four works of synthesis: G. Kitson Clark, *The Making of Victorian England* (1962); A. D. Gilbert, *Religion and Society in Industrial England, 1740–1914: Church, Chapel and Social Change* (1976); Gerald Parsons (ed.), *Religion in Victorian Britain*, 4 vols (Manchester, 1988); and the present book, completed in 1994.

Kitson Clark's review of 'some of the factors which might be said to have created Victorian England' was notable for the amount of space devoted to religion, and also for the paucity of recent research which he was able to draw upon. There was in fact already a considerable body of literature on the 'Victorian crisis of faith', including, for instance, *Ideas and Beliefs of the Victorians* (1949); H. R. Murphy, 'The Ethical Revolt against Christian Orthodoxy in Early Victorian England', *American Historical Review*, 60 (1955); Basil Willey, *More Victorian Studies: Some Honest Doubters* (1956); and various studies of agnosticism by Noel Annan, who has recently returned to the theme with *Leslie Stephen, the Godless Victorian* (Chicago, 1984).

Arguing that these intellectual developments had relatively little impact on the mass of the people, Kitson Clark concentrated on such themes as the religious ignorance or alienation of the poor, revivals, temperance and the rise of Dissent, the reorganisation of the Church of England, the drive to provide a fast-growing population with churches and schools, and the influence of religion on the rise of the labour movement. In doing so he drew, to a considerable extent, on primary sources and on denominational histories, often written many years earlier, but he also made a lot of use of research in progress. For instance, in discussing revivalism, he drew on the work of John Kent, eventually published as *Holding the Fort* (1978), one of the most brilliant, and most sharply critical, studies of Victorian religion – more sympathetic is Richard Carwardine, *Transatlantic Revivalism* (Westport, Conn., 1979).

In his discussion of working-class religion or irreligion he was able to draw on K. S. Inglis's then unpublished work, which became *Churches and the Working Classes in Victorian England* (1963), as well as on E. R. Wickham's study of Sheffield, *Church and People in an Industrial City* (1957). These two books, with their mainly pessimistic assessment of the subject, have had a great influence, and have stimulated a very extensive literature to which I shall refer later. Religion and the labour movement has also been the subject of considerable historical debate. Kitson Clark used the stimulating essay by E. J. Hobsbawm in his collection *Primitive Rebels* (Manchester, 1959). The best of the many more recent studies is Robert Moore, *Pit-men, Preachers and Politics* (1974). In discussing the impact of Nonconformists on local politics, he used A. Temple Patterson, *Radical Leicester* (1954), but not the pioneering work of E. P. Hennock, published as *Fit and Proper Persons* (1973).

In discussing the 1851 religious census he was able to draw on the pioneering paper by K. S. Inglis, *Journal of Ecclesiastical History*, 12 (1960). The most recent contribution to the now very extensive literature, and methodologically one of the most important, is K. D. M. Snell, *Church and Chapel in the North Midlands* (Leicester, 1991). Although the 1851 census was the only nationwide count of church attendance in the Victorian and Edwardian periods, there were also many local censuses: the most comprehensive study of church attendance data is now Robin Gill, *The Myth of the Empty Church* (1993).

Many of the themes highlighted by Kitson Clark became subjects of research in the 1960s. For instance, temperance found its historian in Brian Harrison, author of *Drink and the Victorians* (1971), as well as a series of seminal articles including 'Religion and Recreation', *Past and Present*, 38 (1967). Two books by John Vincent included important material on the interaction between religion and politics, especially at the local level: *The Formation of the Liberal Party, 1857–1868* (1966), and *Pollbooks: How Victorians Voted* (Cambridge, 1967). Kitson Clark himself provided a sympathetic assessment of the Anglican contribution to social reform in *Churchmen and the Condition of England, 1832–1885* (1973), and his Cambridge seminar played a major part in the growth of research on Victorian religion in the 1960s and early 1970s.

In writing his brilliant synthesis, which remains one of the most thought-provoking and most influential interpretations of modern English religious history, Gilbert too depended to a considerable degree on his own research and on older denominational histories. There had none the less been some important developments in the fourteen years since Kitson Clark's book was published. One was the considerable development of the sociology of religion. Gilbert's argument was influenced by contemporary sociologists such as Bryan Wilson and David Martin, as well as by such classic writers as Weber and Troeltsch. He also used some sociological studies of historical topics, such as Kenneth Thompson, *Bureaucracy and Church Reform* (1970). A second development was the systematic study of church membership statistics, pioneered by Robert Currie in *Methodism Divided* (1968). Gilbert later collaborated with Currie and Lee Horsley to produce an invaluable compendium of religious statistics with an extended commentary, *Churches and Churchgoers; Patterns of Church Growth in the British Isles since 1700* (Oxford, 1977). A third was the development of religious geography in such works as John Gay, *The Geography of Religion in England* (1971), and Alan Everitt, *The Pattern of Rural Dissent* (Lercester, 1972). Recently, important work in this field has been done by Paul Ell and T. R. Slater. See, for instance, their article 'The Religious Census of 1851: A Computer-mapped Survey of the Church of England', *Journal of Historical Geography*, 20 (1994), pp. 44–61.

One surprising omission from Gilbert's book was any reference to H. J. Dyos and M. Wolff (eds), *The Victorian City*, 2 vols (1973), a massive and authoritative compendium, including several chapters on religion. And indeed discussion of the urban dimension of modern religious history is one of the weaker aspects of Gilbert's book.

In fact Gilbert was writing on the eve of a flood of major publications, culminating in the annus mirabilis of 1976, which would transform our knowledge of Victorian and Edwardian religion, providing the raw materials for the Open University course, based on the excellent 4-volume collection, edited by Gerald Parsons, *Religion in Victorian Britain* (Manchester, 1988). Most important were a series of major local studies, including Stephen Yeo, *Religion and Voluntary Organisations in Crisis* (1976), based on Reading; James Obelkevich, *Religion and Rural Society: South Lindsey 1825–1875* (Oxford, 1976); and Jeffrey Cox, *English Churches in a Secular Society: Lambeth 1870–1930* (Oxford, 1982).

By the mid-70s the shift of focus, from elite to masses, which Kitson Clark had called for in 1962, had finally become a reality. A shift of a similar kind had happened in the history of irreligion, where Edward Royle, in such studies as *Radicals, Secularists and Republicans* (Manchester, 1980), led the way in the study of working-class secularism. Also important was Susan Budd's comprehensive *Varieties of Unbelief* (1977).

In Catholic history the shift towards 'bottom up' history meant that Irish Catholics were moving to the centre of the stage. See especially Sheridan Gilley and Roger Swift (eds), *The Irish in the Victorian City* (1985), and numerous articles by Gilley, including a contribution to Dyos and Wolff, *Victorian City*, vol. II. Two very different attempts at synthesis were E. R. Norman, *The English Catholic Church in the Nineteenth Century* (Oxford, 1984) and G. P. Connolly, 'The Transsubstantiation of Myth: Towards a New Popular History of Nineteenth-Century Catholicism in England', *Journal of Ecclesiastical History*, 35 (1984). The Open University team could also draw on much new research on the clergy, some of it using statistical evidence, notably Alan Haig, *The Victorian Clergy* (1984) and K. D. Brown, *A Social History of the Nonconformist Ministry in England and Wales, 1800– 1930* (Oxford, 1988). For nuns, see Susan O'Brien, 'Terra Incognita: The Nun in Nineteenth-Century England', *Past and Present*, 121 (1988).

The Jews, who appeared only in a footnote of Kitson Clark's book, and not at all in Gilbert's, were the subject of a chapter in the Parsons collection. Here too, recent research with a social history emphasis played an important part, including notably David Feldman, 'Immigrants and Workers, Englishmen and Jews: Jewish Immigration to the East End of London 1880–1906' (University of Cambridge PhD thesis, 1986), and numerous articles by Todd Endelman, such as 'Communal Solidarity among the Jewish Elite of Victorian London', *Victorian Studies*, 28 (1985), though older works, such as Lloyd P. Gartner, *The Jewish Immigrant in England, 1870–1914* (1960), continued to be important. More recently, a major work of synthesis has appeared: Geoffrey Alderman, *Modern British Jewry* (Oxford, 1992).

The social role of religion and, particularly, the status of the churches as instruments of 'social control', continued to be a subject of lively debate, reflected in the Parsons collection. Two of the most influential studies, written from very different angles, were E. R. Norman, *Church and Society in England 1770–*

1970 (Oxford, 1976), a critique of Anglican social thought; and Patrick Joyce, *Work, Society and Politics* (Brighton, 1980), a highly detailed study of mid-Victorian Lancashire, including a chapter on the links between factory-owners and places of worship. Both books have stimulated considerable debate, and often dissent. See, for instance, the contributions to David Jeremy (ed.), *Business and Religion* (Aldershot, 1988), many of which refer to Joyce; and David M. Thompson, 'The Emergence of the Nonconformist Social Gospel in English' in Keith Robbins (ed.), *Protestant Evangelicalism* (Oxford, 1990), which is partly in response to Norman.

The relationship between religion and party politics was the subject of a regular flow of publications, among the most significant being D. W. Bebbington, *The Nonconformist Conscience* (1982); K. D. Wald, *Crosses on the Ballot* (Princeton, 1984), a statistical study of voting patterns; and G. I. T. Machin, *Politics and the Churches in Great Britain, 1869 to 1921* (Oxford, 1987), which focused on high politics.

Meanwhile the Victorian 'crisis of faith' continued to be a subject of absorbing interest, and, if anything, claimed a disproportionately large share of the space in the Parsons collection. Among the many new contributions were Frank M. Turner, *Between Science and Religion* (New Haven, 1974); James R. Moore, *The Post-Darwinian Controversies: A Study of the Protestant Struggle to Come to Terms with Darwin in Great Britain and America 1870–1900* (New York, 1979); Ieuan Ellis, *Seven against Christ: A Study of 'Essays and Reviews'* (Leiden, 1980); and, more recently, Richard J. Helmstadter and Bernard Lightman (eds), *Victorian Faith in Crisis* (Basingstoke, 1990).

The later 1980s and early 1990s have seen both important twists in old debates, and also the emergence of new themes, or a new centrality for themes that previously were largely neglected. One old area of work which has seen a lot of important research, much of it as yet unpublished, is that of urban religious history, usually with a special emphasis on the working class. Perhaps most influential has been a short polemical essay by Callum Brown entitled 'Did Urbanization Secularize Britain?', *Urban History Yearbook* (1988), pp. 1–14. Brown stresses the central importance of organised religion in Victorian cities, and argues that the extent of working-class involvement was considerably higher than has been generally recognised. He also suggests that the progress of secularisation was slight before the 1890s, and that rapid secularisation has come only in the twentieth century, and more especially since the Second World War.

Important contributions to this debate include Alan Bartlett, 'The Churches in Bermondsey, 1880–1939' (University of Birmingham PhD thesis, 1987); numerous articles by S. J. D. Green, for instance, 'Religion and the Rise of the Common Man', in Derek Fraser (ed.), *Cities, Class and Communication* (Hemel Hempstead, 1990); J. N. Morris, *Religion and Urban Change: Croydon 1840–1914* (Woodbridge, 1992); Mark Smith, *Religion and Industrial Society: Oldham and Saddleworth, 1780–1865* (Oxford, 1994); and the contributions by Callum Brown and Sarah Williams to Hugh McLeod (ed.), *European Religion in the Age of Great Cities* (1995). For an overview of the recent debate see Hugh McLeod, *Religion and Irreligion in Victorian England: How Secular was the Working Class?* (Bangor, 1992). See also the discussion in Hugh McLeod, *Piety and Poverty: Working-Class Religion in Berlin, London and New York, 1870–1914* (New York, 1995).

Among the old themes which have gained a new importance in recent years is that of the relationship between religion and nationalism, patriotism and militarism, and, in particular, the relationship between British imperialism and the great upsurge of missionary activity in the later nineteenth century. An important pioneering contribution was Olive Anderson. 'The Growth of Christian Militarism in Mid-Victorian Britain', *English Historical Review*, 86 (1971). A major synthesis is John Wolffe, *God and Greater Britain, 1843–1945* (1994). Other significant contributions include Susan Thorne, 'Protestant Ethics and the Spirit of Imperialism: British Congregationalists and the London Missionary Society' (University of Michigan PhD thesis, 1990); Brian Stanley, *The Bible and the Flag* (Leicester, 1990); and the numerous writings by J. A. Mangan on elite education, sport and Empire, in which religion often plays a part – see, for instance, *The Games Ethic and Imperialism* (Harmondsworth, 1986).

Another theme of growing importance is that of gender. Again, Olive Anderson pointed the way with 'Women Preachers in Mid-Victorian Britain', *Historical Journal*, 12 (1969), but before the 1980s she found few followers. Since then, there has been a growing volume of work, as is indicated by such collections as Gail Malmgreen (ed.), *Religion in the Lives of English Women 1760–1930* (1986); W. J. Sheils and Diana Wood (eds), *Women in the Church* (Oxford, 1990); Fiona Bowie, Deborah Kirkwood and

Shirley Ardener (eds), *Women and Missions, Past and Present* (Providence, 1993). However, there is as yet no major monograph on the later Victorian period to set beside Leonore Davidoff and Catherine Hall, *Family Fortunes: Men and Women of the English Middle Class, 1780–1850* (1987). While most work has focused on women, there has also been some work on manliness: see, for instance, Norman Vance, *The Sinews of the Spirit* (Cambridge, 1985); and J. A. Mangan and James Walvin (eds), *Manliness and Morality: Middle-Class Masculinity in Britain and America, 1800–1940* (Manchester, 1987).

Finally, some large-scale studies which do not fit readily into any of the categories presented above. While less comprehensive than Parsons and less coherent than Gilbert, Owen Chadwick, *The Victorian Church*, 2 vols (1966–70) remains the widest-ranging study by a single author, and particularly strong on ideas, personalities, church politics and the Anglican parish. David Bebbington, *Evangelicalism in Modern Britain* (1989) is an authoritative synthesis, covering the whole period from 1730 to the present day. James Munson, *The Nonconformists* (1991), is particularly strong on the political dimensions, while Clyde Binfield has made a more diffuse, but equally important, contribution to understanding of the social, cultural and aesthetic dimensions: see *So Down to Prayers* (1977), as well as numerous papers in periodicals and festschrifts, an outstanding example being his chapter on Nonconformist architecture in Keith Robbins (ed.), *Protestant Evangelicalism* (Oxford, 1990).

INDEX

Index

Carlisle, 61
Carpenter, Edward, 120, 132
Chadwick, Rosemary, 62–3, 66
Chamberlain, Joseph, 87, 93, 98
charity, 4, 15, 22, 24–5, 26, 37,
    77–8, 80–1, 131, 143–5
Cheshire, 38
Cheshunt College, 191
church attendance, 6–7, 10, 11–13,
    19–21, 24, 41, 55, 64–70, 78,
    103, 141–2, 157, 169, 170–4,
    178–9, 203, 211
    see also religious censuses
church-building, 20, 24, 72, 126,
    196
church buildings, 13–14, 22, 71–2,
    113–14, 191
church/chapel conflict, *see*
    sectarianism
church membership, 30, 157, 173–5,
    211
Church of England, *see* Anglicans
Church of Scotland, 21, 121
Churches of Christ, 31, 115, 173
cities, 14, 15, 22, 27–8, 61, 144,
    171–3, 175, 204
class, 2, 62–6, 92; *see also* middle
    class; upper class; working class
clergy
    Anglican, 14–19, 26–7, 39, 54, 74,
        85, 86–9, 97, 100, 110–13,
        132, 134, 141–2, 151, 160,
        173, 188, 193–6, 197, 202–4,
        207, 214
    Nonconformist, 32, 85, 91, 96,
        112, 119, 132, 134, 140, 160,
        163, 189, 190–1, 194–5, 210
    Roman Catholic, 39–40, 42, 91,
        112, 132, 157, 160
Colne, 95
Comte, Auguste, 183
Conan Doyle, Sir Arthur, 53
Congregationalists, 28, 30, 33–7, 57,
    66–7, 85, 91, 95–6, 105, 109,
    110, 114–15, 123, 147, 153, 158,
    160, 165, 168, 170, 173, 191–2,
    207
Connolly, Gerard, 41
Conservative Party, 30, 35, 46, 55,
    56, 87, 91–4, 96–100, 109, 113,
    208
Contagious Diseases Acts, 129–30,
    134–6, 164, 215
conversion
    to Catholicism, 39–40
    to Christianity, 146–7
    Evangelical, 140–1

Corke, Helen, 106
Cornwall, 20, 28, 32, 34, 61, 88
Cotton, G. E. L., 111, 151–2
Countess of Huntingdon's
    Connexion, 30, 35
Courtney, W. L., 176–7, 185
Cox, Jeffrey, 3–4, 6–7, 96, 213
Croydon, 106, 195
Currie, Robert, 3, 173

Dahl, Roald, 112
Dale, R. W., 93
Darwin, Charles, 50, 180, 182, 187,
    189, 215
Derrington, Edward, 123
Descartes, R., 187
Devon, 16, 28, 34, 61, 105, 107, 125
Dewsbury, 85, 114, 140–1
Dickens, Charles, 57, 100–1, 132
disestablishment, 92, 217
Disraeli, Benjamin, 94
district visitors, 22, 26, 195–6
Dorset, 20
doubt, 176–7, 179–96
drink, 44, 98, 102, 124, 191, 201
    pubs, 70, 119, 122, 124–6, 140,
        154, 196–7
    temperance movement, 57–8, 85,
        93, 118, 136–7, 140–1, 145,
        154–5, 188
Drummond, Diane K., 95
Durham, 8, 36, 61, 87, 115, 120,
    131

Eastwood, 35–6
Education Acts, 92–3
Edward VII, 11, 21, 128–9
Eliot, George, 51, 132, 183
Ellis, Havelock, 132
Empire, British, 99, 138, 145–9
Essays and Reviews, 183, 190
Essex, 34, 66, 75, 112
Evangelicals, 31, 43, 100, 136–40,
    176, 186, 188, 192–3
evangelism, 140–9, 162, 164–5, 167,
    188

Fabians, 208
family, 102–7, 157–60, 188, 192
farmers, 27, 31, 86, 125, 202, 203
farm labourers, 16, 19, 54–5, 86, 95,
    105, 107, 127, 177–9
Farrar, Revd F. W., 111, 184
Field, Clive, 66, 157
Finney, Charles, 165
Fisher, Archbishop Geoffrey, 112
Flanagan, Revd J., 144

Index

Index

Index